TURKEY
From Empire to Revolutionary Republic

3 August 2007

SİNA AKŞİN

TURKEY
From Empire to Revolutionary Republic

*The Emergence of the Turkish Nation
from 1789 to the Present*

TRANSLATED FROM THE TURKISH BY
DEXTER H. MURSALOĞLU

NEW YORK UNIVERSITY PRESS
Washington Square, New York

First published in the U.S.A. in 2007 by
NEW YORK UNIVERSITY PRESS
Washington Square, New York, 10003
www.nyupress.org

Library of Congress Cataloging-in-Publication Data
Akşin, Sina.
  Turkey: from empire to revolutionary republic: the emergence of
the Turkish nation from 1789 to the present/
Sina Aksin; translated from the Turkish by Dexter H. Mursaloglu.
     p. cm.
  "This edition, including new chapters 31–33, was first published
in the United Kingdom by C. Hurst Co."
—CIP data view.
Includes bibliographical references and index.
  ISBN–13: 978–0–8147–0721–0 (cloth: alk. paper)
  ISBN–10: 0–8147–0721–1 (cloth: alk. paper)
  ISBN–13: 978–0–8147–0722–7 (pbk.: alk. paper)
  ISBN–10: 0–8147–0722–X (pbk.: alk. paper)
  1. Turkey—History. I. Title.
  DR559.A39 2006
  956.1—dc22   2006012757

Manufactured in India

PREFACE AND ACKNOWLEDGEMENTS

The teaching of history in pre-university schools in Turkey is very inadequate. Little world history is taught, and the teaching of Turkish history is also inadequate. The treatment of twentieth-century Turkish history is particularly sketchy and superficial, and generally ends with the death of Atatürk in 1938. The same superficiality and inadequacy afflict the teaching of the humanities and social sciences (but not the exact sciences). It is not easy to describe this situation as accidental; probably it is a consequence of the unfortunate policy of governments unfriendly to enlightenment, which spread its shadow over Turkey after 1950.

It was for this reason that I thought of writing a handbook of modern Turkish history to meet the needs of both general readers and students. The Turkish version of this book was first published in 1996 and is currently in its fifth printing. It has also been printed by the daily newspaper *Cumhuriyet* for distribution to its readers.

The English version of the book is the result of the encouragement and support of the publisher Christopher Hurst. At his suggestion I have written additional chapters (31 to 33) to cover the post-1980 period. I am very thankful indeed for his help and encouragement.

I also thank Dexter H. Mursaloğlu, my expert translator, as well as Marya B. Minor, who edited the translation.

Finally, thanks are due to Elif Akşit, Sarp Balcı, Deniz and Işıl Akşin for their essential help in establishing electronic communication with the publisher.

Ankara, January 2006   SİNA AKŞİN

CONTENTS

NOTE ON TURKISH PRONUNCIATION

c   is pronounced j as in jungle

ç   is pronounced ch as in chain

ğ   only serves to lengthen the preceding vowel

ı   is pronounced as the o in women

j   is pronounced as in French

ö   is pronounced as in German or eu in French

ş   is pronounced sh as in shield

ü   is pronounced as in German or u in French

Present day Turkey

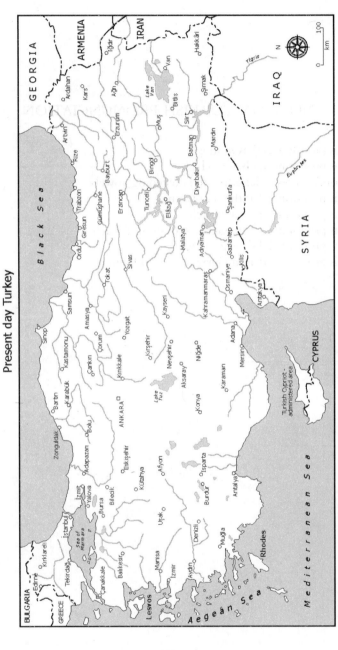

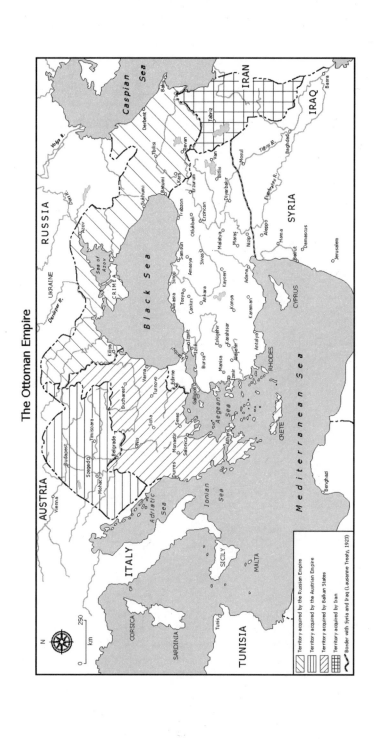

The Ottoman Empire

Territory acquired by the Russian Empire
Territory acquired by the Austrian Empire
Territory acquired by Balkan States
Territory acquired by Iran
Border with Syria and Iraq (Lausanne Treaty, 1923)

Part I

INTRODUCTION
THE BACKGROUND

1

THE PRE-OTTOMAN TURKS

The three homelands of the Turks

The Huns' nomadic kingdom was the first Turkic state to appear on the stage of history (220 BCE to 216 CE). From these dates it may be understood that the Turks were latecomers to ancient history, a relatively "young" people. The following milestones of history afford a better understanding of this point of view.

9000–8000 BCE Beginning of agriculture and the domestication of animals
6250 BCE The city of Chatalhöyük founded in Anatolia
3500 BCE Invention of the wheel in Sumeria and of sailing vessels in Egypt
3000 BCE Invention in Mesopotamia of the Sumerian script—cuneiform, wedge-shaped writing

At the time when the Hun empire was born, ancient Greek civilization and the empire of Alexander the Great had come and gone and the Roman Republic was in its fifth century of existence.

The region where the Huns first held sway, their first homeland called by the Turks 'Central Asia', is an area north of China. The Huns were nomadic herders, dependent on their flocks for their livelihood. These horsemen roamed the grasslands of the steppe, living in yurts (tents) and migrating from season to season in quest of better pastures. In summer they moved up to the high plateaux and climbed the mountain slopes; in winter they descended into the plains. They lived as nomadic shepherds because the arid steppe lands were unamenable to cultivation. For them nomadism was necessary for survival. Arable lands lay to the south, in China. A formidable obstacle blocked the nomads' path to the fertile farmlands of China. The Great Wall of Imperial China was the immense barrier guarding the agricultural civilisation of the south against raids by the nomads of the north. It was a 2,400-kilometre (1,500-mile) line of defence, a highly complex defence system studded at intervals with high towers and topped by a road, which enabled garrisoned troops to move quickly to any point under attack.

The nomadic Huns had no written language and no knowledge of urban life. It has been argued that they lacked the attributes of statehood and may be considered to have been merely a confederation of tribes. After their dispersion, the Turkic tribes did not for a long period reach a sophisticated level of organisation. The Göktürk kingdom was established in the first homeland in 552 CE and existed until 745. The one important characteristic that separates the Gökturks from the Huns is the emergence of a written language towards the end of their era. The first Turkish stone inscriptions, dating from 730, were found at the site of Ötüken. That aside, everything that has been said about the Huns was also true of the Göktürks. Following the Göktürk era, large-scale long-range migration began. There is much speculation as to why the nomadic tribes were forced to migrate: drought, extraordinary increases in population, and epidemics among animals have been suggested.

The first wave of migrants established themselves a little to the west of the first homeland, founding the first fully-fledged Turkish kingdom with attributes of statehood. The Uygur civilization (745–940) had both cities and agriculture and also a written language. However, nomadism was still the dominant culture. The Uygurs converted from Shamanism to Buddhism. Some Turkic tribes migrated far to the west, reaching the second homeland of the Turks, Transoxania, an area roughly to the east of the Caspian sea, south of the Aral Sea and north of what is today Afghanistan. This region is known by the Turks as Maveraünnehir, and it was here that they gradually converted to Islam between 900 and 1150. They founded three prominent states: the Karahan or Kara-Khanid state (940–1211), the principality of Ghazna in Afghanistan (963–1186) and the Great Seljuk kingdom (1038–1157). The Karahan era marked the beginnings of Turkish literature. Two major works were Yusuf Has Hacip's *Kudatgu Bilik* in 1070 and the first Turkish dictionary by Mahmut of Kashgar, entitled the *Divan-ü Lügat-it Türk*.

The great Seljuk victory over Byzantium at Manzikert (1071) triggered the migration of the *Oğuz* (Oghuz or Ghuzz) Turks into the Third Homeland—Anatolia and Rumelia. This victory broke the back of Byzantine power in Anatolia, a blow from which Byzantium never recovered. The first Turkish state to be established in Anatolia (Asia Minor) was the Anatolian Seljuk sultanate (1077–1308). The Third Homeland was very different from the two previous ones. Compared to the harsh steppe of the First Homeland, the Second, Transoxania, had been a relative improvement with areas of fertile, arable land, but it too was belted by huge deserts and had a prevailing arid climate. The Third Homeland had no desert wasteland at all; it was truly fertile and wheat could be cultivated everywhere. The Turks settled this land in large numbers, and with the development of agriculture a peasant class evolved. There was one great difference between Anatolia and Rumelia. In the latter lowlands were predominant whereas Anatolia was a land of high plateaux broken by steep mountain ranges. There were vast spaces where tribes and clans could easily revert to their nomadic existence if they so wished. In addition, when from time to time lawlessness and turmoil broke out in Anatolia, villagers weary of being plundered would take to the mountains, become brigands or return to nomadic life. In short, periodic shifts occurred between the nomadic and peasant populations with one or the other dominating certain areas. As late as 1865 the Ottoman government was obliged to send an army, the Firka-yı Islahiye, to the region of Çukurova (Cilicia). The aim of this army was to 'resettle' the Avshars and other clans that had become 'unsettled'. It is said that during this period a section of the Çukurova plain east of Adana, one of the most fertile agricultural areas of Turkey, reverted to grassland owing to nomadism.

The historian Zeki Velidi Togan has touched upon a subject relevant to the settlement of Anatolia by the Turks. According to Togan, Arab raids caused a majority of the Christian inhabitants of Anatolia to flee to coastal areas. This view carries the implication that because Anatolia was relatively unpopulated when the Turks arrived, they therefore did not mix racially with Anatolian Christians—in other words, that they maintained a racial purity. However, it is impossible to determine what proportion of the Christian population had left or remained. In any event marriage, conversion to Islam, *devshirme* (enforced recruitment of Christians for the Janissary corps and government service) and slavery must have resulted in a mingling of races. The fact that Turks do not have a marked resemblance to the Asian descendants of Turkic tribes, and the added fact that even among themselves the Turks of Turkey do not have uniform physical characteristics, seem to be proofs of racial intermarriage. However, racial considerations aside, the Turkish language became the common language of Anatolia. This is an important tie that binds the people of Anatolia to Central Asia.

The ages of history

The French chronology of the history of mankind is widely acknowledged by Turkish historians. The four periods into which the written history of mankind is thereby divided are as follows:

3000 BCE–CE 476 (the fall of the Western Roman Empire): Ancient History
476–1453 (the fall of Constantinople to the Turks and the end of the Eastern Roman or Byzantine Empire): the Middle Ages
1453–1789 (the French Revolution): the New Age
1789 and after: the Modern Age

Turkish historians who favour this chronology emphasise the importance of 1453 from the angle of Mehmet II—Fatih the Conqueror—as a Renaissance prince and the importance of the fall of Constantinople to Islam and the Turks. Although it is certainly true that the conquest of İstanbul ushers in a period of deep-rooted change that may be summarised as transition 'from *beylik* to empire', may we really define this event as the birthdate of a new age for the Turks? It is this author's opinion that we may not. In taking 1453 as the date for the turning-point of a new age, Europeans cast the Ottomans in a negative historical role. According to this evaluation of history Byzantine intellectuals, fleeing from İstanbul after its conquest by the Turks, arrived in Italy and became a major influence in beginning the Renaissance and Humanism. According to this view of European history, the sum total of the Ottoman contribution was simply to propel a group of intellectuals to move westwards.

İbrahim Kafesoğlu was one of the first Turkish historians to point out that this chronology of the ages of history does not clarify and has no direct bearing on vital aspects of Turkish history. At the date when it occurred, did the end of the Roman Empire have any direct impact upon the Turks? The 1789 French Revolution was of great importance for Turkish history, but there was a time lapse before its effects were felt within Ottoman domains, whereas in Western and Eastern Europe its effect was practically simultaneous.

Thus the significance of these events for the Turks of Anatolia and Rumelia may be disputed. A more meaningful chronology of the ages of Turkish history would be:

BCE 220 (the emergence of the Hunnic state) to CE 1071 (the battle of Manzikert; entry of the Turks into Anatolia and Rumelia): Ancient History
1071–1839 (the Proclamation of Tanzimat): the Middle Ages
1839–1908 (Proclamation of the Constitution): the New Age
1908 and after: the Modern Age

This chronology is relevant to the Turks of Turkey in that it highlights the stages of the country's social development. Ancient History was for the Turks an era of nomadism. The Middle Ages were a transitional period of settlement, agricultural development and the emergence of a peasantry. The New Age embodied concerted effort towards westernisation and the rule of law. The Modern Age marks the point where the Turks of Turkey began to head towards extensive urbanisation, capitalism and the establishment of a democratic Republic.

2

THE CLASSICAL OTTOMAN ERA

The first bey or lord of the Ottoman line was Osman, after whom the Osmanlı Empire was named ('Ottoman' is the European version of Osmanlı). Starting out in 1299 as a small beylik near the ancient city of Bursa, the Ottomans eventually conquered the territory of Byzantium and the entire Balkan peninsula: Greece, Serbia, Bulgaria and the regions of Wallachia and Moldavia north of the Danube. One by one, they overpowered all the other Turkish beyliks to become the sole rulers of Anatolia. In the sixteenth century the Ottomans took control of Syria, Arabia and Egypt, including the holy cities of Jerusalem, Mecca and Medina. At its zenith the empire stretched from North Africa to the Crimea, from Belgrade to Baghdad, controlling the eastern Mediterranean and the east-west caravan routes. The Ottomans evolved into a traditionalist but relatively liberal society and created an ingenious and efficient administrative system based on individual merit. During their expansion they had the largest standing army of Europe, supported by the revenues from their own conquests, and a flourishing agricultural economy based on an original system of land administration unlike the feudal system of Europe. Ruling over a diverse plethora of ethnic groups situated in varying geographic regions, they were able to maintain their empire for six centuries, outlasting their arch-enemies the Russian Tsars and the Habsburgs. However, towards the end they fell behind the times; their power structure crumbled and their society was rent by inner strife. They lost all real power in the international arena and were only able to keep the empire alive thanks to the balance of power politics.

Periodisation of Ottoman history

The 'Classical Ottoman' social structure reached the pinnacle of its development in the period between 1450 and 1550. The periodisation of the eras of Ottoman history taught in Turkish schools is as follows.

1299–1453: from Beylik to Empire

Osman Bey, founder of the dynasty after whom it was named, was followed by his son, Orhan, who took Bursa (ancient Brusa) and crossed the Dardanelles, beginning the conquest of the Balkans. During this period the Osmanlı lands expanded rapidly until the battle of Ankara, when 'Thunderbolt' Sultan Bayezit I was defeated in 1402 by Tamerlane the Great. This defeat was followed by a struggle between Bayezit's sons for control of the budding empire. By 1430 the empire had regained its former borders.

1453–1579: the apogee

Beginning with Mehmet II, 'Fatih the Conqueror', who took Constantinople (renamed İstanbul by the Turks), the four consecutive Sultans of this period were invincible as they led their armies to conquer lands from the Euphrates to the Danube and from North Africa to the Crimea. After Sultan Selim I, 'Selim the Resolute' (Yavuz Selim), conquered Egypt in 1517 the Ottoman Sultans assumed the Caliphate. This period includes the reign of Süleyman the Magnificent (Kanuni Sultan Süleyman, Sultan Suleyman I) and ends with the death of the Grand Vizier Sokullu Mehmet.

1579–1699: Stagnation

The empire had reached its limits. During this period this huge empire was ruled by Sultans who had spent their formative years confined to the 'Cage' (an area of the Topkapı palace) from which they emerged either to be executed, to ensure an uncontested succession, or to reign. No longer did they command their armies on the battlefield. The Sublime Porte or High Gate (the Grand Vizierate) kept the wheels of Empire turning, inhibited by internecine rivalry and palace plots.

1699–1922: Decline and fall

The empire was left behind by the Industrial Revolution and in many ways became relatively backward. The question for the Turks was how and to what extent to modernise, while the question for Europe was how to share the spoils of the disintegrating empire.

This chronology is meaningful only from the standpoint of territorial gains and losses and also perhaps in relation to the power and efficiency of the Ottoman state apparatus. It is less significant when applied to the levels of social and cultural development and economic prosperity of the Turkish people. If statistics were available, it might be proved that in the nineteenth century the average Turk had a longer life-expectancy and that there was a higher rate of literacy than at the time of Süleyman the Magnificent (the height of the empire). Although 'the apogee' may boast of such an architectural genius as Sinan, the eighteenth and nineteenth centuries produced many great names in literature. Katip Çelebi and Evliya Çelebi were two great writers and intellectuals of the seventeenth century. Classical Turkish music may be said to have shown real development in and after the seventeenth century. The first Turkish libraries were built in the eighteenth century. If we were to evaluate development on the basis of landmass alone the Turkish Republic would be deemed to have regressed, but it is evident that in practically every sphere, be it civic, economic or cultural, not only is modern Turkish society far in advance of the Ottomans but it also is in a process of rapid and continuing development.

The Classical Ottoman social structure

This may be outlined as follows:

I. The ruling class
1. The executive military
   a. Salaried officials
   b. Timariot *sipahis* (land-holding cavalrymen) and the *zaims* (greater land-holders)
2. The *Ulema*: *kadis* (judges), *muderris* (professors) and *muftis* (doctors of divinity)

II. The *Reaya* (the flock), non-military, ruled by the above

1. City-dwellers
    a. Members of guilds (tradesmen, craftsmen)
    b. Merchants and moneychangers
2. Peasants
3. Nomads

During the Ottoman era there were two main categories of society, the rulers and the ruled. The state, headed by the Sultan, determined who should be in which and under what circumstances. Because the state was organised as a war machine geared for conquest, the ruling classes were all deemed to be part of the military organisation, even if, as in the case of the *ulema*, they had no direct or indirect military function.

As a rule the Sultan was the wealthiest person in the empire, the Grand Vizier being second wealthiest. If any merchant should accumulate extraordinary wealth, confiscation would cut him down to size. Members of the ruling class were ensured a high standard of living and were exempt from paying taxes. Headed by the Sultan, the ruling class included the *ulema* and the executive military, who had *kul* (slave) status, such as members of the Janissary corps. The functions of the executive military were both administrative and military, in other words, they were at the same time both administrators and soldiers. From the Janissaries and the *sipahis* to the Grand Vizier at the top, all were engaged in dual functions and were considered slaves or *kul*.

The *kul* were slaves of the state and 'Their necks were thinner than a hair-thread', which meant they could be 'politically executed' at the Sultan's decree without resort to legal process. A second consequence of *kul* status was the *müsadere*—the confiscation of property on the death of a *kul*. Although the *müsadere* was most likely to be applied to highly-placed government officials whose wealth made it worthwhile, there was a way to bypass it so that wealth could be passed on to the next generation. Heirs were appointed as directors of family *vakıfs* (endowments) supplying public services such as mosques, *medreses* (religious colleges) and *hans* (inns). Since charitable foundations were exempt from the *müsadere*, the heirs of the wealthiest *kuls* would be assured of an income.

The second branch of the ruling class was the *ulema*, who were responsible for the religious, judicial and educational functions of the state and had little to do with government administration. Like the military, they could attain great wealth and did not pay taxes. But unlike the executive military, they did not have *kul* status and in general were not punished without a trial. Hence, they could not be politically executed and their property did not revert to the state on their death. The *ulema* were the children of Muslims who, after graduating from parochial schools generally situated in mosques, were educated at the *medreses* (theological colleges). The upper echelons of the *ulema* could attain great wealth and could transfer their estates to their children. Titles and privileges were obtained for these children while they were still very young, so as to ease their advancement. These children in turn tended to become *ulema*, creating a kind of intellectual aristocracy.

The *kul* were in a large proportion *devshirme*, the conscripted children of Christians. They were the products of the boy tribute system whereby children were gathered from conquered provinces and after formally converting to Islam were educated for branches of the Sultan's service. After being raised and educated as Turks, they were sent to the provinces to rule the Empire and expand its frontiers even further. They could, according to their talents and after receiving the necessary education, become Janissaries or governors of a province. The system even allowed them to rise to the position of Grand Vizier, attaining great wealth and power. It was an ingenious system of meritocracy. The architect Sinan, Grand Vizier Sokullu Mehmet Pasha and many other grand viziers were *devshirme*.

Ziya Gökalp compared the Enderun, the Imperial School of Topkapı palace attended by the *devshirme*, to the *medrese* attended by the offspring of Muslim families, saying the former took non-Turks and made them into Turks whereas the latter took Turks and made them into non-Turks (in terms of their cultural orientation). In fact, in the imperial schools such as the Enderun the language of academia was Turkish, whereas the language of the *medrese* and the scholar was Arabic. From a modern viewpoint the irony of the situation does not end here. In a non-secular state of an overtly religious bent, those of Muslim ancestry were not involved in military or government affairs, whereas those of Christian ancestry were directly responsible for the fate of the country.

The executive military was divided into two categories: the salaried military, such as the *kapıkulu* and Janissary corps, and the land-holding cavalrymen, the Timariot *sipahis* and greater land-holding *zaims*. There were major differences between these two categories with drawbacks and advantages to each. In an economy where there was lack of hard currency, where the main source of revenue was the *ashar* or tithes paid by the peasants in kind, the salaried military had the advantage of being paid in coin of the realm. But when their salaries were not paid on time and/or when they were paid in debased coinage, they became a group of malcontents, ever ready for rebellion.

The *sipahi* were horsemen who had inherited the *gazi* tradition of warring for the Faith. The aim of these horsemen was to be allotted a military fief, called a *timar*, and to become the Sultan's *sipahi*. The Sultan owned all the land and had claim to all taxes. He lent revenues from these fiefs to his cavalrymen, according to their merits, and in return the Timariots were expected to muster in wartime with a number of men proportionate to the size of their fiefs. The status of the Timariot and the *zaim* was similar to feudal overlordship. Though not legally the owners of the land they occupied, they drew a large portion of their income from the peasantry in the form of taxes paid in kind (*ashar*) and were, in fact, the sovereign power of their areas.

The class of society which was ruled was called the *reaya* (the flock). Production was their sphere, but they could also be recruited for war. They were burdened with paying taxes. As a Platonic state the Ottoman Empire was based on a social order in which the administrators prospered more than the administered. The state was for the rulers, not for the ruled.

The main group of urban *reaya* was the *lonca*, the guild tradesmen or craftsmen. They either produced and marketed their own wares or were traders only; each was a small economic unit functioning within the rigid framework of the guilds, who imposed strict codes of behaviour, regularising the relationships between apprentice, qualified craftsman and master craftsman. Care was taken both by the state and by the guilds themselves to ensure that no unit should expand or develop too far. In other words there was no open door to capitalism from the guilds. Other urban *reaya* who did business on a larger scale were the *sarraf* (moneychangers) and the merchants who did international business. These groups were allowed to accumulate wealth, because the nature of their professions made it impossible for them to function within the restricted confines of the guilds.

The Ottoman state preferred peasants to nomads, the obvious reason being that peasants, who were settled, paid taxes and could be recruited for the army, whereas nomads, who were not settled, disliked and avoided both. As an armed and mobile group, the nomads were unruly and difficult to bring into line, and the Ottomans struggled throughout their history to settle them and turn them into peasants.

3

CHANGES IN THE CLASSICAL OTTOMAN SYSTEM

What we have called 'classical' Ottoman socio-political institutions began to change from the middle of the sixteenth century onwards. The factors influencing this transition were as follows.

The impact of inflation in Europe; the musket

In the centuries under discussion negotiable currency was coined from precious metals. Hence the output of existing gold and silver mines determined the relatively limited number of coins available in Eurasian markets and new sources of silver or gold were needed to increase output. Following the discovery of the New World the Spaniards conquered the Aztec, Mayan and Incan civilisations, plundered their treasuries of silver and gold and worked their mines. Great quantities of Spanish-American silver flooded the money markets of Europe and Asia, giving rise to increased monetisation and rising prices in countries all over the world. Inevitably, the Ottomans felt the effects of this trend. Although the partial increase in monetisation of the Ottoman economy did not transform the peasant into an active participant in the market economy, because peasants still could not transform their produce into cash, it still had an effect because their taxes, paid in kind as a portion of the harvest, could be converted into hard currency by the tax-farmer.

A fief that had no proprietor, if not re-allotted to a new *sipahi* or *zaim* overlord, would be put up for auction and the highest bidder became the tax-farmer (generally for a period of no more than three years). The tax farmer had to pay the state in hard currency but received *ashar* (tithes) from the peasants as produce. The drawback was that in areas where the tax-farming system applied there was no *zaim* or *sipahi* overlord who could be the eyes and ears of the government and be responsible for law and order in their areas of influence. The tax-farmers undertook no such responsibility, did not live on their land and only visited it at harvest time when they came to collect their *ashar.* Consequently, in fiefs belonging to absentee tax-farmers, the *ayan*, provincial notables with wealth, positions of influence and military power, took over, becoming the dominant class in their regions. The state came to depend on them as intermediaries for tax collecting and recruiting men for war. As their power increased, the *ayan* became a kind of squirearchy, similar to the feudal aristocracy of Europe. The empowerment of the *ayan* meant that the central government lost control over the provinces and the centralism ensured by the *timar* system gave way to a decentralised system. However, the abolition of the *timar* system and its replacement by tax farming was a slow process, which took centuries to accomplish. During the reign of Mahmut II, at the beginning of the nineteenth century, there were still Timariot landholdings in existence.

Tax farming was a continual and major source of income for the state, enabling it to pay the wages of additional Janissaries and other classes of salaried foot soldiers in the metropolis. The need for infantry resulted from the development of firearms, muskets in particular. *Sipahis* could not use the heavy musket (the provincial *timar* armies were all cavalry), which was therefore a weapon of the infantry. This development made it necessary to abolish the Timariot *sipahi* system and increase the numbers of the infantry, defrayed by the flow of cash from the tax-farming system.

Increases in the European population, especially
in the Mediterranean area

Population increases in pre-capitalist economies could lead to extremely negative developments because parallel increases in production were much more difficult to achieve than they are today. The results of increased population were hunger and destitution. Brigandage followed in their wake. This was particularly so in the sixteenth century Mediterranean region where, perhaps because there had long been no epidemics, a population explosion took place. In the Anatolian regions of the Ottoman Empire the ensuing chaos was called the 'Jelali Revolt'. This rebellion peaked in 1590–1650 and petered out towards the end of the seventeenth century, probably as a result of the lessening pressure of the dwindling population. During the reign of Süleyman the Magnificent (1520–66) the population of the Empire increased from 12 to 22 million.

Decrease in importance of international caravan trade routes

After the discovery of the sea route to India, the ancient caravan routes through the Middle East, such as the Silk Road, were gradually abandoned. International trade was redirected on to the ocean and the Eastern Mediterranean area became a backwater. Cities and towns whose income was largely generated by overland trade lost their former prosperity. In pre-capitalist times alternative areas of production could not easily compensate after a setback such as this, so economic depression became chronic.

Reaching the limits of conquest

Manpower and animal power turned the wheels of the war machines of the old empires. As they grew they became unwieldy and organic power proved insufficient to protect frontiers.

At its outset the Ottoman state was an extremely successful war machine. It was capable of easily sending armies, ten of thousands strong, to any frontier at a moment's notice. The Ottoman army overcame all obstacles and could counteract any threat. It conquered not only fortresses, towns and cities but whole regions. Conquest was a lucrative business. In Europe feudalism had created a relatively independent aristocracy that was divided by rivalry and had difficulty in gathering a united force equal in power and numbers to the Ottoman army. However, with the passing of time, and as the frontiers of the Empire grew wider, it took longer and longer for the army to reach the borderlands. The speed of the infantry determined the pace at which the army could advance and as war was waged in summer, it was necessary to set out in the rainy spring season to reach the frontiers in time to return home for the harvest. As the empire grew the army was so long on the road that there was little time left to wage war. Furthermore, the Ottomans' European rivals were becoming centralised and therefore capable of gathering great and powerful armies. Victory in the field of battle was becoming more difficult than of old. Consequently as the disadvantages of warfare grew increasingly apparent, interest in warfare and in the army which waged it waned, which resulted in the 'degeneration' of the army. However, for a society with state mechanisms geared for war to suddenly become acclimatised to peace is not easy. Finding no outlet in foreign lands, the lingering inclination for warfare probably had a share in provoking the bloody internal conflict known as the Jelali Revolt.

Influence of the 'Laws of Ibn Khaldun'

Ibn Khaldun of Tunisia lived in Egypt in the fourteenth century and is designated by some as the father of sociology. In his analysis of Islamic history, the *Muqaddimah*, he came to conclusions worthy of serious consideration. According to Ibn Khaldun, Islamic society is the arena for conflict between two divergent forms of society: *medeniyet*-civilised society (*medine* means city in Arabic)—and *bedeviyet*-nomadic society, clans or tribes bonded by kinship. The Bedouins (nomads) possess a high level of solidarity called *asabiyet*. They are a warlike, honest but crude, uncivilised people. The civilised are settled, citified and agricultural societies. Civilised states are under constant attack by the Bedouins and those that have become weak are vanquished by these attacks. A new state thereby arises, ruled by the chieftain of the Bedouins. In the cities of their new country the Bedouins gradually become assimilated by the civilisation they have vanquished. As their level of civilisation increases, they lose their warlike qualities and their solidarity. In four generations (100–120 years) they become sufficiently 'soft' to be vanquished by a new wave of Bedouins. History thus repeats itself over and over again.

According to Niyazi Berkes, the Ottomans were an 'Ibn Khaldun-type' state. Theoretically they should have collapsed in 120 years or so. However they did not come to their 'natural' conclusion, because there was no sufficiently powerful nomadic force to strike the death-blow. The European Great Powers were reluctant to carve up the Empire in case another of their number should capture İstanbul and gain control of the strategically vital Bosphorus and Dardanelles

Straits, and therefore did not allow the Ottoman state to collapse but were content to exploit it. Thus the Empire dragged on, like an aged and terminally ill patient waiting for the end.

Hikmet Kıvılcimlı is another historian who accepts the Ibn Khaldun theory. His sub-theory is that the Ottomans met their end, in accordance with the Ibn Khaldun model, at the battle of Ankara when the Ottoman Sultan Bayezit was defeated by Tamerlane in 1402. Their resuscitation by Mehmet I (Mehmet Çelebi) gave rise to a 'new' or 'second' Ottoman Empire.

Intellectuals of the Ottoman era were familiar with the Ibn Khaldun theory. Accepting the treaties of Carlowitz (1699) and Passarowitz (1718) as proof that the state had grown too old and feeble to wage war, they began to give increasing importance to cultural aspects of life, and beginning with the 'Tulip Era' (1718–30) the Sultans took the lead in encouraging cultural development.

4

PROBLEMS IN THE CULTURAL LIFE OF THE OTTOMAN TURKS

There were many areas in which the Ottomans excelled. Among these were poetry, architecture, ceramics, the art of miniaturisation and classical Turkish music. The ability of the Ottomans for over 400 years to govern the Balkans, whose indigenous population was Christian, and many other provinces and peoples was a triumph of statesmanship and organisational ability. Viewed from the twenty-first century, the Ottomans may not seem to have been liberal in their attitudes, but when their dominion was at its height they represented religious tolerance and were extremely broad-minded in their treatment of vassal peoples and ethnic groups. They became the protectors of the Orthodox Church and shielded Orthodox Christians as well as Protestants from Catholic persecution. They also welcomed Jews fleeing the Spanish Inquisition. In all probability the *timar* system of land tenure, which took the place of European-style feudalism, was less oppressive and did not exploit the peasants to the same extent. It would be illogical and unfair to contend that an administration distanced from its vassals by both language and religion could have ruled the Balkans for centuries by the sword alone. These are significant and positive aspects of the Ottoman regime.

In contrast to their achievements, however, the Ottomans were markedly lacking in certain important aspects of cultural life. Their attitude towards the printing press is a case in point. They thought of books as handmade 'luxury' items, similar to hand-woven carpets, to be possessed by the wealthy alone. It was not considered desirable that they should be printed by presses and come within the means of everyman. Nor was there a demand for such an innovation. Education was generally based on rote learning, without much need for books. Printing presses were established in İstanbul by the Jews in 1493 (in 1495 in Salonika), by the Armenians in 1567, and by the Greeks in 1627. The first Ottoman printing press was established by İbrahim Müteferrika and Sait Çelebi in 1729, 279 years after its invention by Gutenberg and 236 years after the first press began operating in İstanbul. Even at that late date there must have been little demand because the plant shut down in 1742 after printing no more than seventeen books, an average of one a year. When demand finally arose, this same press belatedly resumed production in 1784. The difficulties of cultural and scientific advance for a society lacking a printing press are obvious.

Another glaring cultural deficiency was that of the parochial mosque-schools of the *medrese* system, attended by Muslim Turks. The general situation was that Turkish children, who spoke no Arabic, rote-learned passages from the Koran and a few prayers and were taught precepts of religion with a dash of arithmetic, all in Arabic, presided over by a *hodja* who probably had no real understanding of the Arabic language. No Turkish reading or writing was taught in these schools. Those who did manage to acquire knowledge of their own language did so elsewhere, at home or in the master-apprentice relationship of government service. There were no secondary schools to fill the gap between parochial schools and the supposedly advanced-level *medreses*. Although in the early years of the Empire some *medreses* offered courses in mathematics, medicine, astronomy and science, they were later discontinued and the schools became institutions of religious study only. The language of instruction in the *medrese* was Arabic but since rote learning was considered sufficient, the majority of students and *müderris* (professors) probably had no real understanding either of their subjects or of Arabic.

Compared to the *medrese*, education was much more productive in the Enderun school of Topkapı palace and in other imperial schools. In these institutions, along with religious instruction, courses were taught on military and other subjects, including Arabic, Persian, literature, history, geography, music and art, and the medium of learning was Turkish. The fact that luminaries of eighteenth-century Ottoman culture such as Katip Çelebi and Evliya Çelebi had attended Enderun schools is evidence of the efficacy of these institutions.

Part II
AN EMPIRE IN TRAVAIL

5

THE ROAD TO TANZIMAT

The first decisive steps towards Westernising and modernising Otto-man-Turkish society came with the Tanzimat Proclamation (the Reorganisation), also known as the Rescript of the Rose Chamber or the Gülhane Hatt-ı Hümayunu (the Gülhane Imperial Decree) because it was read out to Ottoman notables and the ambassadors of European states in the rose garden adjacent to the Topkapı palace. The Tanzimat reforms were momentous steps, which were to lead to human rights, the rule of law and freedom and democracy for the Ottoman Turks. This is the point at which the Turks left medieval society behind and entered the New Age. We shall begin with an outline of the events leading to this turning point in Turkish history.

Reform, called *Islahat*, began with the Tulip Period of Ahmet III (1703–30) and continued throughout the eighteenth century. At first attempts at reform were half-hearted and had no results. For example, institutions founded in the eighteenth century were little more than training schools, but named so as to suggest that they were technical colleges. Real reform (the *Islahat*) began after 1789, when Selim III ascended the throne, fostered by Sultan Selim's reformist leanings and also by the faint but potent echoes of the great European upheaval, the French Revolution.

During the reign of Sultan Selim the state was confronted by two grave problems. The first was a serious threat to the unity of the nation presented by the *ayan* (the squirearchy or provincial warlords)

20

who had reached the peak of their power; large and small, they had become prominent in all areas of society. The greatest of them were 'dynasties' on the brink of independence. The Ottoman government had come to depend on them as intermediaries for tax collecting and army recruitment. At the beginning of the nineteenth century two of the great *ayan* were only a breath away from declaring their independence: Tepedelenli Ali Pasha, *ayan* of Janina in Epirus, and Mehmet Ali Pasha, *ayan* of Egypt. Both had enhanced the efficiency and strength of their armies by employing European officers. Mehmet Ali, with the aid of a French officer, had founded a military academy. He had massacred most of the Memluk beys and had become the sovereign lord of all Egypt. He had effected exemplary and major reform in the fields of education, industry and agriculture. Both of these *ayans* had ongoing if unofficial relations with European states. It was evident that these developments curtailed the Sultan's authority and constituted a dire threat to the unity of the Empire.

A second problem of major proportions was posed by the Janissary corps (*the yeniçeri*), which had become a liability. After the state relinquished its policy of conquest, the army lost its position of primary importance and was neglected. A blind eye was then turned to Janissaries who undertook various trades when they could not make ends meet. Busy with their mercantile concerns, they were not inclined to spend their time drilling on the parade ground, whereas the technical development of firearms had heightened the importance of a fully trained army. Battle tactics were still based on two armies facing each other in the field. When the enemy opened fire, the sight of comrades falling on all sides was extremely daunting, and untrained soldiers, no matter how brave, were quickly and easily routed. For the Janissaries to concentrate on training in their barracks instead of earning money in the marketplace, they would have had to receive sufficient pay. Military reform was necessary, not only for success against foreign armies but also to curb the rebellious tendencies of the *ayan*.

Selim III began military reform after consulting his advisers and studying their reports. In 1793 the core of a new disciplined army, the Nizam-i Cedid, was established. It is noteworthy that this name is the Ottoman equivalent of the 'New Order' of the French Revolution. Selim III was careful to move gradually, so as not to excite the wrath of the Janissaries, who were prone to 'overturn their cauldrons' (meaning the Sultan's bounty, rejection of which signified revolt). Additional taxes were imposed as a separate source of income for the separate treasury that was to finance the new army. This was the downside of the Nizam-i Cedid for taxpayers. After the Ottoman victory over Napoleon Bonaparte at Acre in Palestine, the Nizam's strength was increased to 10,000. In 1806, after the Sultan decreed in 1805 that units of the same army should be formed in Edirne (Adrianople), some of the *ayan* of Rumelia rebelled. As the Nizam set off to suppress this rebellion, the Sultan was forced to call them back to control a second rebellion in Tekirdağ (Thrace). The following year a Janissary revolt took place, headed by Kabakçı Mustafa. When Selim hesitated to order the Nizam-i Cedid army into action, things got out of hand and Selim was deposed (1807). Mustafa IV (1807–8) ascended the throne and the Nizam-i Cedid was disbanded.

Sened-i İttifak (the Deed of Agreement)

The surviving reformists fled to the safety of Ruse (Rusçuk), the territory of Alemdar Mustafa Pasha. Finding a pretext to visit İstanbul, Alemdar went to the Topkapı palace with the intention of restoring Selim III to the throne. Sultan Mustafa IV, realising Alemdar Pasha's true intentions, had the palace gates shut and immediately decreed the execution of Selim III and Mahmut, the last two male aspirants to the Ottoman throne. Selim III was executed but Mahmut managed to evade his pursuers, gaining time while Alemdar Pasha was forcing his way into the palace to save him. Mahmut became Sultan Mahmut II (1808–39) with Alemdar Pasha as his Grand Vizier. Alemdar, as kingmaker with his own military forces, was a Grand Vizier of formidable power. His first initiative was to organise a new army, the Sekban-i Cedid corps, similar to the Nizam-i Cedid. He summoned the most influential of the *ayan* to a meeting in İstanbul to find a solution to the problem. His underlying aim was to counteract the threat they presented to the stability of the Empire by giving the *ayan* official status and creating a code of the rights and duties of *ayan*ship, which would, in effect, limit their power.

Meetings were held with the *ayan*, resulting in the Sened-i İttifak, a contract bringing order to the relations between the central authority and the *ayan* in their provinces. In summary, the provisions of this document were that

(1) the *ayan* would be loyal to the Sultan but had the right to protest against any violations of the law;
(2) the *ayan* would help recruit soldiers when necessary and a new army would be established;
(3) taxes would not be unnecessarily burdensome, and would be collected regularly; those allocated to the state would be inviolate; and new taxation would be established only after consultation between the great *ayan* and the government; and
(4) state officials and *ayans* would not be punished and no action would be taken against them unless they were manifestly guilty.

This document had important aspects. If this bill had been put into effect, *ayan*ship would have won official acceptance. The Senet, or contract, might itself have become the first 'constitution' of the Ottoman Empire. The principles it outlined of taxation that was both just and levied by consent were taken up by all democratic revolutions throughout history. It may be said that agreement on taxation marked the beginnings of parliamentarism. The principle concerning the punishment of state officials and *ayan* is a basic one in the struggle for government by law, taken up by all declarations of human rights.

It is arguable that certain aspects of the *Senet* were similar to the English Magna Carta of 1215 between King John and the barons, setting down mutual rights and obligations. Though most of its clauses benefited only the feudal nobility, some contained provisions relating to taxes and justice that were the beginning of the struggle for more freedom and democracy.

Turkish historians' evaluation of the *ayan* and the Sened-i İttifak is generally negative because they view the establishment of a feudal order in nineteenth-century Ottoman domains as a regressive or even reactionary development in direct conflict with trends in Europe. But Mahmut II had found himself powerless to suppress the rebellious Mehmet Ali of Egypt without European support. Thus the Ottoman Empire was becoming quasi-dependent on the Great

Powers whereas, within the framework of the Sened-i İttifak, an agreement with Mehmet Ali might have been reached without foreign interference, salvaging the independence of the state. These, however, are speculative views of no historical validity.

Three and a half months after Alemdar Pasha became the Grand Vizier, the Janissaries rebelled yet again and laid siege to Alemdar's residence. After a pitched battle that went on for hours, Alemdar succumbed to the onslaught and died a hero's death. In the face of this struggle, Mahmut II did not activate his Sekban-i Cedid troops. It may be inferred that he was wary of Alemdar's power and of the Sened-i İttifak. After murdering Alemdar Pasha, the Janissaries turned their attack upon the palace. Mahmut II had Mustafa IV executed to protect his throne, as this made him the sole remaining male heir of the Ottoman line. The Janissaries were forced by this manoeuvre to accept Mahmut as Sultan, but they succeeded in disbanding the Sekban-i Cedid. One by one, all who had had a role in its founding and development were killed. Thus this attempt at military reform was crushed, not to be taken up again until 1826.

The Greek Revolution and the Egyptian Question

In the years that followed, Mahmut tried every method in his power to undermine the power of the *ayan* and in general he was successful. In 1820, however, when it was the turn of Tepedelenli Ali Pasha, the *ayan* of Janina, Mahmut found him a hard nut to crack. The Ottoman army was able to bring Ali Pasha to his knees only after a seventeen-month siege, and even then had to resort to a ruse to do it. Ali Pasha was sent news that the Sultan promised him amnesty and wished to come to terms. Ali ceased hostilities and was summarily executed. While the army was struggling with Tepedelenli the Greeks of the Morea staged an uprising, which became the beginning (1821) of their struggle for independence. While the Muslims of the Morea were being slaughtered by Greek rebels, Mahmut concentrated on the struggle in Janina with Tepedelenli. When at last Janina had fallen and the army was able to move southwards, both the Morea and Athens were in the hands of the revolutionaries. Despite a three-year, all-out effort, the Janissaries were unable to subdue the rebels in the Morea and Athens. Mahmut asked Mehmet Ali Pasha, the governor of Egypt, for help (1824). Mehmet Ali sent an army, commanded by his son İbrahim, which quickly suppressed the rebellion, but this victory was of little account when England, France and Russia intervened, sending a combined naval force that vanquished and totally destroyed the Ottoman-Egyptian fleet at the battle of Navarino. War broke out between the Ottomans and Russia, ending with the Treaty of Adrianople in 1829, whereby the Ottomans recognised the autonomy of Greece, Serbia and Romania. Greece became completely independent in 1830.

These events led to the end of the Janissary corps. The Janissaries had overturned one cauldron too many. Steps were taken to establish a new and disciplined army. When the Janissaries duly rebelled, the government was ready with the combined forces of other military corps. The general populace joined the fight on the side of the government and the Janissaries were annihilated in a bloody encounter. This was called the *Vaka-yi Hayriye*, the 'Auspicious Event'. Those Janissaries who did not escape or hide were killed. A trained army called the Asakir-i Mansure-i Muhammediye (the Victorious Mohammedan Soldiers) was established to replace them.

The Auspicious Event paved the way for reform, with the reforms of Egypt as its model. In 1827 the first Turkish students were sent to be educated in Europe, and the Tıbbiye—the İstanbul School of Medicine, the first Western-style institution of higher learning—was founded. In 1831 an official journal called the *Takvim-i Vekayi* (Calendar of Events), the first Ottoman newspaper, was published. In 1833 the Translation Chamber was founded. Up till the time of the Greek revolution, the only foreign languages spoken by Turks were Arabic (the language of science) and Persian (the language of literature). The Phanariots (the Greeks of the Phanar quarter in İstanbul) were traditionally appointed Dragomans to the Sublime Porte (office of the Grand Vizier). After the Greek rebellion the Porte lost confidence in the Phanariots and began to appoint Turks as dragomans (1821). Methodical instruction in the French language for Turks officially began within the master-apprentice system with the founding of translation chambers. The Harbiye (War College) was established in 1834, and the Mülkiye (School for Civil Servants), a third Western-style school of higher learning, in 1859. The graduates of these three institutions, and of others that followed, formed a nucleus of intellectuals who were to become the leaders of modernisation.

The Committee of Union and Progress, the political organisation of the graduates of these schools, brought about the revolution that inaugurated the Second Constitutional Period (1908–18). An interesting point which highlights the inefficiency of traditional Ottoman-Islamic institutions of learning was that the Western-style colleges were obliged to establish their own primary and secondary schools because of the lack of students capable of following the new curriculum of higher learning. The War College (1834) had its first graduates only in 1848, fourteen years after its foundation.

After the suppression of the Greek revolt, tension developed between the Ottomans and Egypt. Mehmet Ali of Egypt finally came out into the open in 1831, sending an army to Palestine. The Egyptian army emerged victorious from three encounters with the Ottomans. In 1833 the Egyptians advanced to Kütahya, and while they were making preparations to spend the winter in Bursa, Mahmut was faced with two equally unpleasant alternatives. He had either to come to terms with Mehmet Ali or to seek the help of foreign powers. Mahmut opted for the second alternative. At that point Britain and France were too preoccupied with each other to pay attention to Ottoman affairs. That left the Russians, to whom Mahmut applied for help even as he quoted the famous adage 'He who falls into the sea will embrace a snake' (whereas, instead of embracing the snake he could have embraced Mehmet Ali…). The Russians reacted with enthusiasm; they came to İstanbul and settled in areas around the Bosphorus. These developments caught the attention of the other Great Powers, creating great agitation in the West. Franco-British intervention resulted in a treaty, signed in Kütahya, under which Mehmet Ali's son İbrahim became governor of Jedda, Damascus, Aleppo and Adana (1833).

The treaty of 1838

For a Sultan as jealous of his authority as Mahmut, this situation was intolerable and had to be 'corrected'. The following years saw the enactment of decisive reforms, which it was hoped would strengthen the Empire and also help to gain European support. Mahmut went even further to ensure British aid and support, and in 1838 the Ottoman-British Trade Agreement was signed, giving

Britain further privileges in addition to those previously ensured by Capitulations:

(1) British products would not be subject to any domestic tax after the payment of import duty of 5% or export duty of 12%. This clause was unfair to native merchants whose goods were subject to domestic taxes.

(2) Certain goods would no longer be the subject to Ottoman monopolies (*yed-i vahit*). Thus British merchants who could purchase such goods directly from the producers, bargaining with each individually, would in effect determine prices.

(3) The British would be allowed to participate in domestic trade within the Ottoman borders.

According to Doğan Avcızoğlu, this treaty brought about the collapse of traditional guild industry and prevented Ottoman society from participating in the Industrial Revolution and developing a capitalist economy, and was therefore a 'death sentence'. Other historians argue that, even without the treaty, classical Ottoman industry could not have withstood the onslaught of the Industrial Revolution. Neither case can be definitely proved, but either way it is certain that the Ottoman-British Trade Agreement played a part in the downfall of traditional Ottoman industry.

In 1839 the Ottoman and Egyptian armies met for a fourth time at the battle of Nizip and the Ottoman army was vanquished yet again, a demonstration of military bankruptcy. It had become evident to all that the Ottomans had lost their military power. Consequently the army lost, for a long period, its influence in matters of domestic policy. Thereafter the Pashas who came to power generally had no practical knowledge of warfare—instead they spoke fluent French and were masters of diplomacy. The Ottoman state was now kept alive not by military victories but by diplomatic agility. As the army was experiencing bitter defeat at the battle of Nizip and the navy fled to Egypt, Mahmut II lay dying. However, this demoralising state of affairs did not last long. The new Sultan, Abdülmecit, chose as his mentor the reformist Mustafa Reşit Pasha. The British gave their full support and the situation at Nizip was reversed. In the end Mehmet Ali lost all the provinces he had gained at Kütahya and had to be content with the hereditary title to the governorship of Egypt.

The proclamation of Tanzimat (the Reorganisation)

At this juncture Mustafa Reşit Pasha was able to convince the Sultan that only by the Proclamation of Tanzimat could the goodwill and support of the West be ensured. The proclamation, also called the *Gülhane Hatt-ı Hümayunu* (the Rescript of the Rose Chamber), declared that by implementing it the country would be well on the road to recovery within five or ten years.

Matters to be addressed by its regulations were (1) security of life, honour and property; (2) abolition of the tax-farming system; and (3) reorganisation of military service, limiting it to periods of four or five years. The proclamation promised that new laws would be promulgated for the good of the people. Bribery was outlawed. Capital punishment without trial was abolished and justice guaranteed for all, equally for both Muslims and non-Muslims, irrespective of race and creed. The proclamation issued an official invitation to European states to stand witness to its tenets.

The section referring to security of life and property was important in that although normal citizens were relatively secure, state officials were still under *kul* status, which meant that they could be politically executed and were liable to confiscation. Although confiscation had been abolished in 1826, Pertev Pasha (Mustafa Reşit Pasha's mentor) had attracted the wrath of Mahmut II and had been politically executed. Tanzimat put an end to *kul* status and gave state officials security of life and property. The abolition of tax farming stood for two years but obstructionist tax-farmers and a disorganised bureaucracy combined to make it impossible for the government to collect its tax income outside the system. Tax farming and tithes were brought to an end only after the establishment of the Turkish Republic (in 1925). The question of military service was also addressed. Tanzimat recruitment had previously been arbitrary with some geographical areas providing the bulk of recruits while others provided none at all. In addition, once a soldier was recruited he could possibly spend the rest of his life in military service. This system was partly if not fully revised.

The provision that brought equality between Muslims and non-Muslims was a revolutionary innovation. During the rise of the Empire the Ottomans had maintained a tolerant attitude towards non-Muslims but after the seventeenth century, with its series of defeats, non-Muslims began to be despised as inferiors and were subject to ill-treatment.

The fact that Tanzimat was officially communicated to the representatives of European states shows that they were to have some role in its implementation, that they were in effect to become its guarantors. Fuat Pasha, one of the foremost statesmen of the Tanzimat era, explained the role of the Great Powers thus: 'A state has two sources of power. One comes from above, one from below. In our country the power from above is crushing us all and it is not possible to muster power from below. For this reason we need to make use of a force like the glancing blows of a cobbler's *mushta* (an iron ball, used for pounding shoes into shape and smoothing their seams). That (lateral force) is the power of the embassies.' The source of power from above, referred to by the Pasha, was the Sultan, and that which should emanate from below was the power of the people. An excellent summary of the dynamics of Ottoman politics, these words describe the great power of the Sultan, the passivity of the people and the impotence of the statesmen. As a result the Pashas were obliged to depend on the support of the Great Powers in order to achieve a relative position of strength against the Sultan. For example, Mustafa Reşit, Hüseyin Avni and Mithat Pasha availed themselves of British support, Âli and Fuad Pashas had the backing of the French and Mahmut Nedim Pasha relied on the Russians.

It should be understood that after the military bankruptcy of 1839 the Ottomans were no longer a truly independent state, but had become a quasi-dependency of Europe. The interesting aspect of the Ottoman situation was that they were not the colony of one specific state, but had fallen into the position of being the collective quasi-dependency of all of the Great Powers of Europe. It is obvious that there were great advantages to being the dependency of several Powers rather than of a single one. The Ottomans benefited from the rivalry between the Great Powers, playing one against the other and thereby finding a certain freedom to manoeuvre to their own advantage. However, Russia attempted from time to time to gain sole predominance over the Ottoman Empire (1833, 1853, 1878), but at each attempt, confronted by the combined forces of the other Powers, it was forced to back down. The Eastern Question was, on the one hand, the story of the struggle between the rival Powers of

Europe against the Ottomans, to gain power or geopolitical advantage in the crumbling Ottoman Empire. On the other it was the history of the Balkan nationalities' struggle for independence from Ottoman rule. In a nutshell it is the story of the dismemberment of the Ottoman Empire.

Many Turkish nationalist writers view Tanzimat with a critical eye because it came at a time when the Ottomans had become dependent upon the goodwill of the European imperial powers. Although it is true that Tanzimat coincided with a low ebb in Ottoman fortunes, 'We should not burn the quilt for a flea.' It must not be forgotten that Tanzimat was the beginning of the Turkish national struggle for civil rights and constitutional government.

6

THE REFORM DECREE AND
THE YOUNG OTTOMANS

In 1853 the question of the Holy Places of Palestine served Russia as
a pretext to supersede the other European Powers and gain control
over the Ottoman Empire. When the Ottomans rose in opposition
to this threat with Anglo-French support, the Crimean War followed. This conflict took place between the Ottoman Empire,
Britain, France and Sardinia on one side and Russia on the other.
Russia was defeated and the Congress of Paris was convoked to
make the peace. In order to strengthen the Ottoman Empire against
Russian aggression, the Treaty of Paris (1856) stipulated that Ottoman independence and territorial integrity would be respected and
that the Ottomans would be sheltered under the umbrella of European law. The Empire was thereby 'Europeanised'. In return the
Ottoman government promulgated the Reform Decree (1856)
which reaffirmed the Tanzimat proclamation and went a step further, establishing detailed edicts making Muslims and non-Muslims
equal before the law. It was not strictly true that the Ottoman
Empire was viewed as a European state and that its territorial rights
were to be respected. This was made evident while the Paris Congress was still in session. The Ottoman representative Âli Pasha
proposed that since the Ottoman state was to be subject to European
law, the Capitulations should be rescinded, but his suggestion was
ignored by all the other delegates. As for 'territorial integrity', it was
to mean in effect that the Ottoman Empire could be broken up and
shared out if and when the Great Powers came to an amicable
agreement among themselves.

Within the Ottoman Empire equal rights accorded to non-
Muslims were greeted with sarcasm: 'The infidel will no longer be

31

called by the name of infidel'. Riots directed against the Christians of Jedda, Lebanon and Damascus got so out of hand that the British and French intervened. Muslims still saw themselves as the masters of the state and were infuriated by the overtly European lifestyles of the non-Muslim minority bourgeoisie, who had grown prosperous through various professions or through commerce and even industrial manufacturing by working in partnership with Westerners and uti-lising their capital. As if this was not enough, they had now gained equal rights. These were the Muslims' reasons for reaction.

The Young Ottomans

In order to understand fully the Young Ottoman movement it is first necessary to consider developments in journalism, because jour-nalists were the movement's most influential members. The first Ottoman newspaper was the official state gazette, the *Takvim-i Vekayi* (1831), followed by the British-owned *Ceride-i Havadis* (1840), which was also semi-official in character. The real beginning of independent journalism came in 1860 with the weekly *Tercüman-i Ahval* owned by Çapanzade Agah Efendi. The eminent writer and poet Şinasi began his career working for it. In the years after 1860 there was a great increase in the number of Turkish newspapers. Circulation was low, but in those days neighbourhood coffee shops, *kıraathane*, served in the evenings as meeting places and reading rooms where newspapers were read aloud to those present, influ-encing a broader spectrum of society than might be supposed from their narrow circulation. Soon competition arose among this variety of newspapers. Articles addressing important issues and critical of the *status quo* to grab public attention were in demand. This devel-opment inevitably caused displeasure in official circles, and in 1864 the government issued the 'Press Regulations'. These opened the way for punitive measures such as closures, fines and imprisonment. The Regulations probably precipitated the founding of Meslek (profession), a secret society of prominent journalists including the revolutionary writer-poet Namık Kemal, with the aim of under-mining the Âli Pasha administration. Membership later rose to 245. The society has been known as the Patriotic Alliance, but Meslek was its true name.

In the past the Turkish word for liberty or freedom—*hürriyet*—
had merely denoted the state of not being a slave, but it now began to
take on new political connotations. For journalists such as Namık
Kemal 'freedom' meant, above all, freedom of the press. In criticising
trends derived from the West, conservatives tritely insist that the
West has been the source only of superficial innovations such as blue
jeans and neckties for men. It may be true that the latter are both
imitative and superficial, but, though perhaps also inspired by
Western trends, the concept of political freedom appears to have
developed in answer to social need.

The year 1867 was pregnant with momentous events. Mustafa
Fazıl Pasha was a member of the Kavalalı dynasty that ruled Egypt;
he was the brother of Egypt's governor İsmail Pasha and next in line
for the governorship. While Mustafa Fazıl Pasha was in state service
in İstanbul he fell into disfavour with Fuat Pasha, one of the most
powerful government figures, and was consequently relieved of his
duties and exiled to Europe. Shortly after this the hereditary governorship of Egypt was changed to a system of primogeniture, elimi-
nating Fazıl Pasha from the succession. Greatly provoked, Fazıl Pasha
wrote and had published an open letter in which he analysed the
problems besetting the Ottoman state. This letter referred openly to
the 'Young Turks' and reached the conclusion that only through
constitutional monarchy could the Empire's problems be resolved.
Thus a new concept of freedom emerged, beyond freedom of the
press, encompassing a demand for constitutional government. The
word 'Young' symbolised and denoted loyalty to the principles of
the French Revolution—Liberty, Equality, Fraternity—and opposition to feudalism and absolute monarchy. When in later years
Mustafa Kemal Atatürk, founder of the Turkish Republic, entrusted
the new Turkish Republic to its 'youth', it was very probably these
ideals that were in his mind. (During this period there were also
'Young Italy' and 'Young Germany' movements in Europe.) In this
system of constitutional monarchy, an elected legislative body was
entrusted with limiting the power of the government and the
monarch.

Fazıl Pasha's open letter to the press had far-reaching repercussions. The government was awakened to the danger posed by the
liberal movement. Namık Kemal, Ziya Pasha and Ali Suavi were

ordered to leave İstanbul, and a government takeover organised by the Meslek Society failed. Fazıl Pasha called upon the Young Turks to continue their struggle from the safety of France. In Paris eight members of Meslek, including Namık Kemal, Fazıl Pasha, Ziya and Ali Suavi, established the Young Ottoman Society and began to publish a newspaper. In the liberal environment of Europe these young revolutionaries gained the opportunity to develop their ideology and have their ideas published freely.

The most distinguished of the Young Ottomans was Namık Kemal. His writing and poetry had far-reaching, revolutionary impact, not only on his own generation but also on the next generation of which Mustafa Kemal Atatürk was a member. Namık Kemal gained renown as the poet of 'the motherland and liberty'. We have referred to the evolving concept of liberty, let us now take up the subject of the motherland, the idea of 'belonging' to a country. Before this period of Ottoman history, a person's land was merely the place where he happened to have been born and where he resided—his native region or town. People spoke and thought of themselves as being from İstanbul or Ankara, not as citizens of the Ottoman Empire. All the land was considered to be property of the Sultan; people were loyal not to the land itself but to him and if necessary were expected to fight for him and/or for their religion, not for their country.

Namık Kemal with his poetry and prose changed this mode of thinking. He widened the concept of *vatan* or motherland, which took on deeply emotional overtones. One's country was not simply an area of land but a beloved place for which great sacrifices could willingly be made and for which one might lay down one's life.

Namık Kemal returned to İstanbul in 1870, and in 1873 his play *Vatan Yahut Silistre* (The Motherland or Silistre) was staged. Audiences were electrified by the concepts portrayed, by the idea that they, the people, had an independent claim to their country. Spontaneous demonstrations took place during the performance and overflowed into the streets after each performance. The play was banned and its author exiled to Magosa, Cyprus. We do not know the exact motive for this but it is certain that Sultan Abdülaziz and his government were unsettled by the new ideas being propounded. Love of country, viewed in this light, implied loyalty to something other than the Sultan, relegating him to second place. It implied that the people had a proprietary interest in the land which the Sultan considered his own property. This was an individualistic and democratic mode of thinking, irreconcilable with the values of absolute monarchy. A further point was the idea of a country having a separate entity. Even under the harshest absolutist regimes in Europe, the country had a name separate from the dynasty by which it was ruled (Russia, Prussia, France), whereas the Ottoman state bore the name of the line of Osman. The name 'Turkey' first emerged in Europe and was officially adopted much later by the Turkish Grand National Assembly during the War of Independence.

Namık Kemal took the ideology of the French Revolution and clothed it in terms acceptable to and easily assimilated by Muslims. For example, he cited the *biat* (oath of allegiance) ceremony as an Islamic parallel of Jean-Jacques Rousseau's theory of the 'Social Contract'. In the *biat* ceremony subjects accepted the authority of the Sultan and in return were deemed to have a contract with him in which he promised to refrain from oppression and to be just in his dealings with them. It could therefore be maintained that if there was injustice they had the right to resist. Political rights and the parliamentary system were interpreted as being analogous to the *meşveret* command of the Koran which orders the faithful to 'take counsel'. Other concepts introduced to the Turkish people by Namık Kemal were:

— All men are born free.
— The state is not an entity separate from the people and cannot have interests separate from theirs.
— Education should be in the Turkish language. Liberation from the yoke of Latin had helped European development, and development of the Ottoman state would likewise be helped by liberation from Arabic.

'Our future is secure. *Fıkıh* [Muslim canonical jurisprudence] states "Judgements change with the passage of time *kad tegayyürül ahkâm betebdilil zaman*"]. We are obliged to accept the fruits of progress. It is not permitted for us to return to the past or remain unchanged in the present.' (from Namık Kemal's article 'Our Future is Secure')

According to Namık Kemal, all who lived in the lands of the Osmanlı were Ottoman, no matter what religion they professed or what language they spoke. This was called 'the unity of nationalities', also Ottomanism or Ottoman nationalism. This concept was undeservedly ridiculed during the Republican era. Switzerland is an excellent case in point. In Switzerland as many as four languages are spoken: French in Geneva, Vaud, Neuchatel, Fribourg and Valais; German by two-thirds of the population; Italian in the canton of Ticino bordering Italy and Romansh in the canton of Grisons. But Switzerland is certainly a nation, accepted universally as such, and even a power-mad tyrant such as Hitler never seriously entertained the idea of annexing or 'liberating' its German-speaking cantons. Belgium is another such example. From this it follows that the concepts of nationality and nationalism exist in the mind of the individual, separate and independent of language, religion and, in some cases, the geographical limits of the land itself. If a human being believes himself to be of a certain nationality and is loyal to a certain country, the fact that he does not speak the language of the country or is of a different creed from the majority of its population is irrelevant to his belief. The British historian A.J.P. Taylor argues that the Austro-Hungarian and Ottoman Empires collapsed not because of their mixed ethnic structures but because they were defeated in the First World War.

7

THE FIRST CONSTITUTIONAL MONARCHY AND THE GREAT CRISIS

Financial crisis opened the way for Turkey's first period of constitutional monarchy, called the First Meshrutiyet (*Birinci Meşrutiyet*). This is an interesting example of history repeating itself. Many a breakthrough in mankind's struggle for freedom has taken place as a result of financial crises. In Britain such a situation arose in the Revolution of the 1640s. The insistence of King Charles I on increased taxation and additional levies, coupled with the irresponsible manner in which these were used, gave rise to an armed struggle between monarchy and Parliament. In France the States-General, which had not been convened since 1614, was summoned in 1789 by the French King who was in need of funds and had no alternative but to reconvene it. This same assembly launched the French Revolution. Another case in point was the American Revolution, sparked off by unfair taxation.

In 1854, with the start of the Crimean war, the Porte began to borrow from Europe; bonds were issued by financial institutions and sold to investors in the money markets of Europe. However, only a very small part of this credit was apportioned to public projects or productive schemes such as railway-building; most was wasted on luxuries for the court and non-productive areas such as the purchase of arms. During the reign of Sultan Abdülaziz the Ottoman navy became the second largest in Europe measured by tonnage. For the marriage of one of Abdülmecit's twelve children, Fatma Sultana, to Ali Galip, the son of Mustafa Reşit Pasha, 2 million pounds in gold were spent on a wedding celebration which continued for fifteen days. In time money spent in this way created a vicious circle of debt incurred to pay former debts. As confidence in Ottoman financial

37

policies decreased, credit could only be obtained on increasingly unfavourable terms at ruinous rates of interest. Officially one-fourteenth of the state budget was allocated to palace expenses, but it was rumoured that the palace was actually spending one-seventh of all income. Famine in certain rural areas (people had died of malnutrition in the Ankara area) hastened the inevitable end of this situation. Grand Vizier Mahmut Nedim Pasha was forced to declare the bankruptcy of the state with the Reduction of Interest Decision, taken on 6 October 1875. This reduced interest on bonds that had been issued on behalf of the Ottoman government; only half would be paid for a period of five years, and bonds with an annual yield of 5% per annum would be given in lieu of unpaid interest.

Thus after economic (1838) and military (1839) bankruptcy the Empire had become financially bankrupt and more dependent on European goodwill than ever before. The bond-holders' 50% loss of revenue led to furious protests from British and French creditors who held a large proportion of these bonds. Public opinion in Europe now turned against the Ottomans. Until the Reduction of Interest Decision, there had been sympathy for their plight and a belief that they were doing their best to make progress. This was now reversed and the Ottoman state was viewed as sunk in barbarism.

In the early months of 1875 a major uprising broke out among the Christian peasants of Herzegovina. In the Balkans generally there was an accumulation of enmity towards the unprogressive Ottoman administration. Nationalist sentiment among the Slavs was on the rise, and Ottoman rule was seen as an intolerable burden of injustice. Russia was doing all in its power to fan the flames. Austria-Hungary viewed this nationalist trend with anxiety, since it harboured the intent to extend its sphere of influence south towards Salonika. If Bosnia were to unite with Serbia, Montenegro might also join this union, creating a large and powerful Serbia with a numerous population which could possibly become a source of instability and furthermore obstruct Austria's southward expansion. For these reasons Austria wanted to get hold of Bosnia-Herzegovina. It had instigated the Herzegovina revolt, and when it quickly spread the Powers intervened with demands for reform.

In May 1876 the Bulgars also rebelled against Ottoman rule, and after the slaughter of a great number of Muslims the revolt was suppressed, with much loss of life on both sides. According to our sources, 1,000 Turks and 4,500 Bulgars were killed. Westerners generally ignore the Turkish losses and dwell on those of the Bulgars which they insist numbered 15,000. In Britain the leader of the opposition Liberal Party, W.E. Gladstone, took advantage of the anti-Ottoman sentiment aroused by the Reduction of Interest Decision and initiated a campaign against the Conservative Party, which was then in power and had supported the Ottomans.

On 30 May 1876 the newly empowered Muterdjim Rüştü Pasha government forced Sultan Abdülaziz to abdicate the throne (he committed suicide four days later). The Sultan was blamed for inept administration and held personally responsible for the disastrous financial situation. The new Sultan was Murat V. In this new reign, two government factions presented viable alternatives which would bring about government control of palace profligacy. The reformist group leader Mithat Pasha insisted that constitutional monarchy was the best solution because only an elected parliament could control palace spending. Another influential government minister, Hüseyin Avni Pasha, and his group were in favour of different measures, arguing that the Sultan must be relegated to the position of a symbolic figurehead with no political power and that all authority must be vested in the government. 'Constitutional Monarchy is not for us,' he stated. The government initially adopted the second solution, but at this juncture Hüseyin Avni was murdered by Abdülaziz's adjutant and it became evident that Murat V was mentally incapacitated. These events opened the way for constitutional monarchy, to which the heir apparent, Abdülhamit, meeting Mithat Pasha, promised to accede if he were allowed to succeed to the throne. Murat V, who had reigned for only three months, was dethroned.

The Tersane Conference

The new Sultan Abdülhamit decreed that work should begin on a constitution, thus keeping his promise to the government and also hoping to prevent European intervention. All the Ottoman peoples or *millets* were to elect representatives to Parliament which would enact the necessary reforms. Meanwhile the Great Powers had already organised an international conference of ambassadors in İstanbul who were to discuss Balkan reform. On 23 December 1876, just as the ambassadors' conference was about to begin at Tersane (the Dockyards), the roar of cannon fire announced the advent of the Constitution, and of the new system of constitutional monarchy called *Meşrutiyet*. The Foreign Minister Saffet Pasha took the podium, declaring that since the Ottoman people, through the establishment of a constitutional and representative government, had assumed control of state affairs themselves there were no matters left for the conference to discuss. The delegates stonily ignored this *fait accompli* and went on with their discussions without any signs of recognition of the new constitutional government. At the conference a comprehensive plan for reform was prepared that would carry Bulgaria and Bosnia-Herzogovina towards autonomy. The Ottomans were warned that in the event of this plan being rejected all ambassadors would leave İstanbul and in all probability Russia would declare war.

After consultation in an extraordinary council the Ottoman government rejected the foreigners' plan, and the ambassadors accordingly quit İstanbul. Sixteen days after the conference Abdülhamit relieved Grand Vizier Mithat Pasha of his duties and sent him into exile. But 'the arrow had left the bow' and there could be no turning back from constitutional monarchy. Under the Constitution Parliament was to consist of two assemblies: the Chamber of Deputies elected by a two-stage system and the Chamber of Notables (the Senate) appointed by the Sultan. Elections were held and on 20 March 1877 the first Parliament was convened. After a two-month term a new parliament reconvened towards the end of 1877, and at the beginning of 1878 another two-month sitting took place. The fact that Ottoman society was able to establish an elected parliament in 1877 was a landmark in Turkey's move towards democracy (Russia, for example, had its first elected parliament as late as 1906).

For a country experiencing democracy for the first time the Chamber of Deputies acted with noteworthy maturity. Though almost half of its members were non-Muslims, the body showed exemplary Ottoman solidarity in the face of war. Examination of official records of the Chamber gives the clear impression of a government and administration wallowing in the depths of ignorance, corruption, incompetence and oppression. In striking contrast, Parliament was generally progressive, libertarian, rationalist and determined to uphold government by law on all occasions. Its criticism of government incompetence was objective and made with loyalty to the state as its over-riding concern.

After the rejection of the Tersane conference decisions, the Great Powers met in London and modified their demands, but Abdülhamit and his government again rejected them with the ratification of Parliament. This was a brave stand since it was apparent that Russia was spoiling for war.

The Ottoman government must have been over-confident regarding the strength of its army and in its expectation that if the worst happened the British would come to its aid as they had done in the Crimean war. The country was united by what may only be described as a nationalist spirit. On 24 April 1877 the Russians began the 1877–8 Russo-Ottoman war, known in Turkish history as the '93 war' (1877 was 1293 according to the Muslim calendar). Although the war ended in defeat for the Ottomans, the army proved, with its successful defence of Plevne in Bulgaria (with troops commanded by Gazi Osman Pasha) and of Erzurum in Anatolia (commanded by Gazi Ahmet Muhtar Pasha), that the 1839 'military bankruptcy' was a thing of the past.

With the Russian army in sight of İstanbul, the Treaty of San Stefano was imposed upon the Ottomans. Romania, Serbia and Montenegro, till then autonomous, gained total independence. Bulgaria became an autonomous principality with a coast on the Aegean sea, thereby cutting off Ottoman land access to Albania and Macedonia. Russia annexed the regions of Kars, Ardahan and Batum; Austria gained control of Bosnia-Herzegovina. Britain considered these conditions excessively harsh, and its navy entered the Sea of Marmara. On this development Germany intervened and the Congress of Berlin was called by the German Chancellor, Bismarck. The Treaty of Berlin (1878) created a smaller autonomous Bulgarian principality and a region with special status, the province of Eastern Rumelia, centred around Plovdiv. Macedonia was returned to the Ottomans, thereby ensuring the integrity of Ottoman territory. All other conditions were as before.

In declaring war against the Ottoman empire, Russia perhaps had in mind an aim beyond its traditional pursuit of territorial aggrandisement and regional domination. In this instance it was making war on the ideological challenge presented by the Ottoman constitutional government. Ever since the French Revolution Russia had become a defender of absolute monarchy and never had any hesitation in activating its armies in its defence.

As the Russian army neared İstanbul, Abdülhamit suspended Parliament. But this was not exactly the end of the first period of constitutional monarchy because, although Parliament was not reconvened, Abdülhamit acted as though constitutional government was to be restored. All laws were enacted with the provision that they would be 're-debated when Parliament was in session' and new members were appointed to the Senate. In April 1880, however, Britain held a general election and Gladstone's Liberal Party came to power. Because it was openly anti-Ottoman, it seems probable that Abdülhamit decided there was nothing to gain from keeping alive the pretence that he was going to recall the Turkish Parliament. Thus after 1880 the Ottomans were condemned to a downward slide into an increasingly repressive absolute monarchy.

8

THE ERA OF ABDÜLHAMIT II

Abdülhamit was Sultan for the very long period of thirty-three years. His sultanate is known for having been a police state, but although this is certainly true, the repressive regime evolved gradually. Abdülhamit's first major abuse of power was the destruction of Mithat Pasha, an outstanding governor who had realised many developmental projects during his governorships of Bulgaria and of Baghdad. He was also the founding father of several long-lasting Turkish institutions, some of which still exist today: the Agricultural Bank of Turkey (*Ziraat Bankası*), the Social Security Fund and the institution of Vocational and Industrial Schools. Highly regarded by liberals and conservatives alike, Mithat Pasha became the personification of constitutional government in the minds of the people. Abdülhamit first sent him into exile in 1877, but pardoned him the next year and allowed him to return. He was made governor of Syria, but was prevented from initiating any projects or distinguishing himself in any way. In 1880 he was made governor of İzmir and then arrested on the charge of having conspired to murder Sultan Abdülaziz. After a rigged trial which took place in a tent within the grounds of the Yıldız palace he was found guilty and condemned to death, but under pressure from Western public opinion the sentence was commuted. But while incarcerated in Taif, today a city of Saudi Arabia, he was strangled by prison guards. Despite Abdülhamit's protestations that he gave no such order, there is no doubt that he was, at least, politically responsible. Thus Abdülhamit resurrected in an underhand manner the practice of 'political execution'.

During Sultan Abdülhamit's reign it became imperative to bring some kind of order to the chaos born of the 1875 bankruptcy. With the 1881 Muharrem Decree the revenue from certain taxes was allotted to the Ottoman Public Debt Administration (OPDA), established under foreign auspices, which was to be responsible to European bondholders for payment on their bonds. It collected certain taxes in the same way as the Ministry of Finance, but distributed this income directly to creditors. To avert bankruptcy in future, Abdülhamit closely supervised palace expenses. His policy of economy resulted not only in a decrease in the national debt but also in an immense increase of his personal fortune, making him one of the richest men in the country.

Another positive aspect of Abdülhamit's reign was the great advances made in education. For example, from 1867 to 1895 the number of Muslim students attending secondary schools increased fourfold to 33,469 students. However, despite this increase more than twice this number of non-Muslim students attended secondary schools (76,359). Since the total Muslim population was three times the non-Muslim population, it follows that the ratio of educated non-Muslims to Muslims was six to one. In short, advances were made in the field of education, but they were insufficient.

Foreign financing became available for various projects after the OPDA had restored confidence in the financial stability of the Empire. Progress was made in transport by major extensions to the railways. Railways in the Ottoman domains were generally built by foreign capital, with Germany in the dominant position with its Haydarpasha-Baghdad-Basra project. However, the Damascus-Hejaz railway was built by the Ottomans themselves to convey pilgrims on the *Haj* to Mecca.

Abdülhamit was of an excessively suspicious and morbid nature verging on mental disorder. This was reflected in the extreme importance he put on his secret police organisation. People were encouraged to report 'suspicious behaviour' to the Palace, and informers were rewarded even if their reports later turned out to be baseless. An atmosphere of fear and suspicion prevailed. Stringent government censorship was applied to the press. Cartoons or humorous references were prohibited. Newspapers sent all news and articles to the censor every evening. Prohibited sections were deleted and newspapers were often printed with large blank spaces. Censors, afraid of dire consequences to themselves, took no chances in their application of censorship rules and were even more strict than the Sultan himself (the fact that the Sultan's nose was large was sufficient cause for them to delete the word 'nose'). The state's official gazette, the *Takvim-i Vekayi*, was shut down in 1890 (the state was without an official organ till 1908) owing to a printing error which was somehow thought to show the Sultan in a bad light.

The birth of the Committee of Union and Progress (CUP)

In 1889, the hundredth anniversary of the French Revolution, five students of the İstanbul Military School of Medicine established a secret society called the Ottoman Union Association. The best known of its founders were Abdullah Cevdet and İbrahim Temo. The main activity of this fledgling society consisted of reading the works of Namık Kemal and other writers of liberal persuasion. It was a kind of secret discussion group. In 1895 the association made contact in Paris with the Positivist Ahmet Riza, who gave them the idea of calling themselves the İttihat ve Terakki Cemiyeti (Committee of Union and Progress—CUP).

The Armenian movement

It was in 1895 that the Armenian Question exploded on the political scene of İstanbul. After the Congress of Berlin there were no non-Muslim subject peoples other than the Armenians in the Ottoman domains who had not attained either autonomy or independence, and American missionaries, who had established many schools and hospitals in Anatolia, were encouraging the Armenians towards the same goal. Furthermore the Treaty of San Stefano contained an article ensuring reform under the supervision of the Great Powers in six provinces of Anatolia (Van, Bitlis, Elazığ, Diyarbakır, Erzurum and Sivas), a huge territory historically known as Armenia. The Treaty of Berlin also contained this provision. However, the circumstances of the Armenians were complicated by two aspects in which they were different from the other Christian groups of the Empire. One was the geopolitical situation of 'Armenia': the region was inaccessible to the Great Powers, being isolated by mountainous terrain. The second consideration was that the Armenians no longer constituted a majority group in the historic region of Armenia; plying various trades, they lived scattered throughout the Empire.

Even in Bitlis, the most densely populated area of Armenian habitation, they amounted to only one-third of the population.

Armenian revolutionary societies—the Hinchak established in 1887 and the Tashnaksutyun in 1890—organised their revolts along the lines of what may be called the 'Bulgarian model': bloody rebellions which were suppressed in turn with much loss of life, thereby attracting the attention of the Great Powers and ensuring their intervention. Incidents broke out in Musa Bey, Erzurum and Kumkapı in 1890, in Merzifon, Kayseri and Yozgat in 1892–3, and in Sasun in 1894. Following the rejection of the Armenian reform plan prepared jointly by Russia and Britain, bloody encounters broke out in the streets of İstanbul between Muslims and Armenians, lasting for three days. These riots were exacerbated by the action of Abdülhamit in pulling the police forces off the streets. In the face of these events that seemed to herald the demise of the Empire, the Committee of Union and Progress was goaded into action. In two declarations pasted on walls throughout İstanbul, it asserted that the Armenians were right to defy the Abdülhamit regime, but that instead of standing alone they should unite with all the other Ottoman peoples under the flag of the CUP. With the CUP in open defiance of the administration, pressure on all liberals and intellectuals was intensified. CUP members fled the country, many to France. Those who stayed behind tried to stage two more anti-government coups in 1896 and 1897, but both were discovered at an early stage.

The CUP codified its regulations in 1895. Several points of interest emerge from this code. Structurally, this secret society was divided into separate 'cells' so that if members were caught by the police they would not endanger the whole organisation during interrogation. The fact that the CUP declared its opponents to be enemies of the homeland shows that from its outset it saw itself as an organisation whose goals were sacrosanct and which would brook no differences of opinion from anyone. The CUP felt itself justified in going to any lengths to accomplish its mission of modernising Turkey as quickly as possible. Another striking characteristic was that it was actively liberal in its stand on women's rights, putting women members on an equal footing with men and giving them the same rights and duties. This position was noteworthy because, at the time, governmental guidelines for the segregation of women were draconian. A woman was not allowed to be seen in the streets accompanied by a man, even though he might be her brother, husband or father. In such a society the fact of a revolutionary association such as the CUP welcoming female members and giving them equal rights highlights the degree of its ideological liberation.

Ahmet Rıza and Positivism

In 1889, as the CUP was being established, the young Ahmet Rıza went to Paris to visit the Exhibition marking the hundredth anniversary of the French Revolution. He stayed in Europe till 1908, becoming a follower of the Positivist movement started by Auguste Comte (1798–1857). The French Revolution had at one point exalted rationalist philosophy to the position of an unofficial religion, synonymous with the Revolution, but after Napoleon's defeat at Waterloo there was a reversion in France to pre-revolutionary conditions which gave rise to a reaction against rationalism. Comte argued that revolutionism and rationalism were two separate concepts which should be considered individually, and that sociology made it possible to discover the rules that governed society, thus making it possible to reshape society scientifically and ensure its advance without resorting to revolution. The two principles of Positivism—order and progress—envisaged the 'orderly progress' of society. The principle of progress had great influence on the Ottoman liberal movement, causing it to change its name from the Ottoman Union Association to the Committee of Union and Progress. According to Ahmet Rıza, Ottoman society was to be saved more by the creation of a new type of human being than by the Constitution. This new man would be one who 'earned his bread by the sweat of his brow' and did not 'seek advancement to the detriment of another'. This could only be brought about by the domination of science and a higher level of education in general.

The liberal movement lost momentum for a period after 1897. Its ineffective attempts to overthrow absolutism on the one hand, and the prestige gained by Abdülhamit from the 1897 victory of the Ottoman army over the Greeks on the other, caused the liberal movement to sink into passivity. Swayed by Abdülhamit's offer of amnesty and other insubstantial promises, Mizancı Murat, who had replaced Ahmet Rıza as head of the CUP Paris organisation, concluded an 'armistice' and returned to İstanbul. The CUP was to be reactivated through the influence of Prince Sabahattin.

Prince Sabahattin

Prince Sabahattin was the son of Damat* Mahmut Pasha, and his mother was a sister of Abdülhamit. As the German-built Baghdad Railway reached Konya, the British were making a bid to undertake the construction of an alternative Alexandretta–Baghdad–Basra railway, and Mahmut Pasha was given the job of selling the British project to the Sultan. At this juncture (1898) Kaiser Wilhelm II made an official visit to Abdülhamit, which was sufficient to ensure that the Germans got the job because Abdülhamit was being boycotted by all other European sovereigns owing to the Armenian situation.

Thwarted, Damat Mahmut Pasha fled to France, taking his two sons with him. The news that the Sultan's brother-in-law and nephews had fled to Europe on grounds of lack of freedom made the headlines in European newspapers. Abdülhamit claimed that his nephews had been kidnapped. This incident partly revived the liberal movement. In 1902 Prince Sabahattin and his brother convened the first 'Young Turk Congress' in Paris. Forty delegates from various regions of the Empire discussed the problems facing the Ottoman people. İsmail Kemal, an Albanian notable, advanced the argument that publishing propaganda, which till then had been their sole activity, was getting them nowhere and insisted that the use of military force was necessary. Armenian delegates even thought that that would not be enough and that their object could only be achieved with European intervention. Prince Sabahattin took both these views to heart, the condition being that the intervening states should be democratic, namely France and Britain. Ahmet Rıza and his supporters (Dr Nazım and Yusuf Akçura) opposed these decisions.

Thus the Young Turk movement was divided into two factions. Prince Sabahattin and his supporters began preparations for military intervention in accordance with the decisions of the Congress. The

---

* *Damat* means son-in-law. Commoners who married Ottoman princesses bore this title.

governor of Tripoli, Recep Pasha, agreed to give them troops so that they could forcibly depose Abdülhamit; the plan was for these soldiers to be transported to İstanbul on ships procured by the British. However, Recep Pasha changed his mind, and with no troops available the plan had to be abandoned. Prince Sabahattin then turned his attention to social science, espousing the theory that there were two types of society, individualist and communitarian. He cited the British as a premier example of individualist society: their children were encouraged to be self-sufficient and active, and as a result tended to become entrepreneurs and aspire to adventurous lifestyles. Such societies have decentralised governments, their cities, towns and villages providing for their own needs. By contrast, in communitarian societies children are not encouraged to be independent and become civil servants when they grow up. The system of administration is centralist. Communities are not self-sustaining and expect the central authorities to provide for them. According to Prince Sabahattin, the only way for Ottoman society to survive was to make the transformation into an individualistic society. In Paris he founded an Association for Private Enterprise and Decentralisation.

The Russo-Japanese war

These years were full of far-reaching developments in the Far East. A power struggle over Manchuria and Korea had arisen between Russia and Japan, which was newly emerging as a world power. Their rivalry led to war (1904–5), and to the astonishment of the whole world Japan defeated Russia on both land and sea. The defeat of a European power by an Asian country was totally unexpected. The effects of this debacle were felt in Russian internal affairs, opening the way for the first Socialist Russian Revolution (1905). In order to suppress this revolution, the Tsar was forced to engage the support of liberals, i.e. the bourgeoisie, by declaring constitutional monarchy. In 1906 the first elected Russian parliament, the Duma, had its opening session. Since Russia had long been a fervent and aggressive defender of the unalterable rights of monarchy, this about-face in the order of things had far-reaching international repercussions. Iran in 1906 and China in 1908 also declared for constitutional monarchy. The Ottoman declaration of constitutional government in 1908 may be construed as a part of this international movement.

In 1905 Mustafa Kemal graduated from the Turkish War Academy as a staff captain and was posted to Ottoman Fifth Army headquarters in Damascus. There he came into contact with a secret society, Vatan (Motherland), headed by Dr Mustafa Cantekin. Mustafa Kemal became first a member and then head of this society, changing its name to Vatan ve Hürriyet (Motherland and Freedom). Because Damascus was not fertile ground for furthering the cause, he managed to travel secretly to his home town of Salonika where he established a new branch of the society, but he was unable to stay in place long enough to develop it. A more effective revolutionary organisation in Rumelia was the Ottoman Freedom Association (Osmanlı Hürriyet Cemiyeti), founded in Salonika in September 1906 by İsmail Canbolat, Talat, Rahmi and seven other members. Its founders and members were both civilians and military officers; membership was divided into cells. Candidates for membership swore loyalty over a Koran and a gun in the presence of three masked men at midnight, and were told betrayal would be punishable by death. In 1907 this organisation joined with the Paris CUP, and took the name of the latter.

In 1907 the Second Young Turk Congress convened in Paris, attended by Ahmet Rıza and his supporters, Prince Sabahattin and his supporters, and Armenian representatives. This time Ahmet Rıza was the dominant figure. A declaration was prepared listing the negative aspects of the Abdülhamit administration. The Congress approved the use of armed force to achieve revolution.

The Macedonian Question

The 1908 Revolution broke out in Macedonia, and to understand the situation from which it evolved, we must dwell briefly on the Macedonian Question. The region called Macedonia by Europeans consisted more or less of the three provinces under Ottoman dominion, Kosovo, Salonika and Monastir. Their population was made up of 1.5 million Muslims, 900,000 Bulgarians, 300,000 Greeks, 100,000 Serbs and 100,000 Vlachs (like those of Wallachia). Among the Muslims Ottoman statistics made no ethnic differentiation. They constituted the majority of the population, but Balkan nationalism and European public opinion in general branded Muslims as 'invaders', ignoring the fact that this had been their homeland for hundreds of years. From this point of view, with Muslims not taken into consideration, the Bulgars were the majority group. Although the Treaty of San Stefano had apportioned the region to Bulgaria, the subsequent Treaty of Berlin changed this state of affairs. An additional complication was that these groups did not inhabit clearly defined areas but were multi-ethnic communities. The Bulgars established gangs called *comitadji* for 'ethnic cleansing', to repress and evict other peoples from the region by terrorising them. In turn Greeks and Serbs organised their own *comitadjis* in self-defence. Ottoman forces rushed from one area of conflict to another, trying to maintain the peace. (It must also be pointed out that today, the people then designated as and calling themselves 'Bulgarians' would be known not as Bulgarian but as Macedonian.)

In 1902 the Bulgars organised a general uprising, which lasted a month and caused Hüseyin Hilmi Pasha to be appointed General Inspector of all three provinces. Their second uprising occurred in 1903 and lasted for three months, following which Russia and Austria prepared a programme of reform. According to this plan each of the Powers would send to designated regions of Macedonia gendarme officers who would act as consultants to Ottoman gendarmerie, with the exception of Germany which did not participate in the plan in order to maintain its good relations with the Ottomans. Abdülhamit preferred to send Military School graduates to the area, both as being better equipped to keep the peace and as a ploy to keep them away from İstanbul for his own security. Thus a concentration of educated officers came into being in the Balkans. These officers, whose salaries were paid only once every two months, had the illuminating experience of observing at first hand the relatively luxurious lifestyles enjoyed by officers from other armies and the bloody assaults made by the *comitadji* on people who were their co-religionists in the name of nationalism.

The Declaration of Freedom

On 3 March 1908 Britain sent the other Powers a circular calling for the appointment of a single governor for the three provinces and a decreased Ottoman military presence in the area. The CUP evaluated this development as leading dangerously towards Macedonia becoming a separate entity and sent a circular to all consulates in the Macedonian area, other than the Russian, stating that the CUP would put an end to tyranny and should be supported. Thus the CUP at last came out into the open, declaring its views. Abdülhamit tried through various measures to suppress its action but to no avail. In Monastir Adjutant Major Niyazi Bey, the mayor and superintendent of police, took to the mountains with 200 soldiers and the same number of civilians. Şemsi Pasha, sent there to suppress this movement, was killed on his way. The Albanians of Firzovik were tricked into sending Abdülhamit a telegram demanding constitutional monarchy. Events escalated to a point where constitutional government was declared in all the great centres in the Balkans on the same day, 23 July 1908. A total of sixty-seven telegrams were sent to the government saying that it should do likewise. Abdülhamit had already realised that he had no choice in this matter. A few days earlier he had named Sait Pasha Grand Vizier. On 24 July the newspapers published the order for elections to be held. Thus the Ottoman Empire entered the period of the Second Constitutional Government (the İkinci Meşrutiyet).

9

STRUCTURAL CHARACTERISTICS OF
THE C.U.P. AND THE 31 MARCH
INCIDENT

We have already expressed the opinion that the Second Meshrutiyet (the second period of constitutional monarchy) was the Turkish equivalent of the French Revolution, a period that catapulted the Turks into the modern age, and which greatly influenced subsequent Turkish history. The historian Tarık Zafer Tunaya has called the Second Meshrutiyet 'a political laboratory' inasmuch as many of the policies which came to maturity during the republican era had already been under discussion during the Second Meshrutiyet. It is significant that Mustafa Kemal, founding father of the Republic, became active in politics and in the Committee of Union and Progress (CUP) movement at this time.

We should seek to define the five definitive characteristics of the CUP:

(1) *Turkism: the ideology of Turkish nationalism.* The great majority of CUP members were Muslim. Most of the few non-Muslim members had joined the CUP before the Declaration of Freedom and were either Jews or Vlachs who had no aspirations to separatism or nationalism. Most Muslims were either ethnic Turks or, even if they were not, saw themselves as such and were in sympathy with the Turkist cause.

(2) *Youth.* It is frequently the case that young people are the dominant force in a revolutionary society, especially when the organisation's activities are illegal. In general, the young and single more eagerly undertake the dangers and responsibilities of revolutionism.

(3) *The ruling class.* The majority of CUP members were civil servants or military officers.

(4) *Education.* The majority of CUP members were either students or graduates of one of the Western-type schools of higher learning.

(5) *Bourgeois attitudes and ideals.* The main aim of the CUP was to modernise first the Turks and secondly the whole of Ottoman society so that they should be on a par with societies of developed European countries. Since these were capitalist countries, the CUP's aim was therefore to transform their own country into a capitalist, bourgeois society.

Ottoman society was traditionalist, and in such a society it is not acceptable for the young to rule. As a result the CUP was unable to form a government peopled by its own members after constitutional monarchy was declared. Although some CUP members such as Talat and Cavit were appointed as ministers, up until 1913 no Grand Vizier was a CUP member. But it should not be supposed that the CUP was not in power. It was able to impose its will on the government by giving orders as to what should or should not be done. This state of affairs was more 'supervisory government' than full governmental power.

Another fly in the political ointment was that although the CUP was responsible for the Declaration for Freedom in the Balkans, Sultan Abdülhamit was responsible for this declaration in Anatolia and the Arab countries. Therefore, since Abdülhamit had become part and parcel of constitutional government, the CUP was obliged to allow his Sultanate to stand. For years the linchpin of CUP campaigns had been opposition to his repressive regime, so that acceptance of Abdülhamit placed the CUP at odds with its own basic policies. To deliver itself from this dilemma the CUP evolved the theory of the 'imperial circle'. According to this theory Abdülhamit was a well-intentioned sovereign who had evil advisers in his circle and who had been deceived into acting wrongly by their bad advice. The CUP thereby masked its own deficiencies and penalised with heavy fines, thinly disguised as 'donations', those who had been Abdülhamit's councillors in the past and who had not found the chance to escape abroad.

With the advent of constitutional government the social scene was greatly enlivened. On 24 July 1908 the press refused to send copy to the censors. A deluge of newspapers, magazines and books began to be published. Women's movements established their own societies and publications, and workers' movements arose and organised strikes. During this time Prince Sabahattin returned from his self-imposed European exile. Immediately after the Declaration of Freedom, the CUP had merged with the Prince's Association for Private Enterprise and Decentralisation, but when Sabahattin later became disillusioned with the CUP, he and his supporters broke away and founded the Liberal Union Party. There were preparations for elections, but those took time because of the many complications of the two-stage election system. On 17 December 1908 Parliament convened with brilliant ceremony. Ahmet Rıza became President of the Chamber of Deputies.

The CUP won a good number of seats, but the majority of them went to the independent deputies. Non-Muslim candidates had been included on some CUP lists. The CUP had come to a pre-election agreement with minority groups over the number of seats they were to hold, and minorities selected candidates who were then included in CUP lists. In advance of the elections the CUP urged voters not to divide the vote, arguing that if Muslim CUP candidates did not get a sufficient percentage of the vote, minorities would win a disproportionately large number of seats. In these circumstances the Liberal Union Party's lack of success at election time came as no great surprise. Just as the Patriarchates and the Rabbinate represented Greeks, Armenians and Jews, the CUP was to represent Muslims (Turks in particular). In fact the election success of the CUP was misleading because although in the Balkans CUP support was solid and well-organised, in the rest of the Empire its base of supporters was haphazardly organised after the Declaration of Freedom. Outside the Balkans the CUP was obliged to welcome all who called themselves 'Unionists' and selected its candidates from among people who did not necessarily have 'Unionist characteristics': many were neither Unionists nor progressives but unprincipled opportunists. Consequently many Deputies of the CUP majority were Unionists in name alone.

A short while after the Declaration of Freedom the CUP decided that Sait Pasha was unacceptable as Grand Vizier and had him replaced by Kâmil Pasha from Cyprus. These two elderly Pashas were well-known as pro-British ministers of the previous Abdülhamit regime. Kâmil Pasha resented having to take orders from the CUP and insisted on using his own initiative, a situation that escalated until a motion for his censure was raised in Parliament by Hüseyin Cahit, an influential Deputy and the leading columnist of the *Tanin* newspaper. Later the Unionists decided to keep Kâmil Pasha in place and he therefore received a unanimous vote of confidence. This development encouraged Kâmil Pasha in his defiance of the CUP. He replaced the ministers of War and the Navy without consulting it, and again defied the Unionists when he tried to send certain army units (brought to the capital by the CUP to underline their power) back to the Rumelian provinces from where they had come. The CUP became anxious about his independent attitude and had a second vote of confidence raised in Parliament which it won by a large majority. Having lost this vote of confidence, Kâmil Pasha was forced out and retired on 13 February 1909. During the debate certain officers had come to Parliament to protest at the discharge of the previous Minister of the Navy. This created the impression that the present minister, Kâmil Pasha, was being removed because of military pressure.

The background to the 31 March Incident was the fact that all officers were Unionists. This had been ensured by the dismissal, after the Declaration of Freedom, of any officers who were not graduates of a military school; 1,400 officers were relieved of their duties in the First Army in İstanbul alone. The War College produced graduates from 1848 onwards, but in both the civilian bureaucracy and the army graduates and non-graduates had been ranked equally. *Alaylı*—a term first used in the army, meaning 'risen from the ranks'—later gained wider usage with reference to the bureaucracy. It denoted lack of education; people who had not been educated for their stations. Able privates could rise to the rank of sergeant and their discharge papers were 'left open', meaning that they could continue in the service and, through the favour and goodwill of their superiors, become officers at some future time. The result was that men who could hardly read and write were able to become officers and even aspire to the highest rank of Pasha (general). Although the Sultan and his councillors were well aware that the 'educated' were the better officers, they preferred the *alaylı* for their loyalty. They were presumed to be especially loyal because they had 'risen from nowhere' and owed everything to the favour of those who had preferred them. A similar philosophy regarding preferment prevailed in the bureaucracy.

The Unionists accomplished a revolutionary reform by ridding the army at a stroke of these *alaylı* and making the 'educated' supreme. After this reform nearly all officers were inevitably Unionists. The opposition, being aware of this, encouraged groups of noncommissioned officers to stage a revolt with the overt aim of forcing Parliament to recall Kâmil Pasha. The events which followed were called the 31 March Incident.

The 31 March incident

The ostensible cause of this event was the murder of Hasan Fehmi, senior columnist of the *Serbesti* newspaper (known for its hard-line opposition stand), at Galata bridge on the night of 6 April 1909. It was rumoured that his assailant had been wearing an officer's cloak, and although there were police stations on both ends of the bridge, no suspect was arrested. The furious opposition had no hesitation in holding the CUP responsible for the crime, and the CUP, by making little effort to refute the charge, was deemed to have implicitly admitted guilt (years later it became known that the Unionists had indeed organised this crime). Hasan Fehmi's funeral turned into a great mass protest. Five days after the funeral, on 13 April (31 March 1325 by the Roman Islamic calendar), revolt broke out.

In the early hours of the morning of that day, Sergeant Hamdi of the Fourth Hunter Battalion and other sergeants and privates of the Tashkishla barracks near Taksim Square arrested their officers and incited other battalions to do the same. Later the same day they held a meeting in front of Parliament in Sultanahmet Square. Their slogan was 'We want Sharia law!' Their other immediate demands were amnesty for all those taking part in the rebellion; the resignations of the cabinet, Ahmet Rıza (President of the Chamber of Deputies) and other Unionists; and the dismissal of certain senior military officers. Other demands included the reappointment of Kâmil Pasha as Grand Vizier, Nazım Pasha as Minister of War and İsmail Kemal as President of the Chamber of Deputies.

The Hüseyin Hilmi Pasha government first tried the classic Ottoman ploy of placating the rebels with fatherly counsel, but with no success; instead the rebellion spread. The cabinet, Ahmet Rıza and Mahmut Muhtar Pasha, commander of the First Army, had no alternative but to resign. Prominent Unionists went into hiding, fleeing from İstanbul to the Balkans. The fact that the rebel soldiers had gathered in Sultanahmet Square showed that they had accepted the authority of the Chamber of Deputies. Ironically, not only prominent Unionist members but also other deputies had felt intimidated by these events and had absented themselves from Parliament. Thus İsmail Kemal and other opposition deputies had not been able to achieve a sufficient majority to take control of Parliament and of the situation in general. Sultan Abdülhamit stepped in to fill this gap in authority. An announcement was made to the rebel soldiers that they were pardoned and that Tevfik Pasha had become Grand Vizier with Gazi Ethem Pasha, a hero of the 1897 Ottoman-Greek war, who was universally respected, as Minister of War. The pardon was of great importance. The soldiers, overjoyed as the result, went in droves to the Yıldız palace to demonstrate their approval of the Sultan. The Sultan then made the political mistake of showing himself to them on his balcony, which created the impression that he was in collusion with the rebel soldiers. The rebels spent the whole of that night roving the city, firing their guns into the air.

There are three theories as to who planned this rebellion. The first theory, that the CUP was the power behind the rebellion, is based on the fact that its result was to strengthen their hold on the government. It is not unheard of for a party in power to create an incident as an excuse to clamp down on dissident elements. This explanation, however, is unsatisfactory. There is no serious evidence that this theory is true and it would be highly implausible for the CUP to have conceived such a successful plot against itself. The second theory is that the rebellion was planned by Abdülhamit, and this too seems to be incorrect. It cannot be denied that Abdülhamit benefited from the short-lived gap in power, and that if the army had not intervened at a later stage he might have both kept his throne and strengthened his political position. Whether he would have used this power to reinstate his former regime of repression is a matter of conjecture, but these circumstances do not prove that he was responsible for the revolt.

The responsibility appears to lie with the Opposition headed by Prince Sabahattin. If this is so, the question must be asked why they did not take advantage of the opportunity it presented. The answer is that they had expected the non-commissioned rebel soldiers to stage a more disciplined show of force, but instead the incident developed into a bloody rebellion. In two days the insurgents killed over twenty people, most of whom were War College graduates. Among those killed were a Deputy who resembled Hüseyin Cahit and the Minister of Justice, Nazım Pasha. Prince Sabahattin did indeed make an attempt to get the rebellion under control. When, on the second day, he realised that the second aim of the coup, the bid to dethrone Abdülhamit, had had the undesirable result of strengthening the Sultan's hold on the throne, he employed the alternative strategy of asking naval officers to frighten him into abdicating by threatening to shell the palace. Although they all seemed to accept this plan, only one, Commander Ali Kabuli, commanding officer of the battleship *Asar-ı Tevfik*, took action on the third day. As Ali Kabuli began preparations for the attack, sailors who were in contact with the rebels arrested him and took him to the Yıldız palace. Abdülhamit again appeared on the balcony, signalling for them to take Ali Kabuli to the police station, but the rebels lynched Ali Kabuli then and there. This incident was without doubt political material that could be held against Abdülhamit in the future.

It is not totally clear who the true instigator of the rebellion really was, but it is known for certain who and what incited the soldiers. The *Volkan* newspaper, published by Dervish Vahdeti, was one element of provocation. Dervish Vahdeti, a Turkish Cypriot and an active member of the Nakshibendi sect, had been in the employ of the British. He may be described as a modern Islamist working for the opposition. He published soldiers' letters of complaint in his newspaper. Together with Said-i Kurdi—who was later to gain fame as Said-i Nursi, founder of the Nurcu religious sect—he established the Mohammedan Union, in honour of which event a *mevlit* prayer had been said in the Hagia Sophia mosque on 3 April 1909.

A second group known to have encouraged the soldiers to rebel were the *softas*, students of schools of religion—the *medreses*. Previous to the Declaration of Freedom, only students of the *medrese* and residents of İstanbul were exempt from military service; the only way for provincials to do so was for them to become students of religion, and hence the *medreses* were full of people whose only aim was to evade military service. The CUP sought to close this loophole by establishing an examination for the *medrese*; those who failed it could be inducted into the army. Inevitably this made the *medrese* students enemies of the CUP.

A third group of instigators were the officers 'from the ranks', the *alaylı* officers, who had been discharged. The fourth group of instigators were the Albanian nationalists who complained of the CUP's Turkist policy.

In the aftermath of the revolt, many agitators were court-martialled, and Dervish Vahdeti was condemned to death and executed. Prince Sabahattin was arrested, but freed through the intervention of the British Ambassador. It has never been officially determined exactly who the instigator of the rebellion was; one reason for this non-clarification of events may be that the CUP was happy to leave well alone. If Abdülhamit had been declared to be responsible, the investigation which they wished to pursue against the opposition would have seemed repressive. If the opposition had been found responsible, it would have seemed unfair to dethrone the Sultan. Thanks to the indeterminate state of affairs the CUP killed two birds with one stone.

Putting down the rebellion

How was the rebellion put down? The CUP, assessing an attack upon itself to be synonymous with an attack upon constitutional government, took a decided stand in the Balkans where it had solid support. It was immediately decided that an army to be called the 'Hareket Army' (Army of Operation) would be established in Salonika, that Mahmut Şevket Pasha (commander of the Third Army) would be put in command, and that divisions from the Second Army in Edirne and from Salonika would be commanded by Hüseyin Hüsnü Pasha and Şevket Turgut Pasha. On the second day of the rebellion a meeting was held in Salonika attended by all nationalities. The government, the Palace and the Chamber of Deputies were inundated with telegrams of protest. However, in İstanbul the climate of opinion was different. The Palace, the government and opposition journalists felt that the storm had passed and that everything was back to normal, and were content with the new state of affairs in İstanbul, without the CUP. The Chamber of

Deputies was able to convene only on the third day, and was at first in favour of adjusting to the new political situation. However, in the meantime a growing number of Hareket Army units coming from Edirne and Salonika were massing in San Stefano (*Yeşilköy*), and a deputation sent by the Chamber of Deputies to Hareket Army headquarters in San Stefano to advise the army to return to their posts in order to prevent civil war came under the influence of their unswerving revolutionary stand. Reminded that they themselves were also Unionists, if only in name, the members of the deputation remained in San Stefano as supporters of the cause, calling on others to join them.

On 20 April 1909 the Chamber of Deputies was unable to constitute a quorum, and it was henceforth convened in San Stefano under a new name. Under the Constitution the Senate and the Chamber of Deputies had constituted the General Assembly, which was in fact a ceremonial body convoked only at the beginning of each yearly term for the Sultan's opening speech. In San Stefano the deputies and a number of senators assembled together, constituting a body they called the National General Assembly, a name which had no place in the Constitution and was used solely to designate the assembly in San Stefano. The addition of the word 'national' was abandoned after this short period of use and was only officially taken up again on 23 April 1920 with the establishment of the present-day Grand National Assembly of Turkey. It is very likely that the French Revolution inspired this union of the two chambers. It may be recalled that one of the first constitutional acts of the French Revolution had been to unite the three houses of the French parliament, called the States-General, making it into a united 'National Assembly'. No Unionist ever openly declared this source of inspiration, probably because at that time public opinion would not have found a foreign influence of this nature acceptable.

On 24 April 1909 the Hareket Army occupied İstanbul. Although Abdülhamit ordered the rebel soldiers not to resist, bloody encounters took place in some places. On 27 April the National General Assembly held its last session in İstanbul. As a result of a pronouncement (*fetva*) of the Grand Mufti (the *Sheyhülislam*), Abdülhamit was dethroned and replaced by Mehmet Reshat, who was ceremonially girded with the sword of the Ottomans as Sultan

Mehmet V (1909–18). This fatherly and well-intentioned man was a Sultan suitable for a constitutional government because he tended not to involve himself in politics. Thus ended Abdülhamit's thirty-three-year reign, and he had to live a number of years in Salonika. Many young officers of the Hareket Army such as Mustafa Kemal, Kâzim Karabekir and Enver Bey, at this time chiefs of staff to divisional commanding Pashas, were to play important roles in the War of Independence (1919–22).

In this new era of the Young Turks, Hüseyin Hilmi Pasha was reinstated as Grand Vizier. The Chamber of Deputies now proved extraordinarily efficient: within a short period it enacted fundamental legislation necessary for a modern state governed by the rule of law. A significant body of these laws was to remain in force throughout many years of the Republican era, e.g. those concerning freedom of assembly, the press, strikes and associations. Meanwhile Abdülhamit's immense fortune was confiscated, palace spending was subjected to a strict budget, the salaries of high officials were reduced and many superfluous civil servants were discharged. The earlier ban on black slave traffic was extended to include white slaves as well. Most important, the Constitution was comprehensively amended. The 1876 Constitution had made the government responsible to the Sultan, not the Chamber of Deputies, which had no authority to propose legislation. Provisions relating to these and other issues were totally rewritten and the Constitution was democratised to such an extent that the result should be regarded as a new 1909 Constitution.

Another development of the new era was the emergence of a 'strong man', the commander of the Hareket Army, Mahmut Şevket Pasha. He was appointed to the specially created post of General Inspector of the First, Second and Third Armies. More important, he was made military commander of İstanbul, where martial law, which was to last for three years, was declared. He thereby acquired power over all aspects of life in the capital. The CUP must have decided that this was the best way to maintain order. Thus the CUP, a majority of whom were young, had found a father figure ('elder brother' in Turkish parlance) for itself. (This aspect of events had a parallel in the military coup of 27 May 1960 when a retired general, Cemal Gürsel, became president of the junta called the National

Union Committee, the majority of whose members were again young officers. He too was a father figure.) In general, Mahmut Şevket's age and rank caused him to be respected in all quarters. His quasi-leadership of the CUP had major consequences, first in its repercussions on the military and civilian wings of the CUP. The standing of the military wing was strengthened by Mahmut Şevket becoming 'head' of the CUP. Secondly, he had been involved in arms negotiations and foreign relations with Germany during the Abdülhamit regime, which thus tended to reinforce pro-German influences in the CUP. The British had tended to take a positive view of the 31 March Incident, but disapproved of the Hareket Army; the German approach was the opposite. Thirdly, Mahmut Şevket Pasha was more conservative than most of the CUP and therefore was able to check the impetuosity of the progressives. For example, during Hüseyin Cahit's visit to the Sultan on the occasion of a religious festival, his saluting the Sultan by putting the fingers of his right hand to his lips and forehead instead of kissing the fringe of the throne was questioned by the press; Mahmut Şevket forbade any discussion of this matter. A last point is that although the Pasha was a War College graduate and therefore had an affinity with the CUP, he never became a member.

Today the 31 March Incident is remembered on its anniversary as a typical act of the forces of reaction—similar to the Menemen Incident and another outbreak, the Sivas Incident in 1993, when thirty-seven people died in a fire started by fundamentalists. Without doubt 31 March was engineered by reactionary forces; the clamour of the insurgents for Sharia Law, a medieval system, was over-whelming evidence of this. It must also be pointed out that the most important provisions of the Sharia regarding to individual rights, marriage, inheritance and obligations were then still in force and were not rescinded till the enactment of the Civil Code of 1926. It is probable that there was another facet to their reactionary demands. When they shouted 'We want the Sharia', what the soldiers really wanted was to evade the exigencies of new army discipline and revert to the lax ways of the old army where drill could be avoided through the excuse of religious duties. Another of their reactionary preoccupations was probably a return to the old system of 'rising from the ranks' instead of having to fulfil the educational requisites needed to become an officer. Taking a broader view of the situation, it can be said that opposing the power of the CUP, the most effective revolutionary organisation of the time, was in itself reactionary. The destruction of the CUP, regardless of its faults, would have meant reversion to the institutions of the old regime which would have moved to fill the power vacuum.

It has already been mentioned that the CUP applied a model which can conveniently be termed supervisory government. It is clear that a government, especially a revolutionary one, could be hampered by a situation like this, and for this reason the CUP had begun to prepare for full empowerment. The most important of these preparations was a proposal to create a parliamentary under-secretariat. At present in Turkey ministerial under-secretaryship is an administrative position within the bureaucracy, whereas in Britain there are both bureaucratic under-secretaries and parliamentary ones, appointed from Parliament. The CUP, by having its Deputies appointed as parliamentary under-secretaries, intended that they should thereby gain administrative experience and, as a result of their participation in cabinet meetings, experience of government. Mahmut Şevket was the first to oppose this proposition and his stand encouraged the government and the Deputies to join him. It seems likely that all these circles objected to a CUP government as being in some way detrimental to their own interests. As long as Mahmut Şevket was a force in the Chamber of Deputies and could rely on the support of the 'nominal' Unionists, he was able to keep the ministries out of reach of CUP members and thereby block the way to full power for the CUP (until 1912). From time to time the CUP was able to have a few of its members appointed to the cabinet, but this was not sufficient for full empowerment.

Some characteristics of the CUP

The CUP had characteristics not normally encountered in a political party. It has been already mentioned that because many of its members were military officers, it was divided into two wings, military and civilian. Another of its characteristics was its dual structure. On the one hand there was the CUP Association and on the other the CUP Party. The Association had clubs and members all over the country and held local and central congresses. Outwardly it resembled a social and cultural society, and this was the true CUP. The CUP Party consisted of its Deputies in Parliament, in other words it was no more than the CUP caucus. Because many of these deputies were not true CUP supporters and Unionists only in name (till 1912), the CUP Association preferred to keep them at arm's length; for example, only three CUP Party representatives were allowed to attend its annual General Congress. Another striking characteristic was its concept of collective leadership. Some members might have had relatively more authority, their opinions carrying more weight, than others, as in the cases of Talat of the civilian wing and Enver of the military wing, but there was never a single leader followed by all. No matter how prominent Talat and Enver became during the First World War, the Central Committee always retained its decision-making power. To protect itself against power being concentrated in the hands of one man, the CUP did not create the position of chairman till 1913. Whether as secretary-general or after 1913 as chairman, none was nearly as powerful as the head of a Turkish political party today.

Another surprising characteristic was the secrecy involved in the Association's General Congresses. The 1908, 1909, 1910 and 1911 General Congresses took place in Salonika, and were closed to the public and the press. Even the election results of the 1908 Congress, which determined which members were to sit on the Central Committee, were kept secret. Probably because it was thought that the public might find this secrecy strange, two members of the society, Enver and Niyazi, were presented as 'Heroes of Freedom', and posters of the two were to be seen all over the country. Thus the CUP became identified with these personalities. Another facet of the CUP was its resort to terrorism, which may have been comprehensible while they were an illegal society, but not after 1908. It was behind the assassinations of Abdülhamit's head of secret services, İsmail Mahir Pasha, in 1908, and of the opposition journalists Hasan Fehmi in 1909, Ahmet Samim in 1910 and Zeki Bey in 1911. The murder of Ahmet Samim was the subject of a novel, *The Night of Judgment* by Yakup Kadri Karaosmanoğlu (1927).

Why did the CUP feel that it had to rely on secrecy and terrorism, especially in the years after 1908? It made its reasons clear during its 1918 Congress at which it decided to dissolve itself. Even after 1908 it saw itself as a revolutionary organisation still far from its goal of creating a modern society. This had been out of reach because, although backed by the army, it did not have the support of the great majority of the uneducated and conservative public. The 31 March Incident had shown the difficulty of its position. Secrecy and terrorism were proof not of its power but of its weakness. Although its 1908 programme provided for land reform (distribution of land to peasants who were destitute or owned very little land), the CUP was later forced to omit it from its programmes because of its need for the support of the *ayan* (notable) class who were great landowners in the provinces. In the same way, although the CUP was essentially a Turkist association, it was obliged to shape its programmes and pronouncements to accord with Ottomanism. In the opinion of this writer, there was a strong secularist current within the CUP, but it was dangerous to voice such opinions at that time even within the Association itself because the CUP also had members who held Islamist views.

Lastly, there is a matter related to the CUP that has often aroused curiosity: its connection with Freemasonry. At that time, Freemasonry was, in general, a liberal, positivist, progressive and élitist organisation opposed to feudalism, absolutism and religious fanaticism, which made Masons ideologically suitable to be CUP members. Before the Declaration of Freedom, Masonic lodges in the Ottoman Empire were foreign institutions enjoying the privileges of the Capitulations* (for example, the Ottoman police force could not enter their premises unless invited). This was a great advantage for a secret organisation such as the CUP. There is evidence that Freemasonry had some influence on the CUP; however, the great majority of CUP members were not Masons; for example, although Kemal Atatürk and Celal Bayar were at one time Unionists, they were never Masons. The Bektashi sect had a similar connection with the CUP; what can be called their liberal world-view made them more open than others to CUP membership. As a result, many CUP leaders before 1908 were also members of the Bektashi sect.

---

* A system generally applied in semi-colonial countries whereby foreigners and foreign institutions enjoyed certain extraterritorial privileges.

10

THE C.U.P. SUPERVISORY GOVERN-
MENT—FROM THE 31 MARCH
INCIDENT TO 1913

Towards the end of 1909 a matter related to foreign affairs began to shake the foundations of the Hüseyin Hilmi government. The state-owned Hamidiye Company and a British firm, Lynch, were engaged in shipping on the Euphrates river. At this time the Lynch concession was almost at an end and the government was proposing that a new company be established with a seventy-five-year concession and a 50 per cent share of each of the aforementioned companies. Deputies from Baghdad and Mahmut Şevket himself were strongly against this proposal, demanding the termination of the Lynch connection; it is not clear whether the opposition was motivated by nationalist or pro-German sympathies. In the end the administration demanded a vote of confidence from the Chamber of Deputies and received a huge majority. In spite of this affirmation Hüseyin Hilmi insisted on resigning. Hakkı Pasha, who was given the task of forming the new government, did not renew the Lynch concession. The soundness of this decision is questionable; the 31 March Incident had already shown that Britain looked askance at the CUP, and probably the Lynch incident alienated its sympathies even further. This refusal may have been a factor in shaping Britain's negative policy towards the Ottomans, which became apparent during the rebellions and wars which broke out in the months to come.

Two aspects of the Hakkı Pasha government distinguished it from any previous government. First, a greater number of Unionists were members than ever before (Talat—Minister of Internal Affairs, Cavit—Minister of Finance, İsmail Hakkı—Minister of Education, Hayri—Minister of Pious Foundations). Secondly, Mahmut Şevket was made a member of the government as Minister of War. Probably it was hoped that he could be held in check better within the cabinet rather than outside it, but this was a miscalculation. When a disagreement arose over financial policy, Cavit, the Minister of Finance, strove to apply the principle of budgetary unity, but Mahmut Şevket Pasha refused to comply, and would not hand over the 550,000 liras he had appropriated for the Ministry of War from Abdülhamit's (Yıldız) palace. The new budget had apportioned 9.5 million liras to the War Ministry, but when it came before the Chamber of Deputies Mahmut Şevket demanded an additional 5 million liras, and despite Cavit's protests the Deputies acceded. With his budget calculations completely upset, Cavit was obliged to go to France in search of a loan. He applied to the Ottoman Bank (Franco-British), but negotiations came to a standstill when Cavit rejected stipulations for an Ottoman Public Debt Association guarantee against the loan and supervision of its use by the Ottoman Bank, on the grounds that they amounted to foreign supervision of Ottoman internal affairs. The Ottoman Bank, in turn, rejected the credit application. Cavit thereupon reached an agreement with other banks, which the French government then proceeded to obstruct. It became apparent that France was trying to put a stop to CUP aspirations for full independence. Britain supported the French stand. In the end a loan was procured from Germany, which was willing to extend credit on terms Cavit could accept. In addition, Mahmut Şevket refused to allow the Ministry of Finance to supervise the finances of the Ministry of War, and when it persisted he resigned. He was begged to withdraw his resignation but could only be induced to stay at the price of depriving the Audit Department of its supervisory powers over the Ministry of War.

In the wake of the 31 March Incident, the opposition found itself in a difficult position. The CUP chose to assume that 'whoever is not one of us is a reactionary'. Martial law was hard on everyone; still, there were certain organisations which persevered in their activities. One was the Ottoman Democratic Party (ODP), which can be said to have stood for social democratic principles. Its founders, Dr İbrahim Temo and Abdullah Cevdet, were among the original founders of the CUP. The aim of the former was to create a civilised and loyal opposition, but his efforts were impeded by the fact that the party's newspapers were continually being shut down by the martial law administration. According to Temo, Mahmut Şevket shook his walking-stick at the ODP's Secretary General Fuat Şükrü, shouting 'I'll beat you to death'.

A second party, the Moderate Liberal Party, was established by Arab and Albanian Deputies in 1909. According to its programme, which had feudalist characteristics, backward regions in need of reform were to become 'gradually civilised', and to this end provincial assemblies were to have the power to pass regional legislation. First İsmail Kemal and later İsmail Hakkı were its presidents. Impeded by martial law, the party was able to find support only within the confines of Parliament and was not able to appeal to a wider public.

A third one, the People's Party, had an Islamist character. It was established in February 1910 by a group of twenty to thirty Turkish *ulema* Deputies. Its most prominent members were the Deputies from Konya (Zeynelabidin), Balıkesir (Vasfi) and Tokat (Mustafa Sabri). Along with the establishment of contemporary institutions such as chambers of agriculture and commerce, the teaching of science in the *medreses* in accordance with contemporary needs, and the promotion of workers' rights, its programme also included reactionary demands, to be expected from such a party, such as lowering the standards which barred the uneducated *alaylı* from some categories of work and putting increased emphasis on the teaching of Arabic in the *medreses*. Another of its reactionary demands was that candidates for election to the Chamber should have resided for at least five years in the regions they wished to represent and that periods of working as civil servants in those regions should not be counted as residence.

On the night of 9 June 1910 Ahmet Samim, the senior columnist of the opposition *Voice of the Nation* newspaper, was murdered, and Mahmut Şevket, with the 31 March Incident in mind, immediately took action. Rıza Nur and about fifty other oppositionists were arrested for alleged intent to murder Mahmut Şevket and Talat. They were later acquitted of all charges, but the country was rocked by stories of their having been tortured during their interrogation. Meanwhile centralist policies, mostly concerning conscription and taxation, had triggered mounting insurgency in Syria, Albania and

Yemen. In the first months of 1911 a new conservative faction emerged from the CUP, the New Group (*Yeni Hizip*), organised by Colonel Sadık Bey and Deputy Abdulaziz Mecdi Efendi. Among the demands in its ten-article manifesto was that the appointment of ministers from the ranks of the deputies should require a majority of two-thirds of the CUP Party votes. Mahmut Şevket supported this movement and Sadık Bey.

While these events were unfolding, CUP cabinet ministers were being ousted one by one.

The war in Tripolitania (Libya)

Worse was to come with the Tripolitanian war. Italy, only united since 1860, had come away empty-handed from the 1878 Congress of Berlin. The French hold on Morocco and the CUP's steps to upset Italian dominance in Tripoli caused Italy to go into action. With the consent of the Great Powers, it sent an ultimatum to the Ottoman government on 23 September 1911. It is of interest that this document's accusations were specifically aimed at the CUP. Thus Italy was interfering in Ottoman internal affairs. Italy declared war on 29 September.

. The defence of Tripoli was fraught with difficulties for the Ottomans. A major obstacle in the way of reinforcements reaching Tripolitania was the presence of the British in Egypt, who barred the land route between Tripolitania and the rest of the Ottoman Empire. The only way to overcome this was to send them by sea, but the Italian navy was greatly superior to the Ottoman, and had the upper hand in the Aegean and the Mediterranean. It shut off the Dardanelles, occupied the Dodecanese islands including Rhodes, and bombarded Beirut and other Ottoman ports. Exacerbating the situation was the fact that shortly before the war Mahmut Şevket had sent four battalions and a great store of arms and ammunition from Tripoli to Yemen. The situation was saved by the fighting spirit of the people of Tripolitania. Although the Italians, with their strong naval support, could dominate the coastal areas, they were unable to advance inland owing to the opposition put up by Bedouin guerrillas. Volunteer CUP officers made their way through Egypt disguised as civilians, and rushed to the front to help organise the resistance. Among them were Enver, Fethi and Mustafa Kemal. All these young officers (like the whole CUP) had looked on the constitutional government as a rejuvenation of the 'sick man of Europe', but the Tripolitanian war was proof to the contrary—and a warning that not much had changed and that the Empire's disintegration might not have been checked.

Hakkı Pasha resigned when war broke out and was replaced by Sait Pasha, the famous Grand Vizier of the Abdülhamit regime known for his British sympathies. These, however, were not, as extreme as those of Kâmil Pasha. Sait Pasha possessed sufficient authority to neutralise Mahmut Şevket, who had already lost prestige through his mishandling of the situation in Tripoli.

On 21 November 1911, about fifty days after the start of the war, the Freedom and Accord Party (Hürriyet ve İtilaf Fırkası), the FAP, was founded. This was a kind of super-party joining political parties and movements of widely differing views—liberals, moderates, conservatives, democrats and members of the People's Party—under a banner of opposition to the CUP. Its president was Damat Ferit Pasha and its vice-president Sadık Bey, latterly of the New Group, a conservative faction of the CUP. Prince Vahdettin, Damat Ferit's brother-in-law, was a known sympathiser and was even rumoured to be its honorary president. Dervish Vahdeti, fleeing from the Hareket Army, had sought the Prince's protection, which he refused. Although the Freedom and Accord Party had many democrats in its ranks, it was clearly a party to the right of the CUP; one could even say that it was a Palace party. Its programme stated that it would be suitable 'at present' to preserve the two-stage election system and appointment of senators by the Sultan. Its aim was for the Senate to gain increased authority over legislation, government and supervision of the budget. Its conservative tenor became apparent with demands that the Sultan should have the right to veto legislation and be deferred to in matters of government policy.

The Big Stick election

On 11 December 1911 a by-election was held in İstanbul for a single seat in the Chamber of Deputies. The Freedom and Accord Party won the election by one vote and hailed this result as a great victory. Within the CUP there was a defeatist atmosphere. When it put forward a candidate for an empty cabinet seat, Mahmut Şevket succeeded in preventing him from being chosen. But the CUP had come at last to the end of its patience. It took a decision to hold early elections, but the 1909 amendments to the Constitution had made the dissolution of Parliament extremely difficult to achieve. A new amendment was proposed to make this easier, and after long-drawn-out and heated argument the Chamber of Deputies was finally dissolved on 18 January 1912. After this event four CUP members, including Talat and Cavit, were given ministerial posts. The CUP took great care in selecting its candidates for this general election, and did everything in its power to put pressure on voters, to the extent that this election became known as the 'Big Stick election'. Of the 270 members elected, only six were from opposition parties, and of these all but one were elected from Albania. The exception was Ali Galip, an army officer and member of a prominent family of Kayseri, who later became notorious for attempting to raid the Sivas Congress. The president of the new Parliament was Halil (Mente-şe).* Because Ahmet Rıza's relations with the CUP had cooled considerably, he was appointed to the politically less active Senate. After the opposition's success in by-elections, it regarded these results as a great disappointment, and the idea of a coup began to take hold.

Rebellion again broke out in Albania at the beginning of May. In June twelve army officers took to the mountains of Monastir and demanded new elections and a new government, and for those responsible for the Tripolitanian disaster to be brought to trial. Meanwhile a secret military society called the Saviour Officers was publishing anti-CUP declarations. Although it only had five members at this time, it was seen to be speaking for much of the military. No matter what irregularities there had been during the elections, the fact that a rebellion had broken out while the country was engaged in a war with Italy, with officers taking to the mountains to engage in political conspiracies, was generally considered unacceptable. These warning signs showed that the basic consensus which unites a society despite the differences that inevitably arise in all political environments was lacking or seriously

---

* In general Muslims of the Ottoman Empire did not have family names. The surnames mentioned hereafter were adopted after 1934 when the Law of Surnames was enacted.

deficient. On 2 July a law came into force which prohibited military personnel from participating in political activities. Such a prohibition was already in existence, but the CUP, by allowing officers within its own ranks to be politically active even after the Declaration of Freedom, had itself broken the law. In the General Congress of the CUP in 1909 Mustafa Kemal had pointed out the drawbacks of allowing officers to participate in politics, and although his arguments were accepted in principle, they were not put into practice.

Meanwhile, with the advantage of its domination of Parliament, the CUP went into action to free itself of the tutelage of Mahmut Şevket and he was asked to resign from the Ministry of War. He acquiesced without putting up a fight, but the CUP was then unable to come to an agreement with any of the four Pashas whom it offered the portfolio. It seemed that the Pashas were refusing to cooperate in a show of solidarity with Mahmut Şevket. On 15 July Sait Pasha demanded a vote of confidence, but despite receiving a majority affirmation of 194 votes with only four against, he still insisted on resigning two days later. The Sultan offered the position of Grand Vizier to Tevfik Pasha, but this did not work because he would only accept on condition that the Chamber of Deputies was dissolved. The CUP was agreeable to the idea of a supra-party government but threatened that civil war would break out if the Saviour Officers' candidate, Kâmil Pasha, was made Grand Vizier. In the end Gazi Ahmet Muhtar Pasha, commander of the defence of Erzurum during the 1877–8 Ottoman-Russian war, was made Grand Vizier. In the cabinet were Kâmil, Avlonyalı Ferit, Hüseyin Hilmi, Nazım and Gazi Ahmet Muhtar Pasha's son, Mahmut Muhtar. Because it contained so many 'heavyweights' it was called the 'Grand Cabinet'— or the 'Father and Son Cabinet'.

Sait Pasha's resignation from the Vizierate and Gazi Muhtar Pasha's appointment in his place marked the end of the CUP's supervisory government, and the start of a new period that was to continue until the Porte coup (*Babıâli Baskını*). Why had the CUP acceded to this situation despite its position of strength in the Chamber of Deputies? Had it finally grown tired of the protests and accusations that were being made against it from all quarters? This may have been a consideration, but the real motive was probably to avoid the responsibility and shame of signing the peace agreement that would hand Tripoli over to the Italians. The struggle for Tripoli was still going on, but there was little hope of a successful outcome; as its occupation of the Dodecanese islands had proved, Italy was powerful enough to harm the Ottomans in other areas. It could be said that the CUP became the victim of its own propaganda; it could not reconcile handing over Tripoli with its self-proclaimed role of saviour of the nation. However, because of its majority in the Chamber of Deputies it certainly calculated that it could return to power whenever it wished.

Nevertheless, the turn of events proved otherwise. As time passed the government, under the influence of Kâmil Pasha and Nazım Pasha, began to adopt an anti-CUP policy. On 24 July the Saviour Officers sent an ultimatum to the president of the Chamber of Deputies demanding the dissolution of Parliament within forty-eight hours. Meanwhile the government had presented its programme to Parliament and received a vote of confidence of 167 votes to 45, and with this result began to work in opposition to the CUP and suppressed its mouthpiece, the newspaper *Tanin*. Hüseyin Hilmi resigned from the government in protest. At the beginning of August, the constitutional amendment which the CUP had promoted to be able to dissolve Parliament easily was now invoked against it when the Chamber of Deputies was dissolved.

The First Balkan War

Towards the end of 1911 and in the first months of 1912, the fabric of a Balkan alliance was woven to include Bulgaria, Serbia, Greece and Montenegro. The important role of intermediary was undertaken by Russia and Britain. In August Bulgarian organisations committed a number of terrorist acts, and by September events had escalated to the point where war seemed inevitable. Reforms conceded by the Porte were of no avail. On 30 September the Balkan states declared mobilisation and on 1 October the Ottomans did likewise.

On 13 October the Balkan Allies set out their terms:

(1) The Balkan provinces were to become autonomous and have Belgian or Swiss governors.

(2) The Christian population would do their military service in their own provinces, under the command of their own Christian officers; until sufficient officers could be trained they would be exempt from military service.

(3) Provincial legislative councils would be established.

(4) Reforms would be supervised by the Balkan states as well as by the Great Powers.

(5) Reforms would come into force within six months and the Ottomans would cease mobilisation unilaterally.

These demands produced a strongly nationalistic reaction in Ottoman public opinion. It was impossible for the government to give an affirmative answer, which the Balkan Alliance probably did not expect anyway.

On 17 October 1912 Bulgaria and Serbia declared war on the Ottomans, who had concluded a hasty peace with Italy two days earlier. Between 22 and 31 October the Ottoman army suffered one crushing defeat after another: from the Serbs at Kosovo and Komanova and from the Bulgarians at Kırklareli and Lüleburgaz. The Bulgarian army advanced as far as İstanbul's lines of defence at Çatalca and to the Bolayır line on the Gallipoli peninsula. A battle at Monastir on 18 November confirmed the outcome. The fortified cities of Janina, Scutari and Edirne (Adrianople) came under siege. The fate of the Ottoman Balkans was sealed in two weeks.

How did this crushing defeat come about? The Ottomans probably had a supply of arms and equipment equal to that of their adversaries; Mahmut Şevket had spent large portions of past budgets on arms. But events clearly showed that the generalship, communications and supply lines of the Balkan Alliance were superior, and their armies were more highly motivated.

Responsibility for the Ottoman debacle lay with the acting commander-in-chief and Minister of War, Nazım Pasha. Certainly, Ahmet Muhtar and Kâmil Pasha bore the political responsibility for appointing him to such a position and for keeping him in place. They were also especially to blame in that even when faced with a watershed struggle in the Balkans they refused to set aside their grievances against the CUP and thus worked against the creation of a spirit of national unity. We have already referred to a breakdown of national consensus during the Tripolitanian war. The unsophisticated policies towards the Albanians which the CUP thoughtlessly implemented also had a major share in the lack of consensus and the Balkan defeat.

On 29 October 1912 Ahmet Muhtar was forced to resign and Kâmil Pasha became the new Grand Vizier. On 1 November Nazım Pasha, the Minister of War, pessimistic as to the ability of the Çatalca Line to withstand the pressure of the advancing enemy forces, called for a diplomatic solution. The opinion in France was that if the war continued the Ottomans would be unable to safeguard the geographical integrity of their Empire. On 3 November the Ottomans asked the Great Powers to intervene for an armistice on condition that their territorial integrity was ensured. On 9 November the CUP newspaper *Tanin* was banned from publication because of an article by its columnist Hüseyin Cahit calling for Mahmut Şevket to command the Army. On 11 November all the activities of the CUP were suspended. The day before, the Freedom and Accord Party had shut itself down on the advice of the authorities. The number of CUP members under arrest rose to fifty-five. With the Great Powers refusing to intervene, the Porte applied directly to the King of Bulgaria on 12 November, and although the Bulgarians again attacked the Çatalca Line, they did not succeed. They were therefore willing to accept an armistice (3 December), and a peace conference was convened in London.

The London Conference began on 16 December. On the 23rd the Balkan states demanded that they be given all the Aegean islands and the whole of the Empire's Balkan dominions, with the exception of the lands east of a line drawn from east of Tekirdağ and east of Midye, and the Gallipoli peninsula. At first the Ottoman delegation would only agree to the autonomy of Albania and Macedonia, but it later accepted that the future status of Albania and Crete should be decided by the Great Powers and agreed to discuss with the Powers the future status of the Aegean islands on condition that the province of Edirne (Adrianople) up to the Mesta-Karasu border would remain within the Ottoman domains (1 January 1913). The Balkan Alliance declared that if the Ottomans refused to give up the city of Edirne, Crete and the islands, the discussions would be terminated, which in fact happened on 6 January. On 17 January, as the result of a joint decision, the ambassadors of the Great Powers sent a diplomatic note to the Ottomans demanding that they should abandon their demands for Edirne and the Aegean islands. There seemed to be no hope of resolving the situation. Because the Chamber of Deputies had been dissolved, traditional procedures for sharing the responsibility of such a momentous decision were resorted to. The most prominent statesmen of the Empire were gathered to constitute an Imperial Council of State (*Şurâ-yı Saltanat*), which convened in the Palace on 22 January. Kâmil told the assembly that İstanbul and Edirne were under siege and that they must decide for either war or peace. An overwhelming majority decided for peace, which meant that Edirne had to be sacrificed.

The Sublime Porte coup

In these dire straits the CUP effected a coup d'état. On 23 January 1913 a great crowd of Unionists advanced on the Porte shouting slogans calling for the defence of Edirne, and the guards did not stop them because their officers were on the side of the protesters. Two army officers and one police officer who tried to bar their entry were shot. At this point Nazım Pasha came forward shouting 'You betrayed me!', and was killed by Yakup Cemil. (Rumour had it that the CUP had promised Nazım the position of Grand Vizier in return for his support. Of late he had begun to look after the interests of CUP officers and had ensured that certain measures to be taken against the organisation were not enforced.) Enver strode straight up to Kâmil Pasha, dictated his resignation, and took the signed document directly to the Sultan. He had Mahmut Şevket Pasha named Grand Vizier and also Minister of War. Sait Halim Pasha was appointed Minister of Foreign Affairs, Hacı Adil Minister of the Interior, Ahmet İzzet Pasha acting commander-in-chief and Cemal Bey commandant of İstanbul.

The new government set out to create a spirit of national unity. Oppositionists who had been arrested were set free, and on 11 February a general political amnesty was declared; only those who had given material or moral aid to the enemy during the Balkan war were excluded from it. An Association for National Defence (*Müdafaa-i Milliye Cemiyeti*) was founded, and let it be known that it would embrace any hand which was proffered in defence of the homeland. Visits were paid to Prince Sabahattin and all prominent opposition journalists in an effort to win them over to the cause. The Porte Coup received a negative response from Europe primarily because public opinion was against the CUP, perceiving it and its works as a kind of plague. On 28 January the Balkan Alliance declared that the London Conference was at an end. On 30 January the Bulgarian Army high command declared that the armistice, which was to have ended three days later, was over. The Porte replied to the Powers' diplomatic note the same day, stating that Edirne was the second capital of the Ottoman Empire and a Muslim city which would not be given up under any circumstances, but that the lands on the right bank of the Maritza river would be surrendered. The future status of the Aegean islands could be decided by the Powers on condition that the security of Anatolia was safeguarded. There was also a demand for concessions on the part of the Great Powers: recognition of customs independence, trade equality, and taxation of foreigners residing in the Empire. As a first step customs duties would immediately be increased by 4%, foreign post offices would be shut down, and the Capitulations rescinded. Its stand on these matters was the reason why Europe so heartily detested the CUP. Europe wanted the Turks out of the Balkans and Edirne, whereas the CUP was clouding the issue with demands for economic independence.

The Bulgarians duly re-started the war. Young CUP officers wanted to initiate an offensive in order to lift the siege of Edirne, arguing that the objective of the Porte coup had been to save that city. However, neither Mahmut Şevket Pasha nor the acting Commander-in-Chief, Ahmet İzzet Pasha, thought that such an operation would be successful. The Ottoman Bank refused to advance funds to finance such an undertaking, but on the insistence of CUP officers it was decided that an operation in Bolayır should be attempted. As the Special Army Corps (*Mürettep Kolordu*), which was encamped on the Gallipoli peninsula, went into attack, the 10th Corps was to make a seaborne landing behind enemy lines at Şarköy. The Bulgarians were to be trapped between two lines of fire. The Special Corps went into attack on 8 February according to plan, but the Tenth Corps landing was delayed. It was only able to begin its action towards evening, which gave the Bulgarians the chance to stop the first and then the second attack. Fethi was chief of staff of the Special Corps, and his friend Mustafa Kemal was a member

of his staff. Enver was chief of staff of the Tenth Corps. The failure
of the operation caused recrimination between the two corps and
developed into personal disagreement between Enver and the other
two, Mustafa Kemal and Fethi.

There was no hope left on the horizon. During the following
weeks people tried to get used to the idea of abandoning Edirne. On
26 March Edirne surrendered after a heroic defence (stories are told
of people eating tree bark when no food was left). The Powers
insisted on the frontier being between Midye and Enos and thus
excluding Edirne from the rest of the Ottoman Empire. On 1 April
this frontier was accepted and on 30 May the London Peace Treaty
sanctioned the agreement. With the loss of Edirne, Enver, the key
activist in the Porte coup, lost his dominant position within the
CUP, and as the result Fethi Bey came forward and became the CUP
General Secretary.

With the loss of Edirne once more on the agenda, the opposition
again began to plot for a takeover. The CUP had not been able to
save Edirne, and there was also its unpopularity with the Europeans.
The first plot (at the beginning of March) was instigated by Prince
Sabahattin's private secretary, Satvet Lutfi, and was aimed at installing
a decentralist government. Although many people were arrested, the
CUP was careful not to spoil the atmosphere of national unity it had
created by reacting too harshly. For example, Sabahattin was not
deemed to be in collusion with the conspirators, although his house
was searched. The second conspiracy attempt was on 11 June, twelve
days after the London peace treaty. However, like all other opposition attempts to overthrow the government, this too was not well
planned. As Mahmut Şevket was driving from the Ministry of War
to the Sublime Porte, he was forced to stop and murdered by Captain Kâzım, a Circassian, and his fellow-conspirators. However,
nothing came of this plot except the death of Mahmut Şevket Pasha.
Kâzım and his fellow-conspirators were hiding out in the house of a
British woman in Pera, and although the British consulate refused to
issue a search warrant, they were besieged and forced to surrender
after a two-hour shoot-out. Kâzım and eleven other conspirators
were executed, among them Damat Salih Pasha, a French subject.
The CUP had no patience left, either for the Palace or for Capitulations Law. There is no need to go into the details of British and
French reactions to the CUP's new-found belligerence.

After Mahmut Şevket's assassination, the CUP was more than willing to forfeit the atmosphere of 'union and solidarity'. Among the eleven people condemned to death *in absentia* were Sabahattin and Sherif Pasha the Kurd, former Ambassador in Stockholm. Over 200 oppositionists were arrested and exiled to Sinop. A deaf ear was turned to the protests of the British Ambassador when Kâmil Pasha, who had returned from Egypt on 28 May, was placed under house arrest and later forced to leave İstanbul. An important development was that for the very first time a CUP member, Sait Halim Pasha, was asked to form the government. He had not been prominent in the CUP hierarchy, but with his Vizierate the supervisory status of the CUP came to an end. From then on its hold on power was complete.

Overview of the CUP supervisory government

At this point we should review the train of events of this period and evaluate its positive and negative aspects. From a strictly political point of view it may at first appear that this was a period of violent argument and disputes during which the Ottoman state made no headway and was forced to surrender most of its territory in the Balkans. Although to a certain extent this is true, it is not the full picture. Certain advances of a revolutionary nature were made with Turkish society taking definite steps towards a democratic bourgeois revolution—in other words, the modern age.

First there were legislative changes brought about for the dismantling of the old regime and establishment of the new. These are the constitutional reforms already mentioned in detail above. A second area of development was in the intellectual life of the country. No matter how politically oppressive or how jealous a guardian of its political position the CUP was, it basically adhered to a libertarian philosophy. After the long years of the Abdülhamit regime, when all free expression of ideas was restricted and suppressed, the world of letters enjoyed explosive development with a profusion of newspapers, magazines and books being published. A variety of currents of thought were developed and able to flourish. Education also benefited from this new-found atmosphere of freedom. Courses in history were diversified to embrace a broader spectrum rather than being limited, as they were, to Ottoman and

Islamic history. Courses in social sciences and philosophy became part of the curriculum. Like the People's Houses (Halkevi) of the later Republican era, CUP clubs, which were in fact the branches of the CUP Association, assumed an important function, becoming centers of cultural and social activity. The major intellectual currents which emerged in this period and were to continue in later periods will be taken up in the next chapter.

A third area of development was the economy. The right to acquire real estate was granted to corporate entities, and the sale of endowment property that had lost its function was allowed. Internal customs duties were abolished, and machinery and equipment imported for industrial investment were exempted from import tax. In 1911 the Company for the Protection of Fig Producers in the Aegean and, in 1912, the National Consumers' Society were established to increase demand for domestic products. In the twenty-three years from 1886 to the end of 1908 twenty-four industrial companies financed by domestic capital totalling 40.2 million kurush (averaging a 1.75 million kurush capital per year) were established, whereas in 1909–13 twenty-seven nationally financed industrial companies were established with a total capital of 79.2 million kurush (averaging yearly 15.9 million kurush). The number of companies increased fivefold and total capital reached nine times the previous level. In the same period the number and capital of foreign companies increased to only twice their previous total. Up till 1908 Muslims had established only semi-official enterprises. It was impossible, in practice if not legally, for an entrepreneur to establish his own company, and the very suggestion was looked at askance. Agricultural production trends also saw striking increases during the period of the CUP's supervisory government.

The fourth field of development was education. From 1904 to 1908 the Ministry of Education was apportioned 200,000 liras from the budget, rising to 600,000 in 1909, 940,000 in 1910 and 1,230,000 in 1914. In comparing these amounts it must be remembered that during this period the geographical extent of the Ottoman Empire had decreased. At the time of the Declaration of Freedom there were seventy-nine secondary schools, rising to ninety-five in 1914, and there were also great increases in the numbers of teachers and pupils.

11

MAJOR INTELLECTUAL CURRENTS OF THE CONSTITUTIONAL ERA

As has been mentioned above, according to Tarık Zafer Tunaya the Second Constitutional Period was a 'political laboratory' for the Republican era. The intellectual currents of this period should therefore be reviewed.

Islamism

Sultan Abdülhamit was a vigorous defender of Islamic unity and the Caliphate, perhaps more so than any previous Sultan. Although during his reign Islamism already had a mouthpiece in the periodical *Sırat-i Müstakim*, he was careful to allow no intellectual current to develop outside his control. As a result, true development of Islamism only occurred during the Second Constitutional Period. Islamism may be defined as a counter-current against the spreading world domination of Western imperialism and a Muslim reaction against the colonisation of Islamic countries. It was a current for those who sought an Islamic solution for the state of the world.

One group thought that Islam could prevail by wholeheartedly raising the banner of modernity. Namık Kemal was the forerunner of this school of thought: he was the father not only of modern Islamism but also of Ottoman nationalism (Ottomanism). A second forerunner of modern Islamism was Jamaluddin al-Afghani (1839–97), who influenced not only the people of the Ottoman Empire but also those of other Muslim countries. Other prominent modern Islamists were Mohammad Abduh of Egypt, Musa Carullah of Kazan, and Sayyid Ahmad Khan and Muhammad Iqbal of India. A prominent Islamist periodical during the Second Constitutional

Period was the *Sebilürreşad*. Other modern Ottoman Islamists were Sait Halim Pasha, M. Şemsettin Günaltay, İsmail Hakkı İzmirli, Şehbenderzade Ahmet Hilmi and Mehmet Ali Ayni, along with many others. Ahmet Naim and Mustafa Sabri were conservative Islamists of this era.

Westernism

The second major intellectual current of the Constitutional Period was Westernism. Its followers were those who thought the answer to the question 'How to save the Ottoman state?' would be found in Westernisation. Hilmi Ziya Ülken divides the Westernist school into four groups:

— The *Tanzimat Civilisationists*. These believed in Ottomanism, the basic teaching of the Tanzimat Period (1839), and sought to achieve its requisite 'Unity of Nationalities', i.e. Ottoman Nationalism, through Westernisation. They believed that the Ottoman nationalities or *millets* of different religions and creeds could be unified on a basis of Westernist development. Ülken includes in this group those, such as Satı Bey and Emrullah Efendi, who proposed education as a means of promoting Ottomanism. They declared that the only way to keep the Empire from falling apart was to promote pro-Ottoman sentiment in the young through education.

— Those who found fault with the structure of Ottoman society and wished to create an Anglo-Saxon type society. Their most prominent spokesmen were Prince Sabahattin and his followers.

— The *Positivists* were gathered around or had some connection with the periodicals *Servet-i Fünun* and *Ulum-u İktisadiye ve İçtimaiye*. Positivism was the basic world view of the CUP movement and later, during the Republican Era, adherence to this philosophy became a pronounced characteristic of Atatürk's Republican People's Party (the RPP). Ahmet Rıza was a staunch and outspoken supporter, dedicated to promoting positivism. Other CUP and, later, RPP members also adopted it as their world view although they perhaps lacked a full understanding of its implications.

— *Radical Westernists*: uncritical admirers of all that was Western.

The most famous ultra-radical of this school was Abdullah Cevdet, one of the five students of the Military School of Medicine who first established the CUP, and owner of *İçtihat* magazine. Cevdet was an exponent of the Latin alphabet. He and his wife could be seen sporting Western-style hats in the neighbourhood of Sirkeci, expounding the idea of intermarriage with Europeans as a swift antidote to backwardness. Although they did not go as far as Cevdet, other champions of this cause were Celal Nuri, Kılıçzade Hakkı and, to a lesser degree, Rıza Tevfik.

Turkism

Turkism may be regarded as a third major school of thought. As with many other nationalist philosophies, it is possible to analyse its beginnings by studying works in the disciplines of linguistics, literature and history. A majority of these works are relevant to the birth and development of Turcology in Europe, through authors such as Abel Remusat, Silvestre de Sacy, Deguignes and Arthur Lumley Davids. The works of the Polish Muslim convert Mustafa Celalettin Pasha and Leon Cahun as well as the works and public relations efforts of the Hungarian historian and Turcologist Arminius Vambery were of great influence. Awareness of Turkishness was heightened in a broad spectrum of the public by such works as the *Kavaid-i Osmaniye* (1851) of Fuat Pasha and Cevdet Pasha, *Lehçe-i Osmani* and *Hikmet-i Tarih* by Ahmet Vefik Pasha, *Tarih-i Alem* and *Türkçe Sarf* by Süleyman Pasha, *Lugat-i Çağatay* by Sheikh Süleyman Efendi and *Kamus-ı Türki* by Şemsettin Sami. In literature we see examples of simplified Turkish usage devoid of Ottoman stylism in Şinasi's experimental poetry and in a more developed form in the poetry of Mehmet Emin and Rıza Tevfik; also in Ahmet Hikmet's prose and in the defence of the Turkish language by Ziya Pasha and Ali Suavi.

Turkism was transformed into Turkish nationalism by the CUP. Because at first the CUP could not become an outright advocate of the break-up of the Ottoman empire, it was obliged to keep its true objectives secret even from its own adherents and to proceed for a long time with extreme caution. Gradually it underwent a metamorphosis, developing as time passed its own consciousness of being the political organisation of Turkism. *Üç Tarz-ı Siyaset*, a political essay by Yusuf Akçura, was a milestone in this progression. Akçura was the son of an industrialist from the city of Kazan in Russia who had emigrated to Turkey. While still a student at the War College he was exiled to Tripoli because of his affiliation to the CUP, and fled to Paris where he studied political science. After graduating, he returned to Russia and from there sent his essay to Cairo to be published in Ali Kemal's *Türk* newspaper in 1904. In this treatise he made an objective analysis of the pros and cons of Ottomanist, Turkist and Islamist policies for the Ottoman state. Thus for the first time ever these three alternatives were clearly brought to the attention of the educated Ottoman public. The Turks of Russia, such as Ahmet Ağaoğlu, Hüseyinzade Ali and Yusuf Akçura, played an important part in the development of the political aspect of Turkism. This may be related to Russia's more developed socio-economic environment and the fact that they were an oppressed group. The formula of Turkification, Islamification and Europeanisation was first championed by Ali Suavi, and in 1905 it was taken up by Hüseyinzade Ali (one of the five founders of the CUP) in an article for *Hayat* magazine, published in Tbilisi. After Ali Suavi, another champion of this blueprint for the future was Ziya Gökalp who made Turkification, Islamification and Europeanisation bywords.

The first attempt to create a Turkist organisation came after the Declaration of Freedom, when the Turkish Society (*Türk Derneği*) was founded on 7 January 1909. It was a cultural association with Armenians and some European orientalists among its members. On 31 August 1911 the Turkish Homeland Society (*Türk Yurdu Cemiyeti*) was established with the aim at first of providing accommodation for Turkish students. This society published the *Türk Yurdu (Turkish Homeland)* periodical, which influenced the development of Turkism. With the Tripolitanian war one Ottoman disaster after another added impetus to the Turkist cause. On 3 July 1911 the Turkish Hearth (*Türk Ocağı*) began its activities at the Military School of Medicine, which had been the birthplace of the CUP. The fact that Hüseyinzade Ali, a member of the CUP central committee, was a professor of medicine and that Yusuf Akçura taught political history at the War College would have helped prepare fertile ground for the birth and development of these societies.

The Turkish Hearth association was officially founded on 25 March 1912, when the Tripolitanian war had been going on for almost six months and Italy had attacked the Dardanelles only three days before. Among its founders were the most prestigious Turkists—Mehmet Emin Yurdakul, Ahmet Ferit Tek, Ahmet Ağaoğlu and Dr Fuat Salih. The Turkish Hearth became a major influence, especially effective in İstanbul where it sponsored a profusion of activities, including its Friday conferences and theatrical performances with players of both sexes. Its members wrote articles addressing issues of public interest, such as matters of the national economy. These articles were published in *Türk Yurdu*, which became an instrument of the Turkish Hearth association.

In the wake of the Balkan War and with the loss of almost the whole of the Empire's Balkan dominions, it was becoming increasingly apparent that Ottomanist ideology was bankrupt. The turn of events had changed the shape of Turkish politics, creating a new perspective. With Ottomanism being discarded as a viable option, the main obstacle blocking the open development of Turkism and causing it to remain a hidden or unproclaimed ideal, through fear that this would be seen as rejection of a multinational empire, had disappeared. In the face of a threat such as the loss of Edirne, which was considered an essential part of the Turkish homeland, these Ottomanist scruples became a secondary consideration. Events had proved that the concept of being Turkish now had to be promoted as an instrument for the defence of the nation. However, Ottomanist ideals, though of less consequence, were still alive; the drawbacks to the CUP openly declaring itself as a Turkist nationalist organisation had not completely disappeared and as a result the existence of bodies like the Turkish Hearth was still of importance. Despite these developments Turkish Hearth activities up till the 1918 Armistice were concentrated in İstanbul. The membership of its central branch there rose to 2,743, but nationwide it had no more than twenty-eight branches.

The turn of events in the Balkans suddenly and radically altered the ideological perspective of individuals. The composer Münir Mazhar Kamsoy related an incident which took place at the time when he was a student at the Mülkiye School for Civil Servants. Among schools of higher learning the Mülkiye was among the first where a Turkish Hearth organisation was established. Kamsoy and some of his fellow students from Üsküdar (Scutari) had organised a Turkish Hearth branch and were in search of an 'elder brother' figure, a mature and experienced leader and mentor for it. They thought they had found such a person in Hamdullah Suphi, with whom they were familiar from their boat trips across the Bosphorus. One day they invited him to join their society. Hamdullah Suphi, who a short while later became not only a member of the Turkish Hearth but its president, refused to join. He was remembered as saying: 'If Turks become Turkists, this will open the way for other ethnic groups to go their own way and the Empire will disintegrate. In any event, I am a Circassian and am not in sympathy with your cause.'

The pressing realities of actual circumstances and events often make the purest forms of ideology untenable in practice, leading individuals to maintain a judicious mixture of ideals. For example, anyone who was basically an Islamist could adopt certain Westernist and Turkist views. Namık Kemal was essentially a modern Islamist in his writing, but he also published tracts defending Ottomanist, Westernist and even Turkist viewpoints. Modern Islamists could also, to a certain extent, be counted as Westernists, and it was easy for some Westernists, after having contact with Western nationalism, to become somewhat sympathetic to Turkism. Many Westernists, anxious about the loss of identity and/or traditional values, took up a position of 'embargoed' or partial Westernisation. Thus 'the West' was obliged to pass through an intellectual barrier, with its beneficial sides (technology, science) allowed through and its negative sides (extreme individualism, loose family ties) rejected. If humanism and enlightenment are regarded as the highest product of Western thought, they in turn may be equated with unlimited intellectual freedom, without danger of loss of personal, traditional or religious values. But for Westernisation on this level to become widespread an effective educational system has to exist to ensure a substantial cultural background. In Turkey many nationalists have been on the side of 'embargoed', i.e. limited Westernisation. Atatürk's line was both decidedly pro-Western and at the same time nationalist. The basic concept of Atatürkism may be summed up as a high degree of Westernism and a high degree of nationalism.

Socialism

The Ottoman Socialist Party was founded in September 1910, some months after the first appearance of its periodical *İştirak* (Participation). Hüseyin Hilmi (nicknamed Socialist Hilmi) headed the movement. However, it did not have strong support, possibly because of the general lack of socio-economic development of Ottoman and especially Turkish society. There was no developed industrial sector and therefore no organised working class. Of course, social and cultural backwardness was another factor. For example, although Salonika had fewer workers than İstanbul, the socialist movement was much more active there because the city was socially and culturally more advanced.

12

THE C.U.P. IN FULL POWER AND ENTRY INTO THE FIRST WORLD WAR

The Second Balkan War

Nineteen days after the assassination of Mahmut Şevket on 30 June 1913 a 'miracle' took place for the Ottoman Empire and the Turks. After the war the Balkan states began squabbling over the spoils of the Empire. The Bulgarians launched an attack on their erstwhile allies and were defeated. During the conflict they evacuated Eastern Thrace. In accordance with the Treaty of London, the Ottoman army had advanced, at first, to the Midye-Enos Line, as of right, and the question then was whether or not to make an extra effort to regain Edirne. The CUP wanted this to happen. The older generation was pessimistic, decrying this enterprise as trouble for nothing and citing a truism of Ottoman diplomacy, the axiom 'Where once the Cross has entered, the Crescent may not return', meaning that even if the army should succeed in retaking Edirne, the wiles of European diplomacy would prevent it from holding it. The CUP stood firm and carried the day. The Ottoman army was sent racing towards Edirne with the units of Mustafa Kemal and Enver vying to be the first. The race was won by Enver's unit and on 22 July 1913 the Ottoman army entered Edirne and Kırklareli. A deaf ear was turned to the protests and threats of the Great Powers. Members of the Special Organisation (the secret military arm of the CUP) established the Independent Government of Western Thrace, supported by its Turkish majority and headed by Süleyman Askeri. These events culminated in the Treaty of İstanbul (29 September 1913) whereby Bulgaria was allotted Western Thrace with the Maritza river as its border while Edirne and Kırklareli were left in Ottoman hands. The Bulgarians, having lost to the Greeks and Serbs lands they had considered theirs by right, now saw the Ottomans as prospective allies against these two countries and went so far as to initiate talks with them to this end. In the light of the geopolitical situation it would have been unrealistic for the Bulgars to attempt to thwart the Great Powers, Russia in particular, by making a bid for İstanbul, Eastern Thrace or control of the Bosphorus and the Dardanelles.

The recapture of Edirne was greeted by celebration throughout the country. Enver, hero of the Porte coup, had been justified by this outcome and his position within the CUP was strengthened. The appointment that autumn of Fethi as Minister to Bulgaria with Mustafa Kemal as Military Attaché affirmed Enver's hold on power, because duty in Sofia spelt exile from the domestic political scene. Enver and his supporters had their eyes on the Ministry of War. For his services in the Tripolitanian and Balkan wars he was awarded three years' seniority for each war, thereby attaining the rank of Pasha (brigadier-general). With Mustafa Kemal and Fethi out of the way, Cemal emerged as Enver's new rival for power. He too had been promoted and entered the cabinet as Minister of Public Works.

Enver's elevation was perhaps also connected to his having married into the court. After the Declaration of Freedom the CUP had decided that supervision of Palace affairs would be facilitated by having two CUP loyalists marry members of the royal family. Enver was one of the two chosen for this duty, and in 1909 he became engaged to a niece of Sultan Reshat, the Sultana Naciye. At that time he was aged thirty and Naciye twelve. They were officially married in 1911 but only began to live together as man and wife when Naciye reached puberty in 1914 (after the Turks retook Edirne).

On becoming Minister of War, Enver embarked on a new purge of army ranks (January 1914). After the Declaration of Freedom all *alaylı* officers had been retired, and now it was the turn of elderly War College graduates, probably because they were blamed for the Balkan defeat; according to the calculation of General Liman von Sanders, they numbered 1,100. A major reorganisation of the army was initiated (February 1914) and the Ottoman army was largely rejuvenated. Enver (in contrast to Mahmut Şevket) did not use his position of influence within the CUP as a lever to increase the army budget. In 1911, 24.8% of the budget had gone to the Ministry of War, whereas by 1914 this figure had fallen to 17.6%. This may have been due to a growing realisation that economic and social development was more important than a strong, powerful army and that the army's strength would increase in step with the general development of the nation's potential.

Partition of the Ottoman Empire

The devastating and precipitate defeat of the Ottoman army in the Balkan war created a major collapse of morale within the Empire. An article written by Mizancı Murat in November 1912, saying that the Ottomans could only survive as a protectorate of one of the Powers and that this situation would have to continue for at least a quarter of a century, reflected this state of mind. At this juncture Kâmil Pasha espoused the idea of the Ottoman state becoming a British protectorate, and Mahmut Şevket, evaluating the situation from a military standpoint, came to a similar conclusion. Şevket argued that remodelling the army with the help of European advisers had proved ineffective and the only way to revitalise it was to put it under active German command. He carried out this plan, making a formal application to the German ambassador on 24 April 1913. As a result, a five-year agreement was signed in November of that year with General von Sanders, who was to become commander of the First Army Corps in İstanbul and a member of the Military Council, take charge of all military schools and training facilities, and be responsible for the theoretical education of general staff officers and for examinations for the promotion of officers. As the İstanbul Army Corps was to be handed over to the Germans, protests arose from Russia which proposed, to 'equalise' the situation, that İzmir be occupied by the British, Beirut by the French, and Trabzon by Russia itself. In order not to be seen to be backing down, Germany promoted von Sanders to the rank of Field-Marshal, too high a rank for an Army Corps commander. He was given the title of General Inspector.

Anticipating that the German connection would arouse protest, Mahmut Şevket thought to placate the British by requesting their help in enforcing the new 'Law of the Provinces'. They would appoint a British adviser to the Ministry of Internal Affairs and a General Inspector and inspectors of public works, forestry, agriculture and justice for the Eastern General Inspectorate (the provinces of Van, Bitlis, Mamuretülaziz and Diyarbakır) as well as the Northern Anatolian General Inspectorate (the provinces of Erzurum, Sivas and Trabzon), along with a commander for each gendarmerie unit in the seven provinces. Eastern and Northern Anatolia were 'pilot areas' to become in future administrative models for the whole of Anatolia. This British connection was meant to correct the 'mistake' of the rejected Lynch concession. However, there were two aspects of this situation that made it a tragedy for the Ottomans. In the recent past the CUP had refused to accept a loan from the French on the grounds that the concessions involved would impinge on its independence. Now the bitter reality of international politics had brought them to the point of relinquishing control of their army to the Germans and of their internal affairs to the British. A second cloud darkening the horizon was the fact that despite all the concessions made to Britain to ensure that Germany should reform the army, there was still the problem of dealing with the other four Great Powers, which were inevitably also lining up for concessions.

However, the CUP did not give up its struggle to have the Capitulations abolished, and to an extent it was successful. Although in principle the Powers accepted that the Capitulations should be abolished, each continued to block the issue with the condition that 'the others' should first give their consent, a process that could well continue indefinitely.

Thus a situation emerged which Mahmut Şevket had certainly not bargained for. Whereas hitherto geostrategic considerations had precluded the partition of Ottoman lands, the Powers had now manoeuvred themselves into a position where they could agree among themselves on their areas of influence and divide up a major portion of Ottoman lands (masking this under the general heading of railway construction and/or operational rights) while eliciting Ottoman consent to this process. Of course, such highly controversial locations as İstanbul and the Straits were not included in this agreement. The Porte had thought it was making a clever move with its 24 April proposal, juxtaposing the Russians against the British in Eastern Anatolia. However, by coming to an agreement with the British the Russians had turned the tables on the Ottomans and forced them to accept their move into eastern Anatolia. The Russian-Ottoman treaty of 8 February 1914 removed Eastern Anatolia (called 'Armenia' in Europe) from its status of an inter-European issue as determined by the Congress of Berlin and made this region a bone of contention between Russia and the Ottomans, as it had been as a result of the Treaty of San Stefano. In other words, Russia had now finally succeeded in becoming the most influential arbiter of the Armenian Question, if not the only one. If, for example, the Russians did not build railways in Eastern Anatolia, it would be almost impossible to re-contract with another country. Regional military service was established, and the Eastern and North-Eastern Anatolian Inspectorates, which were to have been posts of the British, went to a Dutchman and a Norwegian. However, the outbreak of War in August 1914 prevented these appointees from taking up their posts. In this way the CUP learned the bitter lessons of co-existing with imperialism and the exigencies of governing a multi-national empire.

At the Fifth Congress of the CUP, held on 20 September 1913, it was decided that primary and secondary education should be in local languages with Turkish being taught as a separate language course, whereas in the educational programmes for 1908 and 1909 regional languages had been sanctioned for primary education only. In the Arab world protests had been made in relation to this subject. At the January 1913 Beirut Provincial Assembly decisions were taken for local military service and a generally decentralised administration, with Arabic as the official language for Arab provinces. At the time when the CUP came to power with the Porte coup it had refused to accept decisions of the Beirut Assembly, but in March and April 1913 advances were made towards decentralised administration in Arab provinces, and in addition Arabic was made the official language of the judicial and educational systems. In June a CUP representative attended an Arab Congress in Paris where further demands were made. In August the use of Arabic in the bureaucracy and the employment of Arabic-speaking civil servants were conceded, and when the President of the Arab Congress and four other Arabs were made members of the Senate, it seemed as though an amicable agreement had been reached.

It was rumoured that Sait Halim Pasha had been made Grand Vizier partly to conciliate the Arabs. After the Balkan war some intellectuals evidently envisaged the Ottoman state as a nation of

Turks and Arabs and thought that it should model itself on Austria-Hungary, i.e. as a Turco-Arab empire. Following this line of reasoning, currents emerged and voices were raised urging that Islamism should be espoused by the CUP. This view was expounded in a series of articles written by Ziya Gökalp for the *Türk Yurdu* periodical, entitled 'Turkification, Islamification and Modernisation', the first of which was published on 20 March 1913. It goes without saying that the CUP understanding of Islamism was modernist.

Entry into the First World War

How did the Ottoman Empire become involved in the First World War? It is a matter of common knowledge that towards the end of the nineteenth century the rift between the Great Powers of Europe had separated them into divergent alliances. On one side were the Central Powers: Germany, Austria-Hungary and Italy, and on the other the Entente Powers: France, Russia and Britain, with Italy later joining this alliance. For years the Powers had been preparing for war, but the immediate chain of events that led to its outbreak began with the assassination of the heir to the Austro-Hungarian throne by Serbian nationalists while visiting Sarajevo in Bosnia on 28 June 1914. Much of the population of Austria-Hungary was of Slavic origin, and wary of the influence of Serbia on this ethnic majority Austria-Hungary decided to use this assassination as an excuse to teach Serbia a lesson. On Serbia refusing to comply with its heavy demands, Austria declared war on 28 July. Because Serbia as an Orthodox-Slavic country was to a certain extent a Russian protectorate, this declaration drew Russia into the conflict, causing it to mobilise, not only on its Austrian but also on its German border (29 July). The German Emperor, anxious as to where this mounting tension might lead, took his complaint to his friend the Russian Tsar. The Russian high command informed the Tsar that because Germany and Austria-Hungary were allies, its mobilisation plan included both countries' fronts and at this stage of events could not be revised to focus on Austria alone. German strategy was also geared for war against two countries. The initial German attack was to be directed at France, which would be the quickest to mobilise. After defeating France, Germany would then turn the full force of its army upon Russia. Accordingly, Germany declared war against

Russia on 1 August and against France on 3 August. On 4 August Britain declared war against Germany. The First World War had begun.

As war with Serbia became imminent, the Austrians began to show interest in allying themselves with the Ottomans, but the Balkan defeat had caused the Austrian, and particularly the German, administrations to be wary of an Ottoman alliance, the prevalent opinion being that it could become more of a burden than a benefit. In spite of these views, Germany decided in favour of the alliance (23 July) and talks began (unknown to the Ottoman Cabinet), handled by the pro-German Sait Halim, Talat, Enver and Halil (Menteşe), President of the Chamber of Deputies. A treaty with Germany was signed on 2 August. The German Military Mission would have a strong influence over and actively participate in the organisation and deployment of the Ottoman army, and in return, if it should become necessary, Germany would defend the integrity of Ottoman frontiers. It is of note that the Ottomans signed this treaty after the war had begun, hence the signatories were entirely aware that they were involving their country not only in an alliance but in a war. When the other government members learned of this treaty, there were vehement protests. They insisted that at the very least the alliance should be kept secret and that participation in the war should be delayed for as long as possible. The Ottoman Cabinet went so far as to apply to the Entente with a proposal for a treaty of alliance, but their overtures were coldly rejected with the response that Ottoman neutrality would be sufficient. Of course, their underlying motive in rejecting Ottoman proposals for an alliance was that they did not want as an ally a country which they had already decided to carve up among themselves.

Why was the Ottoman government so eager for an alliance and therefore for the war which it inevitably entailed? The factor that tipped the scales seems to be the hope of redeeming the losses of the Balkan war. Edirne, lost but later regained, was a prime example, feeding hopes of regaining lost territories. All over the country, in the barracks and in the schools, the slogan was 'Revenge for the Balkan war'. It was also feared that if an alliance was not formed with one side or the other, the Powers would inevitably carve up the country. Another factor was lack of funds. In answer to Yakup

Kadri's post-war question 'Why did we get involved?' Cemal Pasha answered, 'To pay people's salaries' (quoted from F. R. Atay, *Zeytindağı*). Throughout the war Germany financially supported the Ottomans.

As hostilities began, the *Goeben* and *Breslau*, two German warships of the latest technology under the command of Admiral Souchon, were in the Mediterranean. Stalked by the British navy, these ships were ordered to enter the Dardanelles strait, and Enver allowed them in without consulting the cabinet (10 August). The government had planned to engage in the war but not before the spring, and in an effort to avoid it for as long as possible, demanded that either the ships be divested of their arms or they quit Turkish waters. When Germany rejected these demands, the Ottoman government announced that it had purchased these ships. The *Goeben* and *Breslau* were renamed the *Yavuz* and the *Midilli*, the Ottoman flag was hoisted, and German sailors donned the fez. On 9 September, on being named commander of the Ottoman navy, Souchon demanded training manoeuvres in the Black Sea. Enver gave his consent without consulting Cemal Pasha, Minister of the Navy. When Cemal Pasha protested at this decision, the German Ambassador announced that the ships were still German. In October the Germans, finding themselves unable to achieve hoped-for victories on the Eastern and Western fronts, began to insist that the Ottomans participate in the war. The Ottoman navy was to stage a surprise attack on Russian ports, and later fronts were to be opened in the Caucasus and on the Suez Canal. Enver accepted this plan and the two other leaders of the CUP, Talat and Cemal, went along with his decision. On 27 October the fleet steamed into the Black Sea. On 29 and 30 October Sebastopol and Odessa were shelled. No other members of the Cabinet had been informed of these decisions. Upon learning of what had transpired, Cavit and three other ministers resigned in protest. Russia on 2 November 1914 and France and Britain on 5 November declared war on the Ottoman Empire. Enver had fallen in with all of Germany's demands, hoping that in the event of a German victory the Ottomans might have a larger share of the spoils. Thus the Ottoman government became a prisoner of German ambition.

On 11 November 1914, the Ottoman state declared war on the Entente Allies and on 23 November a *jihad* (holy war) was proclaimed to the Islamic world with due religious ceremony, but this had little effect. Muslim soldiers fought in British and French armies against the Ottomans, and Ottoman subjects from the Hejaz and many other Arab provinces had few inhibitions about bearing arms against the Ottoman army.

13

THE STRUGGLE FOR FULL INDEPENDENCE

A month into the First World War the Ottoman government took advantage of the Powers' preoccupation with their internecine war and took a historic decision, made public on 9 September (a propitious date for Turkey, on which İzmir was liberated from foreign occupation in 1922). All financial, economic, judicial and administrative Capitulations were totally abolished.

The first seeds of this dependence had been sown in the early centuries of the Empire in the form of a series of privileges and 'capitulations' extended only to foreigners. When the Empire was at the height of its power this system had been meant to facilitate and encourage trade, but in the era of Ottoman weakness it had become an instrument of European hegemony and exploitation. The Ottoman state had become incapable of determining the taxes and tariffs to be collected from foreigners, and economic development was therefore impeded since domestic producers could not compete against foreign goods which flooded the markets of the Empire. The Powers had become a law unto themselves with their own consulate courts of law, postal systems, prisons and a plethora of other privileges. The CUP viewed the Capitulations as the primary obstacle to their goal of modernising the Ottoman state and was determined to abolish them. Having found the opportunity, it was at long last putting an end to this system with the 9 September decision. This was, in effect, a declaration of full independence.

Of course it was not enough simply to declare that the Capitulations were ended. It was also necessary to ensure the official acceptance of the termination by the parties to whom the decision was addressed. However, to the surprise of the Ottomans the Powers were able momentarily to put aside the fact that they were engaged in a deadly conflict with each other in order to formulate a note of protest, delivered by their representatives to the Vizierate, stating that they unanimously rejected this one-sided decision. This bizarre situation continued throughout the war; while Ottoman armies fought against Entente forces at the front, the primary concern of Ottoman diplomacy was to persuade its allies (the Central Powers and Bulgaria) to agree to abolish the Capitulations. At the end of an arduous diplomatic struggle Germany finally agreed to their abolition in January 1917, with the proviso that the German privileges would be renewed if the Entente countries did not give their consent after the war. It was obvious that such a conditional agreement was not of great value, but after further lengthy negotiations the Ottomans finally signed a treaty with the Germans in November 1917, whereby Germany undertook not to sign any treaty allowing the Capitulations to stand.

The development of capitalism

Modernisation of the socio-economic structure and the development of capitalism were an essential aspect of achieving full independence. Measures initiated during the Supervisory Government period for restructuring and accelerating the development of the economy were extended to cover a wider proportion of society. The extraordinary conditions of war added momentum. The process of forming companies is a case in point. In 1913 two members of the CUP, Kâzım Nuri and Topçuoğlu Nazmi, founded the Aydın Fig Producers' Company. In 1909–17, the founding of joint-stock companies followed a generally upward trend:

1909	3	1914	10
1910	13	1915	15
1911	22	1916	15
1912	8	1917	29
1913	5		

The decreases in 1912 and 1913 were due to the Balkan War, but during the years of the First World War it is striking that the business boom continued. Not just joint-stock companies were involved. Kara Kemal, responsible during the war years for food supply, was active in encouraging traders to form companies for their small and medium-sized enterprises. Total domestic capital rose from 3% in 1908 to 38% in 1918. Banks established were the Adapazarı Islamic Trade Bank, today's Turkish Bank of Commerce (Türk Ticaret Bankası) in 1913, the Aydın National Bank (Milli Aydın Bankası) of Kâzim Nuri and Topçuoglu Nazmi in 1914 and the Manisa Bank of Vine-growers (Manisa Bağcılar Bankası) in 1917. On 1 January 1917, the great National Credit Bank (İtibar-i Milli Bankası) was founded with Ottoman shareholders only. Originally founded as a trade bank, it was intended that it should later become Turkey's central bank. As such it would take on the functions of the Ottoman Bank, which was dominated by British and French capital. During the occupation of İstanbul the Entente powers, aware of its importance for Ottoman economic independence, did all in their power to undermine it.

Various measures were implemented to ensure the accumulation of capital. One, enacted towards the end of 1913, was the Law for the Encouragement of Industry. Various incentives were offered such as government land grants for factories, tax exemption and preferential government purchasing. After the Capitulations were abolished, import and export tariffs were redetermined. In March 1916 all companies doing business in the country were obliged to use the Turkish language in their correspondence and accounting. This had the threefold advantage of obliging non-Turks to learn Turkish, facilitating supervision of foreign company activities, and improving the opportunities for Turks with no knowledge of foreign languages to find work. For example, no Turks had been employed by the Aegean railways except in menial positions. To enable Turks to become eligible for these jobs the School for Railway Employees was opened in June 1915 by the CUP representative for İzmir, Celal Bey (who later became Celal Bayar, third President of the Turkish Republic). Wartime shortages were utilised to create opportunities for Turkish enterprise. Because railway car space was largely allocated to the transportation of military matériel during the war, its allocation to Turks (preferably Turks affiliated to the CUP) created a profitable source of income.

The fact that many Greeks and Armenians from Eastern Thrace and Anatolia emigrated or were forced to emigrate was another war-related factor which helped to establish Turkish capitalism. Before the Balkan war almost all the grocery stores in the Aegean region were owned by Greeks, and in many regions commerce and all crafts and artisanship were in the hands of both Greeks and Armenians. Their emigration opened the way for Turks to move into these sectors.

The history of the establishment of companies and capitalism in Ankara is told in the memoirs of Vehbi Koç, one of Turkey's foremost businessmen and industrialists. At the outbreak of the war the Ottoman fleet dominated the Black Sea, but this dominion passed to the Russians when they launched new ships. As a result, Black Sea trade had to be carried out overland. Goods were transported first to Ankara by train, then to Samsun by caravan and from there further east along the coast. This encouraged an economic awakening in Ankara. Koç became a partner in some of the many companies founded in Ankara at this time (many under the auspices of the CUP).

The first book of economic theory to be widely read in Turkey was *Ekonomi Politik* (Political Economy), a defence of protectionism by Ahmet Mithat Efendi (1880). A counter-current defending the principle of free trade had proponents in Ohannes of Chios and Mikail Portakal, professors at the Mülkiye School for Civil Servants. Musa Akyiğit of Kazan, a graduate of a Russian lycée and student of Ohannes, who had graduated with a First from the Mülkiye and became a professor of economics at the War College and at the War Academy, was another proponent of protectionism. He based his arguments on the theories of the German economist List, according to whom domestic industry must be protected for a certain period during its development until it is established. After the Declaration of Freedom free trade became the dominant theory with adherents such as Cavit Bey, Professor of Economics and Minister of Finance for the CUP government.

In 1910 Alexander Helphand, a German Jew known as Parvus, went to Turkey and resided there for five years. Parvus was a Marxist. He became a CUP adviser and author of many articles introducing the concepts of imperialism and exploitation to the Turkish public and explaining exactly how institutions such as the Ottoman Public Debt Association and the Tobacco Monopoly were able to exploit the country. He also emphasised the importance of rural development.

During the war, movements began to develop within the CUP which encouraged traders' associations, cooperatives and even state enterprise. Kara Kemal was active in this. Of greater consequence was the current of statism (*étatisme*, mixed economy), which grew stronger in the later years of the war. It and other currents that found a basis in economic co-operation (solidarism) were inspired by similar developments in Germany. Ziya Gökalp and Tekin Alp (formerly M. Cohen) were active in these areas. Gökalp argued against Manchester economics while Tekin Alp's arguments condemned 'social Darwinism'.

14

THE FIRST WORLD WAR

Major events

It will suffice to outline major aspects and developments of the war from the Turkish point of view without going into detail. The Ottoman state had declared war on 11 November and Jihad-i Ekber (Holy War) on 23 November 1914, thus calling on the Islamic world to side with the Central Powers against the Entente Allies. The Germans and Austro-Hungarians urged the Ottomans to go on the offensive as soon as possible in the east, to relieve pressure on their Western Front. Enver was eager and willing, making plans for the Sarıkamış offensive in Eastern Anatolia against the Russians, over which he personally assumed command, and a Suez Canal operation against the British. Enver's daring Sarıkamış offensive opened on 18 December 1914, promising brilliant results, but ended in total fiasco on 10 January 1915. Even after defeat had clearly become inevitable, Enver stubbornly continued the attack, and nearly all the Ottoman units involved were decimated. The number of dead was estimated at no less than 60,000, a great proportion of whom died not in battle but from exposure, hunger and disease exacerbated by lack of transport. As a result of this rout the opposite of German intentions was realised; the Russians, finding themselves unopposed by Ottoman forces, were able to transfer many of their units to the European front.

Keeping the true facts of the situation secret from the public, Enver decided to return to İstanbul and requested that the battleship *Yavuz*, which had taken him to Trabzon, be sent there for his return trip. Talat, the Minister of the Interior, telegraphed in reply that the *Yavuz* could not be sent into such dangerous waters, an answer which made Enver uneasy about the strength of his position, although he had the backing of the Germans. At this juncture Enver thought of Mustafa Kemal, who had applied to him from Sofia for a field command. If there were indeed political currents running against Enver, it would have been unwise for him to alienate Mustafa Kemal. Enver accordingly ordered that Mustafa Kemal be made a commander of the newly-established 19th Division; coincidentally the British army landing at Gallipoli was to meet Mustafa Kemal's division head-on at Anafartalar. Mustafa Kemal began the battle of Chanakkale as a divisional commander but was to rise in rank dramatically during this struggle to Corps, Army and Army Group commander.

On the second front the Minister of the Navy, Cemal Pasha, was made commander of the 4th Army in Damascus and thereupon embarked on the Suez Canal operation with high hopes of conquering the whole of Egypt. One optimistic assessment of the situation was that when the Egyptians realised that the Turkish army was at the Canal they would rebel against the British. This offensive was launched on 3 February with the aim of overrunning the Canal, but was unsuccessful. As the 35,000 soldiers of the Turkish army depended on camels as their only means of crossing the Sinai desert, this should have come as no surprise. Faced with a hopeless situation, Cemal Pasha at least had the sense to order a retreat.

Encouraged by the Russians, who wanted the Ottoman armies hemmed in on a second front, and supported by the French, the British began their attack on Chanakkale from the sea on 19 February 1915. Meanwhile, the Russians were pushing for British and French recognition of their claim to İstanbul. İstanbul, the Bosphorus, the Dardanelles and the whole of the Marmara region between Midye-Enos and the Sakarya river were thus recognised as Russian territory by the Allied Powers. Having no toleration of rivals in this region, Russia vetoed the offer by Greece to send three divisions and even went so far as to try to keep Italy from joining the Entente. Greece and Italy, evidently having concluded that the Ottoman Empire was at its last gasp, were positioning themselves to grab a share of the spoils. On 26 April 1915, with the Treaty of London, Italy joined the Entente.

Bulgaria and Romania too had their eyes focused on the developments at Chanakkale and were waiting for the outcome. Little war material came through to Turkey from Germany at this time because as neutrals both the two countries mentioned barred the way. Engaged in an all-out struggle at Chanakkale, despite insufficient arms, ammunition and provisions, subsisting solely on their meagre rations of bulgur (wheat), the Turks prevailed and succeeded in repelling the enemy.

This Turkish success was to prolong the war and lead to the collapse of the Tsarist regime by starving it of support. In addition the Turks proved on the battlefield how determined they were to be independent and not become the colony of any Power. Lastly, the myth of the invincibility of the imperialist Powers and the foundations of Europe's colonial empires were shaken by this revelation.

On 18 March 1915 an attempt by the Entente fleet to break through at Chanakkale was repulsed by the Turks. Subsequently a landing took place at Gallipoli on 25 April, but in spite of heavy bombardment of the Turkish positions by the Entente fleet and after many battles resulting in a great number of casualties on both sides, the Entente was forced to evacuate Gallipoli in December 1915 and January 1916. Colonel Mustafa Kemal was hailed as the 'saviour of Istanbul' particularly because of his stand at the battle of Anafartalar in August 1915. The Bulgarians, on this evidence of the strong Turkish stand at Chanakkale, had joined the Central Powers on 6 September 1915. As a result, the Serbs were defeated and the first wartime train from Central Europe arrived at Sirkeci station, Istanbul, on 17 January 1916.

The Ottomans had, for some time, surrounded British forces commanded by General Townshend at Kut-ül Amare, Iraq. The Turkish army gained another victory on its eastern front when General Townshend's forces were forced to surrender on 29 April 1916. This too was a great if temporary boost for Turkish morale.

As if the difficulty of defending the Ottoman Empire's far-flung territories was not enough of a challenge, Enver initiated an operation in Iran. The British launched a new offensive in Iraq and were able to conquer Baghdad on 11 March 1917.

On 11 January 1916 the Russians began their offensive in Eastern Anatolia where the Turkish situation was quickly deteriorating. In six months Erzurum (16 February), Rize (8 March), Trabzon (18 April) and Erzincan (25 July) fell to the Russians. In Arabia the

Emir of Mecca, Sharif Hüseyin, having come to a secret agreement with the British, rebelled against Ottoman authority and took control of Mecca on 2/3 June 1916. Thus a parting of the ways had come for a substantial part of the Arab peoples of the Ottoman Empire. The fact that the CUP was essentially a Turkish nationalist organisation was further highlighted by events.

The situation of the Ottoman railways exemplifies the difficulties faced by the Turks in conducting the war. When the war began, the construction of the Baghdad Railway had been completed only as far as Akçakale (Tel Abiyat beyond Aleppo). Even worse, work on tunnels needed for passage through the mountain ranges of south-eastern Anatolia (37 km. through the Taurus and 97 km. through the Amanos mountains) remained uncompleted. In these areas materials and personnel had to be transported over mountain paths, mostly by pack animals. In the best of circumstances it took twenty-two days to travel from İstanbul to Baghdad, and an uninterrupted rail service from İstanbul to Aleppo only began on 9 October 1918, three weeks before the Armistice.

In eastern Anatolia there were no railways at all. The sea-route east was not safe because the Russians were well on their way to dominating the Black Sea with their new warships. Once past Ulukışla (south of Niğde) only primitive paths led to the front. In the last years of the war, the southern fronts were a scene of barefoot and hunger-stricken Ottoman foot-soldiers, and equally hungry horses and mules, labouring under the harsh weather.

Despite hardships and setbacks a second attempt, commanded by a German, von Kress (again with the underlying aim of lightening the load of the Germans armies in the west), was made on the Suez Canal early in 1916. It yielded no positive results and a retreat followed with many casualties. From the second half of 1916 to the beginning of 1917 select and well-equipped Turkish troops were being sent to the fronts in Romania (three divisions), Galicia (two divisions) and Macedonia (two divisions). In contrast the Bulgarians, keen to protect their own interests, refused to send their troops anywhere except their own fronts and would not even allow Enver to inspect Ottoman troops stationed in those regions.

In this darkening theatre of war hope suddenly flickered on the horizon. In the first half of March 1917 war-weariness gave way to riots in St Petersburg, and the winds of revolution rose to full force. On 15 March the Russian Tsar abdicated, and it was a sign that a new era had begun for Russia when Grand Duke Michael refused the throne. The new Russian government, especially its Foreign Minister Miliukov, was still focused on gaining İstanbul and the Straits and therefore determined to remain in the war. But country people had had enough. Supported by the Germans, Lenin returned to St Petersburg on 16 April 1917 and became the spokesman of the Russian people who wanted peace, bread and land. On 7 November the Bolsheviks came to power with a successful coup. They repudiated all secret treaties and declared that Russia wanted peace with no reparations or annexations. Not content with this declaration, they published those secret agreements and immediately began negotiations for a separate peace. On 15 December the Ottomans signed an armistice with Russia at Brest-Litovsk. While the peace-making process was going on, Russian soldiers began to make their way home to their villages, some selling their weapons. Without doubt this development allowed the Central Powers to take a deep breath, but this was only a temporary respite. As one great Allied power left the war, a greater power, the United States of America, was preparing to enter it (6 March 1917). At this turning point, although America was not yet prepared for war and the Atlantic separated it from Europe, so that its powerful influence was not immediately felt, it was only a matter of time before the inevitable end of the war. In Germany strikes began in April 1917 and a naval rebellion broke out in July, showing that there too war-weariness had begun to affect popular morale.

If only for a short while, there was euphoria on the Central Alliance's eastern front. On 12 February 1918, the Ottoman army began to advance, taking back Erzincan and Trabzon in February, Erzurum and Ardahan in March, and Sarıkamış, Van, Batum and Kars in April. I use the word 'taking' because in place of the retreating Russian army there were now Armenian units putting up a stiff resistance. With the Treaty of Brest-Litovsk, signed on 3 March 1918, the sancaks of Kars, Ardahan and Batum (lost in the 1877–8 Ottoman-Russian war) were returned to the Ottomans. Ottoman operations were not limited to these regions alone. On 28 May 1918 Azerbaijan declared its independence. Its new government felt threatened by the Armenians, the British and the Russians and asked for help from the Ottoman government. Thus the Ottoman army, not content with the three sancaks, began to advance towards Azerbaijan, and on 15 September, Baku was occupied after British withdrawal. The Ottoman army, moving further north, then intervened in Daghestan, entering Derbent on 6 October.

Nevertheless, the end of the war was imminent. On 14 September Austria applied to the Entente for peace and on the 18th the Bulgarian front was overrun. On Germany's Western Front and within the country itself the situation had deteriorated. On 29 September the Germans decided to present their application to Woodrow Wilson, President of the United States, for a peace based on Wilson's Fourteen Points. On 30 October 1918 the Ottoman state signed the Armistice of Mudros (Mondros). In contrast to the Ottoman army's victories in the Caucasus, the situation on its southern fronts had gone from bad to worse. On the Iraqi front the British had taken Baghdad (11 March 1917) and were slowly but inexorably advancing towards Mosul, while in Sinai they were laying railway tracks and water pipelines as they advanced. On 21 December 1916, the British took El Arish; in March–April 1917 the Ottoman army stopped the British advance on Gaza, but on 6 November the Ottoman lines were overrun. On 9 December Jerusalem fell to the British. Despite all their setbacks and deprivations the Ottomans held out on the Palestine front till 18 September 1918, when the British began their major assault. With Arab support, superior British forces demolished the Ottoman defences. The Ottomans established a new front north of Aleppo commanded by Mustafa Kemal, but this was only a few days before the Armistice of Mudros. Henceforth the defence of Anatolia was to begin. It should be pointed out that in 1918 Enver had allocated the greatest part of army resources to the Caucasian front in defiance of German protests. This decision showed that Turkish nationalism had become the government's primary concern, and Arab interests were now relegated to a secondary position, even if only temporarily.

The forcible transfer of the Armenians
It was clear that Turkish involvement in the World War had created an atmosphere of optimism among the Armenians. They apparently

presumed that the Turkish army, which had been so easily routed in the Balkan confrontation, would be quickly vanquished by the vastly superior Russian, British and French forces and that advantages for them would soon be apparent. The 10 January 1915 Turkish debacle at Sarıkamış confirmed these hopes. A month later the confrontation at Chanakkale began, and despite the initial Turkish victory on 18 March, a landing was made by the British at Gallipoli on 25 April. However, Armenian calculations were once again proved wrong. The Turkish army refused to give in at Chanakkale, and the Russians, despite their successes in eastern Anatolia, were slow to occupy the region. In addition to these setbacks to Armenian aspirations, the war was to drag on for four years, in the third year of which the Russian front collapsed in the wake of the Russian Revolution. These developments were not foreseen by the Armenians when they rebelled against Turkish authority in the Van region on 15 April 1915 in support of the Russian attack. Bloody rebellions also took place on 18 April in Bitlis and on 20 April in Van. In the city of Van the Armenian districts put up a stiff resistance and by the middle of May Russo-Armenian units had overrun and taken control of the city. All Muslims were killed and an Armenian state was declared under Russian auspices. Approximately 250,000 Armenians flocked to the Van region, and although Van was retaken by the Ottomans at the beginning of August, the Russians later recaptured it.

This action by the Armenians while Turkey was fighting for its very existence persuaded the CUP that if Turkey were to survive the war, the Armenians had to be neutralised. Consequently their transfer, for the duration of the war, from regions where they could have a negative effect on Turkish fronts—i.e. eastern Anatolia and the Mersin-Iskenderun region—to other regions of the Empire, the interior of Syria and Iraq, was initiated as a precaution. The Armenian rebellion had taken place in April; preparations for the transfer were begun in May, and a provisional law passed on 27 May 1915 gave the army the task of overseeing it. The terms of relocation were made permanent by a cabinet decision of 30 May. Immigrants were to be settled in places evacuated by Armenians, who in return would be compensated for their property and goods, and their previous standards of living would be ensured in the areas where they were resettled. Housing would be provided for the poor. A later pro-

visional law, dated 26 September 1915, ruled that the real property
and goods of the persons being relocated would be liquidated by the
courts and the proceeds distributed in accordance with the reports
of special commissions. Real estate was to be compensated by the
treasury and certain pious foundations; moveable goods were to be
sold. All proceeds were to be given to the transferred Armenians to
whom they were due. To what extent these measures were implemented is a subject for further research.

By far the worst aspect of the relocation of the Armenians was
what happened to them on the way to their places of resettlement.
Lack of transportation, food and shelter, harsh weather and the
resulting diseases caused much loss of life. Revenge and banditry also
caused many deaths. There are varying estimates of the number of
Armenians who died or were killed. Armenians and their supporters have exaggerated the estimates, saying that one million or even
more people died. The historian Stanford J. Shaw places the figure
at 200,000.

Social changes during the war

The dictatorship of the CUP during the war allowed the free application of some of the more radical aspects of its CUP programme
(referred to in previous chapters). This freedom for development
was attained, not only because the CUP no longer needed to be
wary of the opposition, but also because religious fanaticism was
under restraint. During the war the closure of the weekly *Sebilürreşat*
periodical for two years was an example of the CUP's dictatorial
methods. After Sharif Hüseyin unfurled his flag of rebellion, it
became clear that the Arab attitude towards the war was generally
negative. Thereafter the CUP was less inhibited about offending
Arab religious sensibilities and diminishing their war effort. The
retirement of the Islamist Sait Halim and the presence of a broad-
minded Sheyhülislam (the Grand Mufti, head of the Islamic establishment), Musa Kâzim, made progress easier. Consequently, in
accordance with a decision of the 1916 CUP Congress, all Sharia
courts were taken from the Sheyhülislam's jurisdiction and put
under the authority of the Ministry of Justice (Law of 25 March
1917). Born of the CUP's modern and bourgeois outlook, this was
an important step towards secularism. However, while this was

indeed a step towards secularism, it was also taken with a secondary consideration in mind, that of liberation from the system of Capitulations: the existence of religious courts had served Europe as a pretext for its objections to the authority of the Turkish judicial system. Another bold innovation was the Family Law Decree (7 November 1917) which brought into being a system of family law applying to all Ottomans, Muslim and non-Muslim. However, this decree may be considered as being within the boundaries of Sharia law because it was implemented in accordance with a fatwa (*fetva*) and based on rules derived from the four Sunni Muslim sects and deemed most appropriate for contemporary life. In addition, certain entirely new dispositions furthering women's rights, as well as special dispositions concerning non-Muslims, were also included. Another important innovation was brought about by the 1917 Law, ratified after intense dispute, which ended the thirteen-day difference between the Christian and Roman/Islamic calendars. Thus after 1 March 1917 Roman/Islamic and Christian calendars became identical where days and months were concerned, but still the year remained different (for instance, 1 March 1917 became the Roman/Islamic 1 March 1333).

Among other reformist legislation was the Law of the Medreses (*Medaris-i Ilmiye*). This and its related regulations sought to establish a system which would transform the *medreses* (religious colleges) into modern institutions of religious learning. Their curriculum would include the exact and natural sciences and courses in Western languages. Last but not least, efforts were made to revise the old Arabic-based Turkish alphabet in order to make it more compatible with the Turkish language. Sometime around 1911 the Alphabet Reform Society (Islah-ı Huruf) had been established under the auspices of the Turkish Hearth. Hüseyin Cahit, on the other hand, was a proponent of the Latin alphabet. Shortly before the war, Enver had experimented within the army with an application of Arabic characters written separately in the fashion of the Latin alphabet, instead of running together, but this attempt was abandoned for the duration of the war.

Important changes took place in the lives of women. This had been a country where formerly men and women had not been allowed to walk together in the streets because it was not evident at a glance whether they were living in sin or not. The exigencies of war allowed women to enter the workforce. In factories and offices, in agriculture and even in city streets demand arose for women workers (for example, they collected garbage in İstanbul). Naturally the CUP encouraged this development. The Women Workers' Society was established under army auspices, and its members made uniforms, undergarments and sandbags for the army. In the Society's workshops, 6–7,000 women worked for a daily fee of 10 kurush and were given lunch. When necessary, the same number again worked on projects in their homes. The Society was a profit-making association. Furthermore, a women's battalion was established in the First Army. Single women lived the life of their male counterparts, and married women were allowed leave to go home for four nights a week. At the end of 1917 the Society required all of its workers to be married, and to this end instituted a system for them to find suitable husbands. During this period women began to attend a wide range of schools including the University. Although the veil was still worn in big cities such as Istanbul, many women no longer covered their faces. In time the first Muslim actresses began to appear on the stage of the Darülbedayi theatre.

Part III

THE ERA OF ATATÜRK

15

END OF THE WAR AND ARMISTICE (TO 19 MAY 1919)

Defeat at the front

In the autumn of 1918 the Allies mounted their final offensives of the war. The major British assault on Palestine, commanded by General Allenby, began on 19 September. Enver had concentrated most of his resources in the Caucasus, and his successes there were gained at the expense of a relatively undefended Ottoman southern front, which was consequently ripped apart by Allenby's attack. General Liman von Sanders, commander of the Ottoman southern front, at first ordered a retreat to the south of Damascus in order to establish a new front in southern Syria, but on realising that this was not feasible he changed tactics and decided to regroup in Homs. At this point Mustafa Kemal, commander of the 7th Army, pre-empted von Sanders' decision by ordering a retreat to Aleppo near Syria's northern frontier with Anatolia. In answer to the latter's demand that he explain this open defiance of his orders, Mustafa Kemal stated that Syria was an Arab country, whereas it had now become imperative to defend Turkish Anatolia. Von Sanders disassociated himself from this policy and relinquished his command. Thereupon Mustafa Kemal became acting commander and later official commander of the southern front. Arriving in Aleppo, he observed that Ottoman soldiers were being fired on by snipers concealed in the buildings of the city and decided to reposition, moving the new front north of Aleppo. Encompassing the whole of Alexandretta, this new front was able to withstand British assaults. In the words of Mustafa Kemal, this was to be 'the border drawn by Turkish bayonets'.

On 15 September 1918, the time of the British Palestinian offensive, the Allies also initiated a concentrated attack on the Bulgarian front that broke it wide open. On 26 September, realising that the situation was hopeless, Bulgaria sued for peace. An armistice was signed on the 29th and Bulgaria's war was over. From then on, Ottoman prospects took a further turn for the worse because the Bulgarian front had constituted the whole of their western defence. With no Bulgarian front left, the Allies could advance from Thrace to İstanbul without difficulty. This is the truth of the situation, and contradicts the meaningless formula taught to Turkish primary school children: 'We were victorious at Chanakkale but lost the war because our ally Germany was defeated.' By this time Germany too was exhausted, and the German General Staff wanted to make peace while their armies were still in the field in Belgium and France, in the hope that this would secure leverage in the peace-making process. On 4 October the Ottoman Empire, Germany and Austria-Hungary applied to President Woodrow Wilson of the United States to act as their intermediary for peace. On that same day Talat Pasha, who had been Grand Vizier since Sait Halim Pasha retired from the post in 1917, handed his resignation to Sultan Vahdettin.

At his death on 3 July 1918, Sultan Reshat was succeeded by Mehmet VI (Vahdettin) who, unlike Sultan Reshat, took a close interest in politics and was overtly hostile towards the CUP. Though not to the excessive degree of Sultan Abdülhamit, he too was of a paranoid nature—for example, it was rumoured that even inside the Palace he carried a pistol in his pocket.

The United States had entered the war in a spirit of idealism and these ideals were declared in President Wilson's Fourteen Points, which rejected imperialistic objectives, supported self-determination and foresaw the establishment of an organisation which would thereafter ensure that peaceful solutions would be found for international disputes: the League of Nations. The Central Powers, in suing for peace, had asked President Wilson to act as intermediary and the US President had responded positively, saying however that it would be advantageous for these countries to have established democratic rather than military and autocratic governments. This reply shook the foundations of those governments whose peoples already harboured deep resentment at the great and pointless suffering they had undergone. Governments began to fall like a flurry of dead leaves after a storm. In Bulgaria King Ferdinand abdicated in favour of his son Boris (4 October 1918). In Germany Wilhelm II's abdication was not enough to appease public opinion and was followed by the establishment of a republic (9 November). Emperor Karl of Austria-Hungary abdicated his throne, which led to the establishment of the republics of Austria (13 November) and Hungary (16 November). Empires were crumbling and republics arising. Obviously none of these options had any appeal for Vahdettin, who was probably consoling himself with the fact that he had come into his inheritance only a few months before the end of the war and therefore could not be held responsible for Ottoman involvement in the war and its consequences. But ironically, owing largely to his own political miscalculations, Vahdettin in the end lost his throne and a republic was indeed established in Turkey.

The İzzet Pasha government

On 14 October 1918 İzzet Pasha formed a new government, among whose members were two Unionists, Cavit and Hayrı Bey, and two ex-Unionists, Rauf Orbay and Fethi Okyar, making it a latter-day reversion to the CUP's supervisory power model. Telegraphing from the front, Mustafa Kemal suggested that İzzet Pasha form a government of much the same composition, but proposing himself as Minister of War, whereas İzzet Pasha had assumed this position himself, together with that of Grand Vizier. By way of consolation, İzzet Pasha wrote of the vital importance of Mustafa Kemal's present position and also of his hope that they should work together after the establishment of peace. It may be inferred that Vahdettin had been against Mustafa Kemal's appointment, whereas Mustafa Kemal, now that his rival Enver was out of the running and in the light of his previous relationship with Vahdettin, had taken his appointment as Minister of War as a foregone conclusion.

The background of events leading to the above had begun towards the end of 1917, while Vahdettin was still heir-apparent to the throne. The Germans had invited Vahdettin to visit the front and Mustafa Kemal had been appointed his aide-de-camp; during their return trip he seized the chance to suggest that Vahdettin should become commander of the 1st Army Corps which dominated İstanbul, citing the example of German princes who had been appointed to similar positions. When Vahdettin said that he had no credentials for such a position (the German princes were well educated and graduates of military academies) Mustafa Kemal replied that that would be no drawback if he himself were to become 1st Army Corps Chief of Staff. Nothing came of this conversation, although it was rumoured that because of their rapport Vahdettin had proposed to Mustafa Kemal a marriage with his daughter, the Sultana Sabiha, an offer that was refused.

Meanwhile, the British were preoccupied with plans for the dismantling of the Ottoman Empire. It was said that the sun never set on the British Empire because there were colonies in all the four corners of the globe. The population of India alone was ten times that of Britain. All colonial powers, including Britain, employed certain methods to keep their empires under control. One was 'divide and rule'. For example, the Hindus and Muslims in India, the Arabs and Jews in Palestine and the Turks and Greeks in Cyprus were natural candidates among whom ethnic enmity could be fomented. Propaganda to the effect that the British were purveyors of civilisation, safeguarding progress, without whom development would be retarded and misgovernment ensue was also employed. A third method was to terrorise the populace into submission by severely punishing the smallest of incidents. The two victories (at Chanakkale and Kut-ül-Amare) won by the Ottomans, a non-European candidate for colonisation, had caused a bitter loss of British prestige and therefore called for retribution of the same order.

The Turks at the time had no idea of what was being planned, and an optimistic atmosphere prevailed based on totally different interpretations of the international situation. There were those who believed the Chanakkale victory to have been a critical element in the demise of Tsarist Russia and were expecting a gesture of gratitude from Europe for this service to democracy. This was a basic miscalculation in that the Soviets were seen by the capitalist West as an even worse alternative to their predecessors. However, the Turks' optimism had its real basis in the fact that they had become an ally of Germany, largely owing to their antagonism to Russia, whereas the Ottoman Empire had traditionally tended to ally itself with Britain and France. Now that Europe had turned its back on communist Russia and the Turkish connection to Germany had been severed by defeat, it was time for the traditionally close ties between Ottomans, French and British to be renewed and even for an alliance against the Russians, such as had existed at the time of the Crimean war.

Palace calculations

The Palace had its own view of the developing political situation. While Vahdettin was still a prince, he had displayed a close interest in politics. There are indications that he had connections with the Mohammedan Union Association (İttihad-ı Muhammediye Cemiyeti) and with Dervish Vahdeti. His sister, the Sultana Mediha, was married to Damat Ferit Pasha (one-time leader of the reactionary opposition Freedom and Accord Party) and the two brothers-in-law had always been close; thus it is not difficult to surmise that he too was connected to the FAP. While this may explain his animosity towards the CUP, it is a fact that neither Sultan Reshat nor any member of the Ottoman dynasty had ever sided with the CUP; Sultan Reshat had only seemed more benign because he took no great interest in politics and was of a retiring nature. It also appears to be a fact that no member of the dynasty was ever a supporter of democracy (at least not till 1922). Vahdettin's ties to the opposition and rejection of the CUP had no basis in democratic principles. His stand was born of political necessity, in order better to oppose the CUP, but his real loyalty lay with absolute monarchy, as did that of the rest of his dynasty.

Even if Vahdettin had not been opposed to the CUP, he would have had to dissemble his enmity because of the prevalent political situation. Public opinion in Europe and the Entente Allies in particular was against the CUP because of its stand on full independence, which might have set off an explosion of similar demands within their colonial empires. To this was added the treatment of the

Armenian population. The CUP was viewed as being no less of a curse than the Communists. Therefore, to hold on to his throne and secure better results at the peace negotiations, Vahdettin would have been obliged to act as though he were opposed to the CUP, even if he had not been so inclined.

It has already been mentioned that Vahdettin was of an extremely suspicious nature, and as a result he preferred working with politicians to whom he was related by ties of marriage. For instance, when wishing to initiate moderate policies he entrusted the task to Tevfik Pasha, whose son was married to his daughter, the Sultana Ulviye. When he wished harsher policies to be pursued, he would rely on his brother-in-law, Damat Ferit. If the rumours of a proposed marriage of Sultana Sabiha to Mustafa Kemal had been true, Vahdettin would probably have seen this connection as a condition and safeguard of political cooperation with him.

A telltale sign of Vahdettin's state of mind was the speech made in the Senate by Damat Ferit Pasha on 19 October 1918, in which he began by stating that there were two kinds of government, 'the people's government and the government of the élite'. According to the Pasha, the former would be a bad and the latter an extremely good one. In addition, he held that the 1909 constitutional amendments were responsible for the partition of the Empire. But care was taken in his speech not to attack the principle of constitutional government or the 1876 Constitution directly. We are not suggesting that he had any loyalty to democratic principles, but rather, at a time when President Woodrow Wilson was propounding such principles, it would not have been politically expedient to make an all-out attack on the constitutional system.

All these developments show that at the end of the World War Turkey or Turkish society was faced by two different movements whose aim was to turn the clock back. On the one hand the Palace, determined to take advantage of the CUP Unionists' fall from power and unpopularity in the country and abroad after the war, was getting ready at least to curtail the constitutional regime, and if possible to be rid of it altogether in order to reinstate an absolute monarchy. That is to say, the Palace wanted to bring about a counter-revolution. On the other hand, the Entente Allies, as proud victors in the war now preparing to descend upon the Ottomans, were determined to renew the Capitulations, hopefully with additional and heavier clauses, thereby tightening the reins of hegemony and returning the Ottoman state to the status of a semi-dependent colony. The Palace wanted a return to 1908 or even 1907, a time before the beginning of the Second Constitutional era, and the Entente to 1913 or, if possible, 1907 when the Capitulations had yet to be abolished. However, it is not easy to turn the clock back and undo what has been done. From 1908 to 1918 Turkish society had undergone revolutionary change. Even if its transformation was only just beginning, by 1918 a new way of life had begun to emerge. The theme of the Turkish War of Liberation was to stop, with blood and arms, these two different attempts to turn the Turkish clock back.

The armistice of Mudros

The Turks had made armistice overtures on 4 October, and on 30 October an agreement was signed at the port of Mudros on the island of Lemnos. Rauf (Orbay), Minister of Naval Affairs, headed the Ottoman delegation. The Entente representative was the British Admiral Calthorpe (spelt Galtrop in many Turkish documents). Of its many provisions the ones of most consequence for Turkey's future were those opening the Straits and giving the Allies the right to occupy any points they deemed necessary for their security (article 7). Opening the Straits condemned İstanbul, the Ottoman capital, to fall under the control of the Entente army and navy; Rauf had requested that Greek ships should not be included in the naval force to be sent to İstanbul, but no such clause was added to the treaty. The Entente, feeling no need to give any reason, occupied first İstanbul and then Eastern Thrace, the Straits, Mosul, the region of Cilicia (Çukurova) and its adjacent districts including Mersin, Tarsus, Adana, Alexandretta (Hatay) and Antalya. In addition, officials called control officers and/or small military units were posted to other strategically important places such as Eskişehir, Samsun, Konya, Trabzon and Erzurum. The thorough demobilisation and disarmament of the Ottoman army was begun with all speed. Surrendered arms and ammunition were stored in depots guarded by Entente forces where, for example, the breech-blocks of cannon or rifle mechanisms were dismantled so as to make them unusable.

Particularly during the first months of the occupation, the British and French endeavoured to treat the Turks as a people of a subject territory, at times vying with each other in their arrogant behaviour. They allowed only twenty-four hours for evacuating state offices and even private homes. To make it clear that they favoured minority groups, they encouraged minorities to indulge in excesses. They used them against the Turks, e.g. the Armenian Legion under French command in Cilicia and working for the British police force in İstanbul. This policy was to the disadvantage of all and no kindness to the minorities, because the Allies would eventually leave and the peoples of Turkey would be left behind to live together. The Italian occupation of the southwestern regions of Antalya and Burdur was much more civilised, since the Italians made an effort to show sympathy towards the Turkish people. The French conducted themselves with moderation after their paths separated them from the British. It is also held that the British too acted more moderately, notably after the Turkish victory at Sakarya. However, the Greek occupation reached extremes of cruelty, as we will see below.

Mustafa Kemal in İstanbul

On the night of 1 November after the Armistice of Mudros had been concluded, the leaders of the CUP, the three Pashas—Talat, Enver and Cemal—and prominent CUP members such as Dr Nazım and Bahaettin Şakir fled to Russia on a German warship. The opposition was in an uproar, holding the government responsible for their flight. Vahdettin was of the opinion that the İzzet Pasha government was unsuitable to deal with the Entente, and used Ahmet Rıza (incidentally his former neighbour), who had recently cut all ties with the CUP, as his intermediary in pressing the government to resign. Unable to withstand this pressure, İzzet Pasha resigned. The government was replaced on 11 November by the Tevfik Pasha administration, consisting largely of elder statesmen—Tevfik Pasha was seventy-three—with no party connections. On 13 November about 100 warships of the Allied navies, including the Greek *Averof,* arrived off İstanbul in a show of force to the Ottomans. Coincidentally, the man who was to lead Turkey's liberation movement was at that very moment disembarking from a train at Haydarpasha station in İstanbul. Newly arrived from the front, Mustafa Kemal was informed that the ferry service to the European side of the Bosphorus had been discontinued owing to the arrival of the Allied fleet. Finding a rowing boat, he made his way with difficulty to the other side and straightaway visited İzzet Pasha—whose resignation he regarded as a great mistake. In this crisis the government should not have been handed over to the old guard. İzzet had to be reinstated as Grand Vizier, and he himself would be the Minister of War. İzzet Pasha agreed.

On 18 November the Tevfik Pasha government programme was to be read out in Parliament for a vote of confidence. Dressed as a civilian, Mustafa Kemal went early to this session to explain to the gathered deputies the need to vote down the government. The deputies with whom he spoke seemed to acquiesce in his view, but when it came to the vote the government survived. The deputies of this parliament had been elected in 1914, and were thus largely affiliated to the CUP, and were not as lacking in leadership as Mustafa Kemal may have supposed. On 5 November, at its final congress, the CUP dissolved itself, and in its place the Renovation Party (Teceddüt Fırkası) was established four days later. Cavit was its leader and from this time Mustafa Kemal began to cooperate with Cavit. Through their joint efforts, a motion of censure was raised in Parliament, to be discussed during the session on 21 December. That day Tevfik Pasha gave a speech explaining the government's execution of its programme, but at the end of the speech and without allowing any time for discussion, he read out the Sultan's decree for the dissolution of Parliament. All present were thunderstruck. Apparently no one had thought of this eventuality as even remotely possible, because the Parliament of 1914 represented the Ottoman territories of that date with representatives from all over Anatolia and from the Ottoman Arab provinces (Yemen, the Hejaz, Palestine, Syria and Iraq). In a new election it was highly unlikely that the Arab provinces and the occupied regions of Anatolia would be allowed to elect representatives (and indeed they were not). In other words the 1914 Parliament could only have been dissolved if the Sultan and/or the government were enemies of the Constitution, which they unfortunately proved to be. No one had foreseen this disastrous turn of events because of Vahdettin's adroitness in hiding his true intentions.

After a short time Vahdettin became displeased with the Tevfik Pasha government because it was not sufficiently pro-British and did not vigorously pursue the prosecution of CUP leaders for the crimes of entering the war, corruption and the transfer of Armenians. Many of these allegations arose from the Freedom and Accord Party who were thirsting for vengeance and power. With its support Vahdettin was able not only to force the government to resign but also to replace it with one led by Damat Ferit Pasha, supported by and composed of members of the FAP. Both to ingratiate themselves with the British and for the sake of vengeance, the new government initiated a series of arrests and speeded up the investigation of anti-CUP allegations. As a result the Prefect of Yozgat, Kemal Bey, was hanged for his conduct during the Armenian transfer (April 10).

Also needing to be resolved was the question of law and order in the Black Sea region and whether or not Mustafa Kemal should be sent there for this purpose. The government came to the view that simultaneously İstanbul would be rid of a troublemaker and Mustafa Kemal would become an asset, solving the security problems of the region. He for his part had realised that nothing could be accomplished in the capital. His comrades-in-arms Kâzim Karabekir and Ali Fuat Cebesoy had already been in Anatolia for some time. Stationed in Erzurum, Karabekir was commander of the 15th Army Corps, the only Ottoman army corps to have maintained its fighting ability. Ali Fuat commanded the 20th Army Corps, with headquarters in Ankara. Infesting the Black Sea region were bands of Greek and Turkish brigands. Apprehending the Turks was no great problem, but rounding up the Greeks was a delicate matter since it involved the British. On 9 March 1919 a British unit some 200-strong had landed in Samsun. Mustafa Kemal was posted there as Inspector of the 9th Army (later renamed the 3rd Army after general reorganisation). On 15 May, before setting off from İstanbul, he paid a farewell visit to the Grand Vizierate and at that very moment was witness to the confusion that reigned. The Greeks had landed in İzmir.

The occupation of İzmir

This decision had been taken at the Paris Peace Conference. At that time the Italians were boycotting the conference because of disappointment at not being given their full share of the spoils; had they been in attendance they would probably have objected to the Greek occupation since they themselves had their eyes on İzmir. This event had been provoked by the British Prime Minister, David Lloyd George, who had wanted an example made of the Ottomans, but taking İzmir from the Turks was a step too far. It might have upset Indian Muslims and their Hindu sympathisers, leading to disquiet in India. In addition, a Greek occupation was against British Rail Company interests in the region, which required that the Aegean market should not be divided. Nevertheless, Lloyd George was as if motivated by a personal vendetta. In his youth he had been of a religious bent and at one time intended to become a clergyman. Another determinant was that he had belonged to Gladstone's vehemently anti-Turkish Liberal Party and had close connections with a number of Greeks, one of whom was Sir Basil Zaharoff. Zaharoff, originally from the town of Muğla in the Aegean area of Anatolia, had made a fortune and eventually become the head of Vickers Armstrong, one of the world's leading munitions companies. During his term as Minister of Munitions at the beginning of the war, Lloyd George had concluded munitions deals of immense proportions with Zaharoff. Motivated more by private than public considerations, Lloyd George was behind this decision. Quoting from a letter from a British acquaintance of his residing in Athens, which alleged that the Greeks in Aegean Anatolia were being persecuted, he pressed the Peace Conference to authorise the Greek occupation of that region.

Admiral Calthorpe travelled to İzmir to ensure that the Turks would be caught unawares by the arrival of the Greek occupation forces. At the time when the Damat Ferit government first came to power, Nurettin Pasha (Bearded Nurettin) had been both 17th Army Corps commander and acting governor of İzmir, but on coming to power Damat Ferit relieved him of both of these positions and handed the Corps' command to old Ali Nadir Pasha (who had been deemed incompetent and retired by the CUP) and the governorship to İzzet Bey, a former cabinet minister, rumoured to be a British spy who informed them of what went on at cabinet meetings. On 14 May Calthorpe, as commander of the British fleet anchored in the Bay of İzmir, handed İzzet a note stating that the forts of İzmir were to be occupied by Entente forces. İzzet not only did not demur but may even be said to have reacted positively to this news. That evening, after state offices had closed, Calthorpe handed in a second note stating that the Greeks would occupy İzmir the following morning. İzzet had been unruffled by the first note, but the second finally gave him cause for alarm. Government offices in İstanbul had closed and could not be reached by telegraph, the only means of communication. İzzet, left to his own devices, possessed neither the strength of character nor sufficient loyalty to an ideology to take a stand against a Greek occupation. Neither did poor old Ali Nadir Pasha. It is possible that Nurettin Pasha had been relieved and replaced by such a duo with the intention of making İzmir a soft target in the event of an occupation. The situation in İzmir was to be softened up to a certain extent, but for what—occupation by the Entente or by the Greeks? The fact that first İzzet and later Ferit became extremely alarmed when the truth came out seems to point to the former alternative having been taken for granted and the second not having been considered possible.

It is impossible to exaggerate the importance of the Greek occupation. The Turks had experienced the British, French and Italian occupations in the south, the French in eastern Thrace and a joint Entente occupation of İstanbul. No matter how humiliating and exploitative, Western European occupation or even colonisation generally did not totally obliterate hope for future liberation or the right of the native peoples to survive. Greek occupation was a different case entirely. The history of nineteenth- and twentieth-century Balkan nationalism shows many examples of the difficulty of Muslim survival in the shadow of these Balkan statelets. Contemporary examples of ethnic cleansing in this region may be considered as the continuation of this mentality. The Turks had experience of this situation and knew what to expect. No matter how war-weary they were, such a threat could only motivate them to rearm in defence of their right to survive. We have no information regarding the plans of Mustafa Kemal before the occupation of İzmir, but there is no doubt that this event accelerated and fortified the process of Turkey's liberation. Had it not been for this turn of events, the Turks probably would have been more patient and chosen a long-term struggle.

Necip Fazıl Kısakürek's book *Not a Traitor but a Patriot*, puts forward the proposition that it was Vahdettin who made Mustafa

Kemal responsible for the national struggle with an imperial writ and even went so far as to finance this venture to the tune of 20,000 Turkish liras. In the first place, no one has ever seen such a writ. If such a document had existed, would Mustafa Kemal not have made use of it, particularly during the first stages of the National Struggle? Secondly, there is no evidence that he and his comrades had abundant funds, and it is a known fact that they had difficulty in paying their travelling expenses as they journeyed from Erzurum to Sivas. Thirdly, even if this had been true, in the light of his later actions, what difference would this make in a final evaluation of Vahdettin's character? As Ziya Pasha said, 'Actions mirror the man, regardless of his words.' Atatürk relates in his memoirs that as he made his farewell to Vahdettin on 15 May Vahdettin said to him: 'Pasha, you will save this country.' Should not this be taken to mean that Mustafa Kemal, by restoring order in the Black Sea region, would be able to avert a possible Greek landing there?

On the morning of 15 May the Greeks landed in İzmir and a Greek unit began to march down the Kordon, the main boulevard. When the Greeks reached Konak Square, Hasan Tahsin (his real name was Osman Nevres) shot at a Greek standard-bearer and was shot and killed in return. Hasan Tahsin was a gunman for the Teşkilat-i Mahsusa, the striking arm of the CUP. In the past he had (in Romania) shot and wounded the British Buxton brothers who had worked for the formation of the Balkan Alliance. By sacrificing his life Hasan Tahsin probably wished to make a statement that there was no alternative to an armed struggle. But the Greek soldiers were not satisfied with killing him alone. Throwing aside any show of discipline, they charged into İzmir's Muslim neighbourhoods and for two days kept up a state of terror. It is alleged that on that first day alone 2,000 Turks were killed. Ali Nadir Pasha had gathered all the Turkish soldiers in their barracks to await the arrival of the Greek forces. They duly arrived and immediately opened fire on the barracks, totally ignoring the Turks' white flags of surrender. Afterwards, they forced the Turks, led by Ali Nadir Pasha, to walk down the main boulevard with their hands in the air, only to be thrown into a ship's hold. Officers were made to shout '*Zito Venizelos!*' (Long Live Venizelos!) and Colonel Süleyman Fethi, who refused, was stabbed with bayonets and bludgeoned to death with rifle butts. Can Hasan

Tahsin's gesture be said to have provoked these events or were the Greek soldiers pre-conditioned to act in this way?

The latter seems more likely. After the incidents at İzmir no great Turkish reaction occurred at first during the spread of the Greek occupation of the Aegean area. It was even rumoured that the people of Akhisar, in hope of protecting their lives and property, welcomed the Greeks with Greek flags flying. When the Greeks reached Bergama (Pergamon), however, the people put up armed resistance and did not allow them into their town. The events of İzmir were repeated and, in their anger, the same Greek units entering Menemen sought out and killed ten of its most prominent citizens. Outrages were also perpetrated on the general populace. What relation had the people of Menemen with the incidents in Bergama or the people of İzmir with Hasan Tahsin? Perhaps in the eyes of Greek soldiers they deserved the worst treatment possible merely by virtue of being Turks—and Muslims.

İzmir was a city of importance for international trade, and Entente warships were anchored in the bay. But although these events took place before the eyes of the world, England's foremost newspaper, *The Times*, did not mention them for days. When at last the Greeks initiated a disciplinary inquiry, *that* news was reported in *The Times*.

The Turkish people of the Aegean realised that there was no choice but to rearm and engage in a struggle against the Greek occupation. In Alaşehir and Balıkesir meetings of the Rejection of Annexation Society (Redd-i İlhak Cemiyeti) took place and branches of this society were established in other regions. People's defence units called National Forces (Kuva-yı Milliye) were organised and financed throughout the country by the notables of each region. In Ayvalık the 172nd Regiment, commanded by Ali Çetinkaya, and in Nazilli the 57th Division commanded by Şefik Aker began to fight on their own initiative or in support of National Forces, playing an important role at the outset of the national struggle. Anatolian zeybeks, brigands such as Yörük Ali Efe, also joined in the fight. A National Forces Front had now emerged to oppose the Greeks at the perimeters of their areas of occupation.

After the occupation of İzmir Defence of Rights organisations (Müdafaa-yi Hukuk Cemiyetleri) quickly took hold throughout the country. Protest meetings against the occupation were held in many regions. The Allies found it expedient not to take action against meetings held in İstanbul, and at the great Sultanahmet Meeting on 23 May 1919 the female novelist Halide Edip Adivar and other speakers addressed an immense crowd. Damat Ferit resigned and no FAP members were admitted to the new government, which he was to form.

16

FROM SAMSUN TO THE FALL OF THE DAMAT FERIT GOVERNMENT

As Mustafa Kemal set off from İstanbul for Samsun on the ship *Bandırma*, the country was rocked by news of the occupation of İzmir. As the Chamber of Deputies had been dissolved, Grand Vizier Ferit, on 26 May, felt it necessary to convoke an Imperial Council (Şura-yı Saltanat). As has been explained in a previous chapter, this was an assembly of notables of various professions. At the Council all voiced their deep distress and concern over the news from İzmir and it was apparent that many had become totally disheartened at this turn of events, as after the Balkan defeat. Sadık Bey, representative of the FAP, put forward the view that the only way out of this desperate situation was to become a protectorate of one of the Great Powers. The Palace and the FAP were in favour of becoming a British protectorate, while advocates of constitutional government were sympathetic to an American mandate, arguing that it would promote democratic development.

Having landed in Samsun, Mustafa Kemal lost no time in telegraphing four sentences to Damat Ferit describing reactions to the occupation of İzmir. Three of these four sentences mentioned 'the people and the army', and the other one 'the state and the army'. Ferit must have been unsettled by this portentous wording. Mustafa Kemal then travelled on to Havza, and after communicating with Kâzim Karabekir, Ali Fuat Cebesoy and Refet Bele, he sent a circular on 3 June to five army commanders and six provincial governors or prefects, stating that Ferit had proved by his approach to 'certain questions' that he could not represent the nation's true interests at the Peace Conference. Although this despatch had been sent to eleven trusted recipients only, Mustafa Kemal must have known that it could not be kept secret and that news of its contents would reach the government in İstanbul. This circular, therefore, symbolised his unfurling of the flag of rebellion. The British had already come to regret having allowed Mustafa Kemal and his associates to leave the capital and demanded that the Porte recall him. Bowing to British pressure, on 8 June, the government ordered his return—which marked the beginning of the conflict between the government in İstanbul and the Anatolian Resistance. Two days later, on 10 June, Mustafa Kemal sent out a second circular in which he stated that various organisations for the Defence of Rights and the Rejection of Annexation had asked him to become the leader of the national movement and that he had accepted, regardless of the cost. Thus he took up the gauntlet of leadership. That same day he left Havza for a meeting in Amasya to which he had invited some of his fellow officers. He was thirty-eight when he set off on what had become for him a sacred mission.

The Amasya Resolutions

The meeting in Amasya began on 19 June. Besides Mustafa Kemal himself, three men were present: Ali Fuat (Cebesoy), commander of the 20th Army Corps in Ankara, Refet (Bele), commander of the 3rd Army Corps in Sivas and Rauf Orbay, former Minister of the Navy and Ottoman delegate to Mudros. Kâzim Karabekir, commander of the 15th Army Corps in Erzurum and Cemal Pasha, called Mersinli or Küçük Cemal Pasha (Cemal Pasha the Younger or Cemal Pasha of Mersin), Inspector of the 2nd Army in Konya, were consulted by telegraph throughout the meeting. By 21 June the Amasya Resolutions had taken shape. The main points of these decisions can be summarised as follows:

The integrity of our motherland and the independence of our nation are in grave danger, but the İstanbul government has not fulfilled its responsibilities. National independence will only be preserved by decided and resolute action on the part of the nation itself. With this objective, a national congress will be held in Sivas within the shortest period of time possible, to be attended by three representatives from each [sancak]. Before this, however, a regional congress will be held in Erzurum to organise the defence of eastern Anatolia.

Some of the Amasya Resolutions were circulated all over the country. This was the Amasya Circular of 22 June 1919. However, the fifth and sixth articles were not included and were designated a national secret.

The secret sixth article, of the utmost consequence, declared:

(1) From this day forward, military units and national organisations will no longer be disbanded or abolished, but instead will be maintained.

(2) The command of military units will under no circumstances whatsoever be surrendered to another authority.

(3) Arms and ammunition, likewise, will under no circumstances be handed over.

(4) The enemy occupation of any region or province will be a matter *not only* for the military forces of that region but for the armed forces as a whole.

Henceforth, in accordance with article 6, government orders to disband military units or for the closure of national organisations were to be defied and military appointments made by the government ignored. Arms and ammunition were no longer to be surrendered to the Entente, even if this were to mean defiance of armistice conditions. The army was to act as an integrated whole.

Hence, article 6 was an article of rebellion against the Ottoman government, against the Armistice of Mudros and, therefore against the Allied Powers' occupation forces. An organisation of a military nature was established in Amasya, consisting of one naval and five army officers, which was to act as the high command of the national movement (we will refer to it as the Amasya Military Organisation). After Cemal Pasha, the highest in rank and seniority of its members was Mustafa Kemal. Cemal Pasha soon left Anatolia, quitting his official duties in Konya to return to İstanbul and thereby also abandoning his position in this organisation (probably because he found being under the leadership of Mustafa Kemal unacceptable). In any event Mustafa Kemal emerged as the natural leader of the national struggle, owing not only to rank or seniority but to his superior intelligence, cultural background and will-power.

In the later years of the national struggle, differences of opinion were to divide the five original members of this organisation, bringing them to a parting of the ways. Atatürk, in his renowned six-day *Speech* (1927), explained that in its early days the national struggle would have been undermined and doomed to failure by an outright declaration of revolutionary republicanism. This had to be kept a 'national secret', each step towards this objective had to be announced when the time was right. As each of these steps was taken, certain of his colleagues, whose horizons were not broad enough to envisage such a future, were alienated and went their separate ways. It is evident that he was referring mainly to his associates in the Amasya Military Organisation. He was also clarifying the limited extent of their contribution to the cause. Kâzım Karabekir countered this view in his book, *Our War for Independence*, probably using the first person plural in its title to refer to the Amasya Military Organisation. This book endeavours to emphasise important contributions made to the cause, primarily his own, and in second place, the contributions of those other than Mustafa Kemal. Karabekir goes so far as to claim that, at a time when he and Fevzi (Çakmak) Pasha were both in Bursa, Fevzi Pasha had stated that his own and İsmet Pasha's intention had been to make Mustafa Kemal a dictator. This implied that Atatürk's underlying aim had been to use the revolution later as a tool to override his associates and become a dictator.

Aside from this dispute there is another question to be asked. Was the Amasya Military Organisation a junta? It was a secret organisation, composed of military officers, and its intention *was* to gain power; so in that way it conforms to the definition of the word, but it does not correspond fully to such a designation because, though military, it was also an organisation which sought popular support at the Erzurum and Sivas Congresses, adhered to their decisions in demanding parliamentary elections, and ensured that those elections were held. Juntas are not built on popular support though some seek the support of the people once they are in power. Therefore, although the Amasya Military Organisation had some of the characteristics of a junta, the fact that it was in search of a democratic power-base *before* coming to power precludes it from truly being one. Furthermore, even if the Amasya Military Organisation should be held to be a junta, the fact that it was engaged in a struggle for freedom and equality against the feudalism and absolutism of the Sultan automatically makes it more of a democratic movement than not.

Damat Ferit at the Peace Conference

Meanwhile, the Entente had begun to display its first signs of pro-Ottoman sympathy. The French had come to the opinion that allowing the Greeks to occupy İzmir had been too drastic a step. In addition the British were concerned about disquiet in India due to the pro-Ottoman sympathies of its peoples. As a result, an option, which had not been allowed to other members of the Central Alliance, was offered to the Ottomans: they were invited to state their case at the Paris Peace Conference. Damat Ferit Pasha went to Paris in June as head of the Ottoman delegation, and in his speech he expounded views objectionable both to the Europeans and to the Turkish people. He spoke of the Taurus mountain range as a natural border of the Turkish homeland, whereas there were many regions beyond that inhabited by Turks and seen by them as an integral part of their homeland. He also laid claim to Arab lands. He characterised the Unionists (the CUP) as worse than the Bolsheviks, and to heap even further blame upon them, gave an estimate of the number of Armenian dead even higher than that of the Armenians themselves.

Lloyd George had not been in favour of an Ottoman presence at the conference. The French, at this juncture, were seeking a British guarantee against a future German war of revenge and were still hopeful of getting it; for that reason they were willing to accept British demands which conflicted with their own interests. For example, they refrained from protesting against the British takeover of Mosul, a region that had been assigned to them by the Sykes-Picot Agreement partitioning Arab lands. The French Premier Georges Clemenceau, acting as spokesman for the policy of Lloyd George, now answered Ferit in insultingly harsh terms, saying that wherever Turks went, civilisation regressed, and added that Ferit should not hope to avoid blame for the Armenian affair by loading it on to the Unionists. After this speech the Ottoman delegation was asked to leave the conference and go home.

After further deliberation, coming to the conclusion that it had again weighted the scales too heavily against the Turks, the Conference took two decisions on 18 July. The first was that borders were to be specified limiting the Greek occupation. In fact, certain boundaries had indeed been determined at the time when the Greeks were landing in İzmir, but the Greeks had ignored them. The second was that Ottoman allegations concerning their mistreatment by the Greeks were to be investigated by a commission of one Italian, one British and one French officer, headed by Admiral Bristol, US High Commissioner in İstanbul. The commission travelled to the Aegean and listened to all sides. In its report it was determined that before 15 May no oppression of Greeks by the Turks had taken place, and that the Greeks had acted not as a security force but as an invading army. However, although the Bristol Report gave the lie to Lloyd George's previous allegations and to any justification for sending the Greek Army into Aegean Anatolia, as may be seen from the evidence it reviewed, it had no effect on the decisions of the Conference.

The Erzurum Congress

After this we see Mustafa Kemal in Erzurum, receiving repeated government orders demanding his return to İstanbul. When it became apparent that he had no intention of following these orders, the Sultan involved himself in the affair, asking him (in a telegram of 2 July) to take two months' leave of absence from his official duties. This seemed a viable alternative, but on 8 July a second telegram arrived, relieving him of all duties. His official title and position as Army Inspector had secured him influence in all quarters, but what influence would a Pasha have when he had lost official standing? In addition, there was the fact that military officers were held in low esteem by a majority of the people at that time owing to the painful after effects of a war that had ended in humiliating defeat. Weighing up the situation, Mustafa Kemal took the momentous decision to resign from the army. It must also have been an emotionally difficult decision. Why did the İstanbul government revoke its decision to grant him leave of absence? One factor was probably Refet's defiance of Allied authority on the arrival in Samsun of a second British detachment. Refet had evacuated all Turkish soldiers in advance and announced that his forces would resist any attempt by the British to spread further inland from Samsun without government authorisation. Secondly, the approaching national congress in Sivas had been perceived as a national parliament. Mustafa Kemal and his associates' open defiance of Entente authority was probably evaluated by the government in İstanbul as an adventuristic aberration, against which a moderate stand would not be enough to mollify the Allied Powers.

The Erzurum Congress was to begin on 10 July. This was no arbitrary date, being full of symbolism for the nationalist cause since it commemorated the proclamation of freedom in the Balkans and was celebrated as a national holiday. Vahdettin had abolished this celebration as part of his counter-revolution, but when the day came many delegates had not yet put in an appearance in Erzurum. In such circumstances a postponement of a few days would have been normal, but the Erzurum Congress was postponed for thirteen days till 23 July. This was not an easy situation, and incidentally caused embarrassment to delegates who had arrived on time and felt themselves to be imposing on the hospitality of their Erzurum hosts. Why such a delay? Probably the new date was chosen because the 23rd was as symbolic a date as the 10th, being its equivalent according to the Gregorian calendar (23 July 1908). This insistence on symbolism shows that Vahdettin's counter-revolutionary intentions had been understood and therefore the need was felt for a gesture clearly favouring democracy. This is proof that the Erzurum Congress had made a commitment to a democratic-nationalist ideology, and had thus come to resemble the CUP. Although Mustafa Kemal at that juncture sided with these aims, he was in fact far more radically left-wing than the CUP, with his ideal of a secular republic.

In summary, the decisions of the Erzurum Congress were as follows:

(1) The Eastern Anatolia Defence of Rights Association (Doğu Anadolu Müdafaa-i Hukuk Cemiyeti) was established through the union of two regional defence societies: the Eastern Provinces' Defence of National Rights Society and the Trabzon Preservation of National Rights Society.

(2) The provinces of Eastern Anatolia are an integral whole which cannot be separated, one from the other or from the Ottoman Empire for any reason whatever. All Muslims are brothers. These Muslim compatriots who, on the day that the Armistice was signed, are and were the overwhelming majority living within Ottoman frontiers are an indivisible nation. Any intervention or occupation within the borders of the territory under Ottoman control at the

time of the Armistice will be considered as aiming to establish Greek and Armenian sovereignty and will not be countenanced.

(3) No new concessions upsetting political sovereignty and/or social equilibrium will be granted but we reaffirm that the rights of Christians, as previously determined by the laws of the Ottoman state, will be respected.

(4) Scientific, industrial and economic aid offered by any state that does not harbour intentions of invasion against our country and that is in accordance with our national principles within the 30 October 1918 Armistice borders will be welcomed.

(5) In the event that the government, under foreign pressure, is forced to neglect or abandon Eastern Anatolia, a temporary administration will be established. If the Ottoman government should disintegrate, the Eastern provinces will band together with other provinces to organise resistance and, if that is not possible, fight alone to defend their independence. Any negative evaluations or propaganda against the decisions of this congress will be viewed as treason to the nation and the motherland.

(6) This movement is in no way affiliated to the CUP. Elections must be held and the Chamber of Deputies convoked without delay.

These decisions set out the basic and governing principles of the nationalist movement, the concepts of establishing an alternative government and an armed struggle in defence of the motherland. Another important point is that no differentiation was made between good or bad occupation; all were to be identified as detrimental to national interests, aimed at establishing either Armenian or Greek states. Moreover, demands were made for elections and the convocation of Parliament, i.e. for democracy. Lastly, no demands were made in relation to Arab lands; on the contrary, the borders determined by the Armistice are specifically mentioned. This was a decision to relinquish empire—momentous indeed. Unfortunately, no proper documentation of the sittings of the Erzurum Congress is available. It is customary today for a party congress to last for one or two days, but the Erzurum Congress, after a protracted delay, continued for the surprisingly long period of two weeks (23 July–7 August 1919). This must be a sign of lengthy and spirited debate. These people, the last generation to have grown up in the traditions of a 600-year empire, must have come to the realisation that this great sacrifice had to be made to attain full independence in face of the crushing defeat that had been suffered, followed by the very real threat of partition and colonisation. It would have been unrealistic and in conflict with the gravity of the situation to demand full independence for themselves while making demands on Arab lands. In any event, Wilson's Fourteen Points had called for the separation of the Arab countries from the Empire. They were also aware of the insults to which Damat Ferit had been subjected because of such demands. But, no matter how rational, this was an emotionally difficult decision to take, causing bitter and lengthy dispute. The statesmanship and extraordinary ability of Mustafa Kemal as chairman of the Congress, and his dexterity in directing it, played an important role in evolving a consensus. The Congress also elected a Representative Committee that was to organise and administer the Eastern Anatolia Defence of Rights Association, of which Mustafa Kemal was elected chairman.

To illustrate the great divide that existed between Vahdettin's Palace circle and the democratic-nationalist movement of Atatürk and his associates, which amounted to much more than a difference of political viewpoints but was rather a divide of ideology and even of historical eras, we will outline the peace plan offered on behalf of Vahdettin by Damat Ferit Pasha to Admiral Calthorpe on 30 March 1919:

(1) Non-Arab countries will remain directly under the sovereignty of the Sultan-Caliph. The Arab countries will be allowed autonomy but in matters of religion will defer to the Caliph's authority. The Sultan's coin will be the coin of the realm, the Sultan will be named in Friday prayers, and the Ottoman flag will be used for all. The Hejaz will remain in the hands of its previous administrators, but an Ottoman representative with a guard of 100 soldiers will ensure that its foreign relations are in accord with Ottoman policies. An Ottoman general will command a garrison stationed in Medina. Yemen will be administered as before the war. Armenia will be an autonomous or independent republic in accordance with the decisions of the Powers.

(2) Britain will occupy whichever regions (including the autonomous ones) it deems necessary for internal security and to protect Ottoman independence for a period of fifteen years.

(3) Ottoman European frontiers will begin from the Emine Balkans near Burgaz and reach to Samakof and from there to the Aegean sea, west of Enez (Enos).

(4) All fortifications in the Black Sea and in the Dardanelles area will be dismantled and the British will occupy the Straits.

(5) In matters of administration Britain will agree to appoint counsellors to whichever ministries the Sultan sees fit. In every province there will be appointed, for a period of fifteen years, a British consul who will also undertake the duty of counsellor to the governor. British consuls will supervise local and parliamentary elections.

(6) The British will audit the Exchequer in the provinces as well as in the capital.

(7) The Constitution will be simplified so that it will conform with the capabilities of oriental peoples (in accordance with a report submitted by Damat Ferit to the Senate on 15 February 1910). The Chamber of Deputies will vote the budget and inform the central government of regional requirements.

(8) The Sultan will have 'absolute freedom' in the conduct of foreign affairs.

This programme, preserved only in the British archives, shows the state of mind of the Palace. First and foremost the Palace was clearly not amenable to any alteration of the Empire's frontiers. It still cherished unrealistic hopes of holding on to all the Arab lands, including the Hejaz, the 'darling' of the British. Even in the hopeless case of Armenian independence, the option of some kind of autonomy is considered feasible. Moreover, a wish is expressed to extend Ottoman territory at the expense of Bulgaria, which was then in a weak position. In return Britain was to be allowed a wide range of privileges. The Straits and therefore İstanbul, the Exchequer and the administration, through consulates in the provinces and counsellors in the ministries, are all surrendered to the British and for a fifteen-year period they may occupy as and where they wish. After all these concessions, it is a strange paradox that the Sultan should insist on having 'absolute' freedom in foreign affairs. It also seems that a radical limitation of the constitutional regime was intended. The original of Ferit's on report could not be traced, but since the budget was to be 'voted' rather than debated or prepared, with no mention of legislative or supervisory functions, and the *reporting* of provincial needs was mentioned instead, this may be considered sufficient evidence of the mindset involved. Vahdettin's insistence on territory and disregard of nationality denotes a feudal approach typical of the Ottoman mentality. To allow the Capitulations (1740) to stand indefinitely for the sake of territory and allow Britain expansive trade concessions in order to hold on to Egypt (1838) had been ongoing policies of the Sultanate. In this instance too Vahdettin was willing to forgo independence completely in order to hold on to land.

The political approach of the Erzurum Congress and the democratic-nationalist movement was of a much more contemporary nature, in harmony with capitalist mentality. Experience had shown them that capitalism and a capitalist class could not develop in a state of dependence. The nationalists also understood that to gain full independence, claims to sovereignty over Arab lands must be abandoned. To reiterate, this constitutes not simply a difference of opinion but a divergence of mentalities rooted in different eras of history, one in the medieval and the other in the modern age.

The Sivas Congress

The Sivas Congress began on 4 September 1919 and ended on 11 September. Mustafa Kemal was elected chairman. At its outset, things did not go well. First, it was to have taken place as soon as possible after the Erzurum Congress, as specified in the Amasya Circular, but Atatürk and the Representative Committee were delayed in Erzurum for three weeks after the Congress was over. Secondly, when the Sivas Congress finally convened, the number of delegates in attendance was very low. (At the regional Erzurum Congress of Eastern provinces only, fifty-six delegates had been present, whereas Sivas, although it was a national congress, only attracted thirty-eight.) The main reason for this was the difference in approach to defence policies of the provincial defence organisations of the Western (Marmara and Aegean) regions and Eastern Anatolia. The west held that it was unnecessary to create a national defence system by uniting regional defence organisations because each provincial organisation had to deal with the specific problems facing its own region. The threat posed by Armenia headed the list of eastern problems whereas Greece was the foremost enemy facing the west. Another difference in their attitudes was that the eastern defence organisations were totally against occupation by any power whatsoever, whereas the idea of occupation by any member of the Entente (with the exception of Greece) was acceptable to the west. Finally, though the east had democratic demands, such as holding elections and convening the Chamber of Deputies, the west had no such demands. These divergent views may have arisen in part from the fact that the leadership of the eastern provinces was in the hands of the more radical military officers whereas, in the west, the relatively moderate notables had undertaken that role. The Porte, aware that the west was relatively moderate in its views, had begun to look with increasing cordiality upon the western national movement.

At the Sivas Congress 183 delegates should have been present (three from each of the sixty-one sancaks). If we reckon that the Representative Committee of the Eastern Anatolian Defence of Rights Association represented the twenty-one sancaks of the east, even then 120 delegates were to be expected from the other counties. When only thirty-eight arrived, Mustafa Kemal and his associates felt they had been unsuccessful in rallying a majority of the country and decided to organise instead a 'Great Anatolian Congress'. Invitations were sent out for this purpose forthwith. However, despite its unpropitious start, unfolding events were to turn the Sivas Congress into a great success, leaving no need for another congress.

Some of the delegates had come to Sivas with the specific aim of lobbying for an American mandate. In the early days of the Armistice, a group called the Wilsonian Principles Society had emerged in İstanbul, but little came of its activities and it petered out. As a result of the shockwaves created by the Greek occupation, the idea of an American mandate had begun to take hold in constitutionalist circles, countered by Palace and FAP circles which were pro-British. (A 'Friends of England Society' had been established with Sait Molla as its chairman.) The United States High Commissioner, Admiral Bristol, had encouraged pro-American groups and invited them to the American Embassy to further this trend. For some Ottoman intellectuals who had not yet relinquished their illusions of empire (most prominently the novelist Halide Edip Adivar and the journalist Ahmet Emin Yalman) the attraction of an American mandate lay in the hope of holding on to Arab countries such as Syria and Iraq. However, once under the American yoke, it would be necessary to become resigned to the establishment of Armenia in eastern Anatolia. Admiral Bristol was in fact not being totally forthright about US policy, since Washington had not yet come to any decision on whether it would assume the Turkish mandate. Bristol was more or less promoting his own views regarding this question.

Supporters of the mandate came to the congressional podium one after another to extol the benefits and inevitability of a US mandate. Halide Edip Adivar had sent a letter in support of this prospect, describing the high degree of prosperity attained by the Philippines under American administration, which, however, was not entirely true. Interestingly, Mustafa Kemal and his associates did not bother to refute these claims (Raif Hodja of Erzurum alone, his radical eastern sensibilities offended, could not refrain from voicing his protest). Mustafa Kemal and Rauf employed a clever counter-tactic. Instead of making an overt counter-stand, they avoided making the mandate an issue of contention by posing a question which immediately caught everyone's attention: 'Presuming that we want a US mandate, does the US too have such an intention?' Apparently, no one had thought to ask this question. As a result, a motion was passed for a letter to be written, asking for official confirmation from the US Senate of American policy as to a mandate. This tactic was clever in that it obviated loss of all-important American support for the nationalist cause. At a time when the Palace and the FAP were actively courting British support, outright Turkish nationalist opposition to the US mandate proposal might have affronted American susceptibilities. An American called Browne, correspondent for the *Chicago Tribune*, was present at the Congress.

According to another decision taken at the Congress, occupational and invading forces were to be opposed, not by the regular army, but by the National Forces, the Kuva-yi Milliye. This would avoid accusations of violating armistice conditions. By a decision taken on 9 September, Ali Fuat Pasha was made commander-in-chief of the National Forces.

From the moment the Sivas Congress began, the government had been intriguing against it. Despite the Sivas Congress being a legal body, the government was conspiring to disperse and apprehend its delegates by illegal means. Ali Galip, governor of Harput and a fierce oppositionist, was selected for this purpose as the government's agent. He had arrived in Malatya, there meeting with a British Major Noel (a Kurdish expert and fluent in the language) together with members of the Kurdish nationalist movement, Celadet Ali Bedirhan, Kâmuran Ali Bedirhan and Ekrem Bey. Ali Galip was to make a raid with 150 Kurdish horsemen on Sivas and declare himself its governor. To ensure the success of the raid, the governor of Ankara, Muhittin Pasha, was to begin an advance from the west. However, before all this could come about, the matter of remuneration had to be considered. In return for his extraordinary and illegal services, Ali Galip demanded the rank of military Pasha (general) and a financial reward. His bargaining with İstanbul had been going on by telegraph, but the telegraph line happened to pass through Sivas where this traffic caught the attention of the staff on duty. The government codes employed were deciphered in Sivas. As a result, Mustafa Kemal learned of the incipient plot on 7 September and immediately alerted his forces to arrest those involved. Muhittin Pasha was caught, but the others escaped. Mustafa Kemal reported these events to the Sivas Congress two days later.

The Congress reacted strongly against this unwarranted use of force against a legal meeting. In a letter addressed to the Sultan, it described this intrigue of Damat Ferit and demanded that he be removed as Grand Vizier. This document was sent by telegraph. In answer, the Congress was informed that it was impossible to present the Sultan with such a telegram, thus giving him the excuse of being 'uninformed' and therefore unable to take action. The Ferit government remained in place. Thereupon the Sivas Congress took a momentous decision. From that day until the Ferit government resigned Sivas would take the place of the capital and all telegraphic and other communication with İstanbul would be suspended. The whole country was informed of this decision, which put military and civilian officials alike in an extremely difficult position. If they conformed to it, they would be rebelling against the government, and if not they would be approving of Ferit's tactics. The Sivas-İstanbul struggle went on for three weeks. All Army Corps commanders sided with the Sivas decision. Force was used against the governors of Konya and Trabzon and the prefect of Eskişehir, all of whom defied the Sivas decision. The prefect was killed in the resulting conflict. Meanwhile two letters were entrusted to Browne, the American journalist. The first was written to the United States Senate concerning the mandate, and the second was the letter of protest written to the Sultan. When Browne personally took the second letter to İstanbul and handed it to the authorities, the Sultan's excuse of ignorance of the situation lost validity and could no longer be sustained. The Sultan recommended that both sides come to an agreement in a proclamation on 20 September. Various intermediaries were employed. Ferit sounded the British on their willingness to approve the despatch of a force of 2,000 soldiers, but they wanted to avoid any upheaval and declined to give their consent. With nowhere to turn, Ferit resigned on the night of 30 September.

Thus the Sivas Congress, inspite of having an inauspicious beginning, ultimately achieved brilliant success: no Great Anatolian Congress was now needed. The Sivas Congress ratified in full the decisions of the Erzurum Congress and established a nation-wide organisation, the League for the Defence of Rights of Anatolia and Rumelia—LDRAR. As in Erzurum, a Representative Committee was created to assume executive functions with Mustafa Kemal as chairman. The LDRAR was to organise elections. It was to dominate these, and thus the convocation of the Chamber of Deputies was assured.

17

THE THIRD PERIOD OF CONSTITUTIONAL GOVERNMENT

Why should this be viewed as a *third* constitutional period? The reason lies in the fact that Vahdettin had caused the government to deviate from the constitution when he violated the constitutional requirement that elections should take place within four months of the dissolution of Parliament. The 31 March Incident showed that whenever the CUP lost its predominance in governmental affairs, the constitutional government seemed inevitably to fall under the control of the Palace. Vahdettin might stop short of offending British sensibilities by making an outright move to abolish constitutional government completely, but he certainly did all in his power to emasculate and assume control of it. Consequently, with Vahdettin dominating the political situation, we can assume that the Second Constitutional Period had ended. Constitutional government was reborn owing to the political ascendancy of the Sivas Congress, after a year-long interval of absolute monarchy. Mahmut Goloğlu was the first historian to define the establishment of the Turkish Grand National Assembly (TGNA) on 23 April 1920 as inaugurating the Third Constitutional Period. Because at first the Turkish Grand National Assembly recognised the Sultanate and proclaimed its intention to preserve it, this definition was generally accepted, but in view of the civil war situation which developed between the TGNA and the Sultan, and the revolutionary character of the TGNA and its leader Mustafa Kemal, it seems more plausible to consider the convocation of the last Ottoman Chamber of Deputies as inaugurating the Third Constitutional period.

Ali Riza Pasha, deemed 'harmless' by the LDRAR, formed the new government. Another positive development was that Mersinli

143

Cemal Pasha, a former member of the Amasya Military Organisation, became the new Minister of War while Salih Pasha, who as a Military College graduate could be considered predisposed towards democratic-nationalist objectives, was made Navy Minister. Mustafa Kemal wanted to ensure that the new government would accept the resolutions of the Erzurum and Sivas Congresses, and that no decisions would be taken on the future of the country until the Chamber of Deputies had been elected. Furthermore, only delegates who could be trusted to express the will of the Turkish people should be sent to the Peace Conference. Salih Pasha and Mustafa Kemal determined the details of an agreement for cooperation between the LDRAR and the government at the Amasya Meeting on 20–22 October 1919. Ultimately five protocols resulted from their deliberations. One matter of immediate concern that was taken in hand was the geographical location of the new Parliament. Mustafa Kemal thought that the enemy occupation made İstanbul too dangerous, an opinion shared by Salih Pasha. However, when Salih Pasha returned to the capital it became apparent that the Sultan and the government were against any location other than İstanbul, which they argued would not only hinder cooperation between Parliament and the government but might also give the impression that the Ottomans were preparing to abandon İstanbul.

Faced with this dilemma, Mustafa Kemal organised a meeting of an enlarged LDRAR Representative Committee (16–28 November 1919) to be attended by all the members of the Amasya Military Organisation including Kâzim Karabekir, in deference to whom Atatürk referred to it in his *Speech* as 'the Commanders' Meeting'. The final decision of the Representative Committee was that İstanbul was the most appropriate location for Parliament.

The İstanbul government, too, was faced with a dilemma. On the one hand it did not want the LDRAR to involve itself in the coming election; on the other, to avoid embarrassing the Allied Powers it wanted the election to be free of ex-CUP candidates, meaning that intervention was a necessary expedient. The elections took time to organise owing to the two-stage election system and were boycotted by non-Muslims and the Freedom and Accord Party (FAP). Thus when the elections finally did take place, they were almost totally controlled by the LDRAR and inevitably a majority of its members were elected. Mustafa Kemal and Rauf were both elected Deputies but there was a risk that the Allies would not respect their parliamentary immunity if they were to appear in İstanbul. It was therefore decided that they should remain in Anatolia and direct and coordinate the Deputies at a meeting to be organised before the latter left for İstanbul.

On 27 December Mustafa Kemal and the Representative Committee moved from Sivas to Ankara to be in closer contact with İstanbul and the Chamber of Deputies. In addition to this, there was another facet of Ankara that attracted Mustafa Kemal and kept him there. The people of Ankara had embraced the democratic-nationalist cause even before his arrival, and on their own initiative had defied the Sultan's representatives. (Although Ankara had been dominated by the Ottomans for centuries, perhaps it took this independent stand because it had never lost the spirit of Ahi Republicanism.*) A single meeting of all the deputies could not be organised, but instead, as the newly elected Deputies arrived in Ankara, Mustafa Kemal arranged a series of meetings, speaking with small groups to ensure that every Deputy was fully conversant with democratic-nationalist policy.

Mustafa Kemal demanded from the Deputies as they took up their duties in İstanbul

(1) that they ratify and proclaim the programme to be called the National Pact (Misak-ı Milli), which would set out the peace objectives of the democratic-nationalist movement;

(2) that Mustafa Kemal himself be elected *in absentia* as the President of the Chamber of Deputies, because if, as he thought probable, the enemy should dissolve or in some way undermine the Chamber, the title of president would facilitate his convocation of Parliament elsewhere;

(3) that those elected from the LDRAR, i.e., the great majority of the Deputies, should establish a parliamentary group called the Defence of Rights Group;

---

* As the Anatolian Seljuk state faded away at the end of the thirteenth century, many regions of Anatolia began to be ruled by local potentates. Ankara, governed by its guilds as the Ahi Republic, was an exception.

(4) that because the Ali Riza government was obstructing the democratic-nationalist movement, therefore all efforts should be made to overthrow the present government and establish a new government more sympathetic to the cause in its place.

The last Ottoman Parliament opened on 12 January 1920. Vahdettin typically excused himself on grounds of ill-health for not attending.

The National Pact

The National Pact (Misak-ı Milli) was ratified on 28 January 1920. In summary it declared

(1) that all Ottoman territories inside and outside the boundaries drawn by the Armistice formed an indivisible whole. The destiny of the Arab lands, and the region of Kars, Ardahan, Batum and of Western Thrace could be determined by plebiscite.
(2) that a decision arrived at jointly by all concerned opening the Straits to international trade would be honoured, on the condition that the security of İstanbul and the Sea of Marmara should be secured;
(3) that the rights of minorities, as agreed on in the treaties concluded between the Entente and the Allied states, would be confirmed by Turkey on condition that Muslim minorities in neighbouring countries benefited from the same rights; and
(4) that full independence was necessary for Turkey's national and economic development. For this reason the Capitulations were opposed. The settlement of the nation's share of Ottoman debts would be determined in accordance with these principles.

In the draft which Atatürk prepared for the Deputies it had been stated that the regions *within* the Armistice frontiers were to be accepted as an integral whole in accordance with the resolutions of the Sivas and Erzurum Congresses. However, on reaching İstanbul the Deputies were unable to resist the allurement of Empire and gave their support to claims for Arab territories under enemy occupation (at the time when the Armistice was signed) that were outside the boundaries drawn by the Armistice. In later years many Turkish historians have suppressed this fact.

The National Pact is the programme the democratic-nationalist movement declared to the world. Its error in laying claim to Arab territories themselves was lightened by the provision for a plebiscite in the territories, and apart from this it was a realistic programme fully cognisant of the gravity of the political situation.

Parliament, by its affirmation of this programme, had realised one of Mustafa Kemal's objectives, but strangely events were to deny him the accomplishment of his other three staged goals set out in Ankara. A great majority of the LDRAR Deputies did indeed form a parliamentary group, but they named it Felah-ı Vatan as if, by rejecting the title 'Defence of Rights', they were also rejecting their parent body. Reşat Hikmet (who was not even a member of Felah-ı Vatan), not Mustafa Kemal, was elected president of the assembly, and on his death Celalettin Arif, also a non-member, was elected. Lastly, the government was given its vote of confidence. All of this happened although, by a later decision, Rauf had braved the dangers of İstanbul in order to instil some sense of their mission into the Deputies. Either he himself was swayed by the prevalent political atmosphere in İstanbul or he was not persuasive enough and the Deputies ignored his urging. In his *Speech* Atatürk roundly criticised the Deputies' behaviour; as he pointed out, one is inevitably drawn to the conclusion that they came under the influence of the Palace, the Allies and the FAP. Finally becoming part of the establishment in İstanbul, they came to view loyalty to the LDRAR as extremist, adventurist and dangerous, and as a result set aside their leader Mustafa Kemal and even came to the point of rejecting him.

Mustafa Kemal may have been seen as ultra-radical in his views, but his extremism was born of that of his adversaries. On 22–23 December 1919 the British and French had held a meeting in London to discuss the probable conditions of the Ottoman peace treaty, and at it a decision was taken that İstanbul would be taken from the Turks. The only point left for further discussion was where the new Ottoman capital would be. The French thought Konya appropriate, while the British preferred Bursa as being within reach of their navy. This decision was leaked to the press and on 4 January it became a headline in the İstanbul newspapers, and immediately created deep consternation. Even Vahdettin rebelled at the news and began to favour the Americans and the French. Meanwhile, the Entente (instigated by the British) sent an ultimatum demanding the resignations of the Minister of War Cemal Pasha and the chief of the General Staff Cevat Pasha on the grounds that they were in collusion with the National Forces, and both resigned without consulting Ankara (21 January). Mustafa Kemal was greatly incensed, believing that rather than resign they should have resisted. The decision to take İstanbul from the Turks, combined with this ultimatum, provoked Mustafa Kemal and his supporters to aggressive counter-measures. On 25 January the order went out for all-out guerrilla warfare in the southeastern region of Cilicia. Hostilities began in Maraş, Antep and Urfa to great effect. On 11 February the French, unable to withstand the attacks, were forced to evacuate Maraş. On the night of 27 January Köprülülü Hamdi Bey of the Biga National Forces raided the Akbaş arms depot under French guard in Gallipoli, and, snatching a large supply of arms and ammunition, carried it off to Anatolia.

The Allies realised that once again they had gone too far. Another conference in London was assembled, at which on 14 February it was announced that İstanbul was to remain in Turkish hands. Vahdettin thereupon resumed cordial relations with the British, and thus, two days later on 16 February, the second Anzavur rebellion broke out. Ahmet Anzavur was of Circassian origin, an officer risen from the ranks. Declaring that he was acting for the Sharia and the Mohammedan Party (somewhat similar in ideology to the Mohammedan Union of 1909), he with his supporters captured Köprülülü Hamdi and his men, killed them all, and defiled their bodies, dragging them to Biga to display to the general populace and the British. They later attacked Yenice where the arms and ammunition from Akbaş were hidden. Faced by superior forces, Hamdi's brothers-in-arms destroyed the munitions and fled. This was a major setback because they had been earmarked for an offensive operation against the Greeks. It is no exaggeration to say that Vahdettin, by backing Anzavur and other anti-nationalist forces, had betrayed the National Forces in Western Anatolia.

Not knowing which way to turn and under pressure from the Palace, the Entente and Ankara, Ali Riza Pasha resigned his post of Grand Vizier. Deputies who had seemingly turned their backs on Ankara now became anxious that Vahdettin might bring back Damat Ferit as the new Grand Vizier. The power source lay in

Anatolia and the LDRAR. In the words of Atatürk, the Representative Committee organised a 'storm of telegrams' nationwide. The technique of creating pressure by telegraph had been used to good effect during the Declaration of Freedom and the 31 March Incident. Probably because of this pressure, Vahdettin had no choice but to behave in a fashion acceptable to the democratic-nationalist movement. After much hesitation, Salih Pasha was made Grand Vizier (8 March) and Fevzi (Çakmak) Pasha Minister of War.

The escalated occupation of İstanbul

Meanwhile, the Entente resumed their pre-conference deliberations. İstanbul was supposedly to be left to the Ottomans, but the peace conditions were to be very harsh. To ensure that the Turks would submit to whatever conditions the Entente saw fit to impose, it was first necessary to subdue nationalist resistance and cut off popular support for the democratic-nationalist movement by dealing it a series of blows. Stringent measures against the nationalists would also have the advantage of indirectly stiffening support for the Sultan. To this end the British organised a raid on İstanbul on 16 March 1920. Since the city was already under occupation this action can be termed its escalated occupation rather than simply the 'occupation' or 'official occupation'. It took the form of a surprise attack or coup. In the early hours of that day British warships trained their guns on the city, while moving in towards the Galata Bridge on the Golden Horn. Machine-gunners were positioned on rooftops and British forces entered the Ministry of War and other official buildings which had not so far been occupied. Of more consequence, politicians and journalists pinpointed as nationalists were violently arrested and taken from their homes in the early hours of the morning, many in their night clothes. A proclamation threatened execution as punishment for resistance.

When a military building at Şehzadebaşı was raided fighting broke out and there were some deaths. That same day Entente representatives visited the Palace to assure Vahdettin that he was not the target of the coup.

The British, while cowing the populace, did not make a direct attack on Parliament or on the Salih Pasha government but laid down a condition that the latter must issue a proclamation denouncing the nationalist forces. The government stood fast as their patriotic duty demanded, nor did it resign, assuming that if it did Damat Ferit probably would be reinstated. It carefully prepared a proclamation that the people had taken up arms against Greek oppression, thus exercising its legitimate right of self-defence, but that there had been some instances of illegal and extreme measures being employed. The Entente rejected this declaration as being without effect, whereupon the government rewrote the proclamation using stronger language, which was again rejected. The declaration went to and fro between the Allies and the government like a shuttlecock—until the government resigned.

Although in the early morning the British military had forced their way into private homes and offices using their rifle butts, in the afternoon they presented themselves in an orderly fashion to Parliament, giving polite notice at the entrance that they had come to detain Rauf and certain other members. Despite the fact Mustafa Kemal had received advance intelligence of the coup and asked Rauf to join him in Anatolia, Rauf was present that day, perhaps desiring a dramatic encounter which would document for the historical record British disrespect for democracy and the institution of Parliament. He had appeared in Parliament to give the British soldiers this chance to haul him off at bayonet point. However, the respectful demeanour of the British ruined his plan, and he decided to surrender after obtaining from the British officer in charge a signed affidavit to the effect that he was being detained against his will. Even at the moment when the British arrived it would not have been impossible for him to evade arrest and Atatürk, probably with this incident in mind, did not refrain from saying in his *Speech* that some people had preferred the prisons of a civilised country to the danger and uncertainties of the national struggle.

Two deputations, one headed by Rauf and the other by Hüseyin Kâzım, went to the Palace to ask the Sultan not to name Damat Ferit as Grand Vizier. Vahdettin rejected both pleas out of hand. To Hüseyin Kâzim his words were: 'I shall appoint whomsoever I please to the vizierate, be it the Greek Patriarch, the Armenian Patriarch or the Jewish Chief Rabbi.' To Rauf he said: 'Rauf Bey! There is a nation, a flock of sheep. They need a shepherd. I am he.' This description of the people as a flock and himself as a shepherd merely typifies the medieval mindset of Vahdettin.

In protest at Entente aggression, the Chamber of Deputies suspended assembly meetings, but this stand found no support among ultra-right oppositionists and Palace supporters, the majority in the Senate. Their view was that there was no need for any protest at all, with Rıza Tevfik even going so far as to oppose an initiative for the release of a senator whom the British had arrested. His justification was that a great state could not be unjust. This denial of the most basic sense of solidarity illustrated clearly the polarisation in Turkish society that stoked controversy to a point beyond bounds the possibility of reconciliation, so that any chance of a consensus was lost. Clearly these conditions were propitious for civil war, which in fact had already begun.

Mustafa Kemal had foreseen that a coup was imminent and was prepared for it. He immediately went into action, sending a 'storm of telegrams' all over the country protesting against the Allies' actions, proposing that Parliament be reconvened in Ankara, and calling for the cutting of all official communication between Ankara and Anatolia (as during the Sivas Congress incident). Meanwhile, the patriotic Salih Pasha government stayed in place for seventeen more days. During this time General Assembly meetings were not convened, but the Chamber of Deputies was in 'part-time' session. The Minister of War Fevzi Pasha demanded that the army should not sever its ties with the War Ministry. Two Army Corps commanders (Fahrettin Altay of the 12th Corps in Konya and Yusuf İzzet of the 14th Corps in Bandırma) complied with this demand, and thus the Army Corps Commanders' Front, established in September 1919 during the Sivas Congress with no problems, could not be re-established in 1920. These developments are reminiscent of the aftermath of the 31 March Incident, when the Chamber of Deputies sent commissions to dissuade the Hareket Army from entering İstanbul. The government sent a deputation of four Deputies to persuade Ankara to reinstate severed communications. On the other hand, Ankara used force to bring the two rebellious commanders into line. Salih Pasha, unable to withstand the growing pressure applied by the Entente, resigned on 2 April. The Allied Powers had not been at all impressed by the government's condemnation of the National Forces. On 4 April Damat Ferit again assumed the vizierate. Thus, the people were obliged to choose one side or the other, and the sheep were separated from the goats. Meanwhile, former Minister of War Fevzi Pasha fled to Anatolia. On 11 April the Chamber of Deputies was dissolved, after which many Deputies also chose to join the nationalist resistance in Anatolia. The short period of the Third Constitutional Government was at an end.

18

ESTABLISHMENT OF THE TURKISH GRAND NATIONAL ASSEMBLY, CIVIL WAR AND THE TREATY OF SÈVRES

The Turkish Grand National Assembly

From the moment that the British staged their coup in İstanbul, Mustafa Kemal was active organising a new Parliament in Ankara. Its members were to be those Deputies who had been able to escape from İstanbul. Elections were to be held to replace those Deputies who had chosen not to escape or who could not. Another question to be dealt with was the title of the new assembly. It could no longer be constituted as the two chambers of the Ottoman Parliament, first because it was certain that the senators would not be present, and secondly because there was no longer any question of working in cooperation with the İstanbul government or the Sultan. Mustafa Kemal proposed that this new assembly be called the Constituent Assembly (Müessisan Meclisi). Kâzım Karabekir objected, proposing instead the use of the term *Şura* (council) because of its Islamic connotations. The title 'Türkiye Büyük Millet Meclisi' (hereafter referred to as the Turkish Grand National Assembly or the TGNA), conceived by Mustafa Kemal and his colleagues, was finally decided on as being most apposite. Every word of this new title was full of revolutionary symbolism. Turkey (Türkiye) means the land of the Turks whereas in Ottoman times the country had been called 'memalik-i Osmaniye'—the Imperial Ottoman dominions, or lands owned and ruled by the Ottomans. In Europe countries, even if ruled as a kingdom or empire, had names other than those of the ruling dynasty. For example, in the British Isles, the countries themselves were England, Wales, Scotland and Ireland, whether the

153

reigning the dynasty was Tudor, Stuart or Hanoverian. 'Memalik-i Osmaniye' implied that the country and its ruling dynasty were one; that the land was the dynasty's property. In contrast foreigners generally spoke of 'Turkey' and this was indeed a more democratic concept. The word 'grand' or 'great' emphasised that this was not just any assembly but one which had extraordinary powers to meet the needs of the nation. The word 'national' affirmed that the assembly was to represent the Turkish nation. The first use of this word in the official title of a Turkish parliament had occurred at San Stefano, but it was discontinued after the Hareket Army entered İstanbul. Now the word (*millet*) re-emerged as a constant.

The TGNA opened on 23 April 1920. Mustafa Kemal was elected its president and it was decided that he should also preside over the Ankara government that soon would be established. Hereafter the Turkish national struggle for democracy was to gain new impetus.

Civil war

The first business of the Damat Ferit government in İstanbul was to obtain a *fatwa* from the Sheyhülislam (Grand Mufti) Dürrizade Abdullah Efendi pronouncing the nationalist movement a rebellion against the Caliphate and stating that its members should be killed, and that those who took up arms against them would become *gazi* or *şehit* (warriors or martyrs for the Faith). Thousands of these *fatwas* were distributed throughout the country, some said to have been dropped from British aeroplanes. Mustafa Kemal and his associates were court-martialled *in absentia* by the military court of Mustafa Pasha and many were condemned to death (11 May 1920).

These measures amounted to an official declaration of civil war, but by September 1919, during the struggle between the Sivas Congress and the the government, attacks against the nationalist movement had already begun, encouraged if not organised by the Palace and Damat Ferit and supported by the British: the first Bozkır revolt (27 September–4 November), the first Anzavur revolt (1 October–30 November), the second Bozkır revolt (20 October–4 November) and the Sheikh Eşref rebellion (26 October–24 December 1919). After a ceasefire of a month and a half, during which the Allied powers changed their decision to take İstanbul from the

Turks, a more violent and far-reaching second act began on 16 February 1920, with the Second Anzavur rebellion. Turkish historians referring to these popular pro-monarchist uprisings sometimes use the term 'domestic rebellion'—meaningless in that a foreigner cannot rebel against what is not his own state. Although the pro-monarchist movement was an attack on the authority of the TGNA government, from Vahdettin's point of view they were legitimate forces supporting established religious and legal authorities; the Sultan referred to them as the Loyalist Army. If we look at the matter neither from the point of view of the Ankara nationalists nor from that of the İstanbul government this was outright civil war, a bloody domestic struggle with one side fighting to defend the democratic-nationalist revolution and the other for medievalist absolutism and counter-revolution.

The democratic-nationalist movement lost no time instituting counter-measures. On 5 May 1920 the Mufti of Ankara, Rifat (Börekçi) Efendi, issued a counter-*fatwa* in which opposition to the nationalist cause was pronounced treason. Already on 29 April the Law for Treason to the Motherland had been enacted. Any rebellion against the TGNA was to be accounted treason punishable by death. Later, on 18 September, the TGNA established revolutionary Courts of Independence (*İstiklal Mahkemeleri*), with their judges and prosecutors elected from among members of the TGNA, and their decisions to be final with no court of appeal. On 6 May 1920 the TGNA came to the decision that all official communication with the İstanbul government was to cease, and on 24 May all its decisions and undertakings made after 16 March were declared null and void. It was declared that the TGNA's aim was to rescue the Sultan-Caliph from the Allied Powers who were holding him prisoner. The National Assembly was thus proceeding with caution, taking care not to be seen to be directly attacking the Sultanate while at the same time doing what was necessary to conduct a civil war.

Let us now review the major fronts of the Civil War. The anti-nationalist Anzavur rebellion took place in the regions of Biga, Gönen and Karacabey (Bursa). Insurgency in Adapazarı and Düzce-Bolu spread as far as Beypazarı, a sancak of Ankara. Halide Edip Adıvar, in her book *The Turkish Ordeal*, describes how at Mustafa Kemal's nationalist headquarters during this time 'Intermittent gunfire was heard, its source unknown. Security precautions included measures for evacuation and escape at a moment's notice.'

Konya was the stronghold for the Delibaşı Mustafa Rebellion, and the fourth major uprising, the Çapanoglu rebellion, took place in Yozgat. The locations for these rebellions were chosen in order to hem Ankara in on three sides. As a final measure the Sultan established an official army, the Security Force, also called the Army of the Caliphate, commanded by Süleyman Şefik Pasha. Its aim was the annihilation of the nationalist movement. On 25 June 1920, National Force units under Ali Fuat Pasha halted and defeated this army at Geyve. Throughout the summer of 1920 and on into the autumn, the fighting created havoc in Anatolia. It continued for a full year from the autumn of 1919 with a break during the resolution of the İstanbul question. Sultan Vahdettin rather than Damat Ferit must be held responsible because Ferit was not in office for much of this period. The Anzavur, Düzce-Bolu-Adapazarı and the Çapanoglu rebellions were all suppressed by the so-called Mobile Forces, an autonomous unit of the National Forces commanded by Ethem the Circassian (Çerkez Ethem). The TGNA emerged victorious from the civil war largely through the efforts of the National Forces rather than those of the regular army.

The Treaty of Sèvres

While the people of Anatolia were preoccupied with these conflicts, developments of great moment were taking place in foreign affairs. Following a series of meetings in the Italian town of San Remo (24 April 1920), the Allied powers gave final shape to the Ottoman peace treaty. They then requested the Ottoman government to send its representatives to the Peace Conference. The terms of peace were handed to the Ottoman delegation in Paris (11 May) as a *fait accompli*. The head of the delegation, Tevfik Pasha, shocked by this vindictive document, telegraphed İstanbul that the treaty not only denied Ottoman independence but was not even compatible with the concept of statehood. The whole country, including the Sultan, was plunged into consternation.

The main points of the Treaty of Sèvres were as follows:

(1) Eastern Thrace was ceded to Greece and preparations were to be made for the İzmir-Manisa-Ayvalık region to be annexed to Greece within a period of five years.

(2) Armenia was to be recognised and its borders with the Empire determined by President Wilson. (Wilson did later undertake this task, and fixed frontiers that would take in a large portion of Anatolia, including Tirebolu, Gümüşhane, Erzincan, Mush, Bitlis and the territory east of this line.)

(3) An autonomous Kurdistan was to be established in those eastern and southeastern regions of Anatolia left over from Armenia and, if it were so decided by this entity in the future, it too would become independent.

(4) Passage through the Straits and the Sea of Marmara was to be administered by a Straits Commission, an independent international body with its headquarters in İstanbul and its own flag and police force. The Straits and the coasts of Marmara, with a generous hinterland, were to be demilitarised. As long as the Ottoman Empire conducted itself in accordance with accepted norms, it would be allowed to retain İstanbul as its capital.

(5) Mardin, Urfa, Antep and Ceyhan would be annexed to Syria.

(6) The number of soldiers and gendarmerie allowed to the Ottoman armed forces, inclusive of Palace guards, was not to exceed 50,700.

(7) The Capitulations were to be reinstated.

(8) French, British and Italian representatives were to form a Finance Commission, and the Ottoman budget would be drawn up in accordance with its decisions. The Commission was to supervise the treasury and control the amount of currency in circulation. No debts would be incurred and no concessions granted without its permission.

9) The seventh article of the armistice agreement was to stand; that is, the Allies were to occupy any areas they deemed necessary (art. 206).

According to a Tripartite Agreement between the Entente Powers, an Italian zone of influence comprising Antalya, Silifke, Niğde, Aksaray, Akşehir, Afyon, Balıkesir, Aydın and Muğla and a French zone comprising Mersin, Adana, Maraş, Diyarbakır, Silvan, Elazığ, Arapkir, Sivas and Tokat were to be constituted. The Ottoman government's objections were almost totally disregarded. The only concession made was that if Turkey were admitted to the League of Nations, an

Ottoman representative, with one vote, would become a member of the Straits Commission. The Allies, realising that even the Sultan was reluctant to put his signature to this treaty, activated the Greeks. On 22 June 1920 the Greek army went on the offensive: it invaded a huge area of western Anatolia and captured Bursa on 8 July and Uşak on 29 August. Yalova, Bursa, Uşak and Buldan were now in the new region of occupation. Despite some resistance, the Greeks also occupied Eastern Thrace on 20 July. The National Forces of western Anatolia not only were unable to stop the Greek advance, but could not even put up any resistance worthy of the name. The National Forces had worked miracles in southern Anatolia, but were ineffective in the Aegean region. This is not difficult to explain. At the time of the Greek attack, the Turkish people of the west were fully engaged in the Civil War and in these circumstances the Greek victory was not surprising. Since the Civil War had been instigated and to some extent directed by Vahdettin, it is no exaggeration that the Greeks owed their victories to him. However, he could not have been pleased by the defeat of the National Forces, since this left him no choice but to accept the Treaty of Sèvres, which gave the death sentence to Ottoman rule. After a meeting of an Imperial Council, which had no function other than to document the impotence of the Ottoman state (there was only one vote against), on 10 August 1920, the Ottoman delegates Riza Tevfik, Reşat Halis and Hadi Pasha signed the Treaty at the Paris Conference. This was perhaps the darkest moment of Turkish history.

This is not to say that Vahdettin had no recourse but to sign. Acting with courage and resolve, he might have refused Ottoman affirmation or even have declared a *Jihad*. The consequence of such a stand might have been his removal from the Palace to exile as was the fate of Napoleon Bonaparte, but Vahdettin obviously did not have the strength of character necessary for any such firm action. Mustafa Kemal and his colleagues, the TGNA as a whole, displayed superior fortitude; they threw caution to the winds and openly declared their defiance of the treaty, resolving that whoever accepted it was a traitor. The day the Greeks occupied Bursa the podium of the TGNA was covered by a black cloth which was to be only removed when that city was liberated.

The Treaty of Sèvres was a traumatic blow to the Turkish psyche. Allied to Balkan nationalism, Europe had shown with words and deeds that it was decided in its aim of evicting the Turks from the Balkans as a political force and even as an ethnic entity, and by 1913 the Ottoman state had relatively small territorial claims left there. The Turks were perhaps prepared for a treaty further limiting their dominion in Eastern Thrace. However, the Turks totally failed to anticipate that the treaty would also initiate the process of their eviction from Anatolia. Without any investigation of which people were the majority group in any given region, and basing its decisions solely on historical claims, the treaty allowed the creation of an Armenia with an Armenian minority and an Anatolian Greece peopled by a Greek minority. The phrase 'process of eviction' is used here advisedly because Balkan history shows that the process would not have stopped with this treaty. There was no guarantee that in the near future a Greek state or statelets would not be created in the Black Sea region (the Greeks of Samsun, Bafra, Amasya and Tokat did indeed stage an uprising in December) or in Central Anatolia or the Mediterranean region. Far from being a remote contingency, this was highly likely to happen in the near future and almost certain to do so in the long term. The history of colonialism and imperialism has been littered with instances of tyranny, injustice, exploitation and repression, but it is rare that a colonialist or imperialist power says to a native people, 'This land is mine. You are not wanted here. Go elsewhere.' This extraordinary treatment was reserved for the Anatolian Turks, as it was later for the Palestinian Arabs. This was a shock for the Turks.

The Turks demolished the Treaty of Sèvres with their bayonets, and their victories achieved the Peace of Lausanne. The revolution of Mustafa Kemal Atatürk was the continuation of this process. It brought about the Turkish nation's advance towards the forefront of civilisation, the reaffirmation of the validity of Lausanne, and it made the Treaty of Sèvres null and void in perpetuity. The Atatürk revolution is the security and guarantee of Lausanne. As a nation that survived the Treaty of Sèvres, the Turks are well aware of this reality and therefore, although many decades have passed since Mustafa Kemal's death, the principles on which his revolution was based are upheld and safeguarded along with all of its institutions.

As for the Civil War, its last front was that of the Delibaşı Mehmet rebellion which broke out on 2 October 1920 and spread like wildfire. The rebels were able to capture Konya, but regular army units flushed them out in a few days. On 16 October the TGNA army entered Bozkır. The next day, on 17 October, Damat Ferit resigned from the Grand Vizierate in İstanbul and his political life thereby came to an end. Why did Vahdettin and therefore Ferit wait so long? Was it still their hope that the Delibaşı revolt would spread throughout the country? It seems that Vahdettin did not give up hope that the Civil War would produce a positive result for the monarchy until this last rebellion ended in defeat. Faced by this reality, Vahdettin removed his 'hawk' Damat Ferit from the fray and thereafter till the end of the Sultanate he employed the services of another of his relatives, his 'dove' Tevfik Pasha.

19

THE REGULAR ARMY'S ROAD
TO VICTORY

The regular army had its first successes in the east. Armenia had been agitating on Turkey's eastern frontier since June 1920 in an effort to take advantage of its preoccupation with the Civil War and the Greek invasion in the west. On 24 September the Armenians moved into a large-scale offensive. General Kâzım Karabekir's 15th Army Corps, which had retained its fighting capability in defiance of armistice measures for disarmament, was stationed in Eastern Anatolia and it not only stopped the Armenian offensive in its tracks but also proceeded to take back Turkish territories. The Armenians were forced to sue for peace. With the Treaty of Alexandropol (Gümrü) signed on 3 December 1920, Oltu, Sarıkamış and Kars were returned to Turkey, and Armenia was obliged to declare its non-recognition of the Treaty of Sèvres.

It is impossible to estimate the degree of success the National Forces would have had against Greece if there had been no civil war. However, there is no doubt that domestic upheaval severely undermined its fighting potential. As may be remembered, the National Forces were established at the beginning of the War of Liberation to avoid accusations of defying the conditions of the Armistice of Mudros and consisted of volunteers, though in some places the soldiers were paid. At that time too, recruiting for the regular army was difficult because of the war-weariness of the population. Some irregular soldiers, such as those of Ethem the Circassian's Mobile Forces, pillaged and plundered their way to a lucrative income. As the Greek invasion spread unchecked over Eastern Thrace and western Anatolia, the overt lack of success of the National Forces in the west gave rise to popular support for a regular army capable of

defeating the enemy. This made recruitment possible and reorganisation of the regular army a priority. The western front had been
established in June 1920 with Ali Fuat in command. Left over from
the days of the National Forces' irregulars and having acquired their
habits, he was a general who carried a rifle on his shoulder and had
no badges of rank on his uniform. A new man was now needed for
the new era. On 8 November Ali Fuat was relieved of his military
post, appointed ambassador to Soviet Russia and replaced by Colonel İsmet Bey. Efforts were made to incorporate the National Forces
into the regular army as it was reorganised and expanded.

The new order went against the grain of the irregular commanders Demirci Mehmet Efe and Ethem the Circassian (Çerkez Ethem).
The 11 December Demirci revolt was defeated by forces under
Refet Pasha and Demirci surrendered. A series of meetings was held
to persuade Ethem the Circassian to join forces as a division of the
regular army but to no avail. He too openly rebelled on 1 January
1921. As the army entered his Mobile Forces headquarters in Gediz
on 5 January, Ethem fled and sought refuge with the Greeks. Historians hold divergent opinions of Ethem the Circassian's place in
Turkish history. Some call him a traitor while others interpret his
actions more sympathetically. None dispute the extraordinary service he rendered to his country during the Civil War. He may be
criticised for refusing to join the regular army but not condemned as
a traitor solely for seeking refuge with the Greeks to save his life and
liberty. The question is whether or not he worked against his country *after* taking refuge with the Greeks, a matter on which doubt
remains.

The new Tevfik Pasha administration of İstanbul sought to re-
establish contact with Ankara for cooperation between the two governments. A meeting was held on 5 December 1920 at Bilecik. İzzet
Pasha and Salih Pasha (both former Grand Viziers) came as emissar-
ies of İstanbul while Mustafa Kemal, together with Colonel İsmet,
represented the TGNA, but no positive results ensued.

Events in Greece

Meanwhile, Greece was the scene of events of consequence for
Greco-Turkish affairs. King Constantine was reigning when the
Great War began in Europe in 1914. He had been educated at the

German War Academy and married to a German princess, sister of Kaiser Wilhelm II—circumstances that made him sympathetic to Germany. Greece had therefore chosen to remain neutral, whereas Venizelos, the Greek political leader from Crete, saw neutrality as a mistake. He believed that the Entente powers would win the war and that if Greece were to throw in its lot with theirs, advances could be made towards the realisation of the *Megali Idea* (the Great Idea of establishing a greater Greek realm). In 1917 the French invaded Thessaly and forced the abdication of Constantine and the accession of his second son Alexander. Venizelos was made Prime Minister and Greece entered the war on the side of the Entente. Alexander died in October 1920 as the result of a bite by his pet monkey. Venizelos called a general election, sure of its results after his great service to Greece. The opposition favoured the restoration of King Constantine. However, the electorate voted for considerations other than that of the *Megali Idea*, Venizelos was defeated at the polls, and Constantine returned. Aware of French opposition to him, Constantine sided with the idea of a renewed military offensive to force the Turks into accepting the Treaty of Sèvres and thus win over the French. The consequences of these events were the battles of İnönü and Sakarya.

The first battle of İnönü and its repercussions

Colonel İsmet's forces met the Greek army in battle on 6–10 January 1921 at a place called İnönü near Eskişehir. This battle came on the heels of the operation against Ethem the Circassian. Though greatly inferior in numbers and equipment, the Turks defeated the Greeks in a pitched battle, forcing them to retreat. This battle is sometimes downgraded as a reconnaissance operation of the Greeks involving a small number of their forces. Nevertheless, throughout history a battle's importance has been determined by its consequences rather than the number of soldiers who took part. During the birth of Islam, battles no bigger than a large neighbourhood skirmish had great repercussions and were therefore important.

The victory at İnönü opened the eyes of the Allied Powers to the reality that they had gone too far. They decided to convene a conference in London at which Turkey would be represented. An invitation was sent to Grand Vizier Tevfik Pasha with the request that representatives of the TGNA be included in the Ottoman delegation. When Tevfik Pasha informed Ankara of this development, Mustafa Kemal sent him a categorical refusal, declaring that this change in Allied policy was a product of the perseverance and sacrifice of the Turkish people and the determination of the TGNA never to accept the Treaty of Sèvres. It was impossible for a government which had signed that treaty to obtain results beneficial to the nation. *All* delegates to the conference should be selected by the TGNA, and the İstanbul government should refrain from interference. On İstanbul's rejection of these arguments, the Ankara Assembly demanded a separate invitation for an independent delegation of its own and the Allies were forced to agree.

The London Conference began on 23 February 1921. When Tevfik Pasha's turn came to speak, he deferred to the leader of the TGNA delegation, the Foreign Minister Bekir Sami, stating that the people's representatives had the right to speak for the nation. This recognition on the part of the İstanbul government greatly enhanced the standing of Bekir Sami. However, as the conference continued, it became clear that the Allied proposals were merely a slightly altered version of the Treaty of Sèvres, incompatible with the principles of the National Pact. The conference therefore ended without any result (11 March). However, Bekir Sami did sign treaties with the Italians and the French and an agreement for release of prisoners of war with the British, but the TGNA repudiated all three of these agreements on grounds of incompatibility with the National Pact. Although no concrete results came of the London Conference, it had one positive result: international recognition of the TGNA government.

After the first battle of İnönü, major developments occurred in Turkey's relations with Soviet Russia. In the spring of 1920 the first step in establishing good relations had begun with correspondence between Lenin and Mustafa Kemal. The democratic-nationalist movement had little affinity with socialism; the bond between them came from the fact that both countries were targets of West European enmity, which made it natural for them to develop closer relations. On 11 May 1920 a Turkish delegation headed by Bekir

Sami was sent to Moscow, and its meetings resulted in Soviet recognition of the National Pact (June 3). Although Ambassador Ali Fuat had been in Moscow since November, this major development in foreign affairs came only after the first battle of İnönü. The Turkish-Soviet Treaty of Friendship, signed in Moscow on 16 March 1921, determined Turkey's borders with Soviet Russia. Batum was left to the Soviets, who promised to provide Turkey with war materials and financial aid. This border, which still stands, was later reaffirmed by the Treaty of Kars, signed by Turkey, Georgia, Armenia and Azerbaijan on 13 October 1921.

Friendly relations with the Soviet regime awakened interest in socialism and Communism in certain circles of Turkish society. For example, Ethem the Circassian was a member of the Green Army Organisation. On 14 July 1920 the Turkish Communist Party was established in secret, and in December the same year it was legalised as the People's Socialist Party of Turkey. Mustafa Kemal was uneasy about where these activities might lead, and in order to keep the movement under control he encouraged a group of his colleagues, including Celal Bayar, to found the 'official' Turkish Communist Party (October). All of these organisations were shut down after the Çerkez Ethem rebellion. In September 1920 Mustafa Suphi founded a Turkish Communist Party in Baku, and in January 1921, he and his associates visited Turkey. They were assassinated by Yahya Kâhya in waters off Trabzon for reasons which have never been fully clarified.

The first İnönü victory paved the way for yet another development in foreign affairs, the Turco-Afghan Friendship Pact, signed on 1 March 1921. As may be concluded from the above, the first battle of İnönü, though undervalued by some, gave rise to three major advances in Turkish foreign affairs.

Defeat in the battle left the appetite of the Greeks for war undiminished. They were convinced that they could take Eskişehir and then advance on Ankara, an opinion shared by the British Prime Minister David Lloyd George. The Greeks launched their offensive on 31 March and the second battle of İnönü was fought on 31 March and 1 April 1921, ending in an unequivocal victory for the Turks. İsmet Pasha (who later adopted the place of the battle as his surname) had been promoted to full general after the first battle of

İnönü. With this second victory Mustafa Kemal congratulated him saying: 'You defeated there not only the enemy but also the misfortune of the nation.'

The Italians withdrew from Marmaris in May and from Antalya in July. The French evacuated Zonguldak in June. Earlier, in April, the Ottoman Prince Ömer Faruk, in an attempt to visit Ankara, had landed at the Black Sea port of İnebolu, but Mustafa Kemal politely but firmly sent him back to İstanbul. Vahdettin's hopes of reaching a compromise with the nationalists were dashed after the failure of all his undertakings, at the Bilecik meeting, the London Conference and this last attempt in İnebolu.

The battle of Sakarya

Though twice defeated at İnönü, the Greeks remained undaunted. They mustered all their forces in preparation for a great attack. The Greek campaign began on 10 July and started off well. The Turkish army was beaten back from Eskişehir and Kütahya, and the Greeks took Eskişehir, Kütahya and Afyon—an extensive advance. Mustafa Kemal ordered a retreat to the east of the Sakarya river that surrounded the plain of Ankara, having decided that this good defensive position would offset the superiority of the Greek army. The TGNA was gripped by anger and panic. A deluge of civilians flooded the road from Ankara to Kayseri as the government considered whether it too should evacuate its offices to Kayseri.

On 25 July the Turkish army took up its position east of the Sakarya river. The TGNA wanted Mustafa Kemal himself to command the army. He accepted on condition that he be granted full power. On 5 August 1921 the TGNA conferred on Mustafa Kemal the function of commander-in-chief and authorised him to exercise full powers in the name of the Assembly for a period of three months (these powers were to be renewed several times until the Great Offensive). He made immediate use of this power on 7 and 8 August when, in his 'Orders for National Taxation', he declared an extraordinary mobilisation of the whole country, involving every citizen in the war.

In the words of Mustafa Kemal, the coming engagement would be 'not two armies fighting against one another but two nations which are both risking their existence and which summon for the fight all of their resources, all their possessions and all their material and moral forces... In future wars also the decisive element of victory will be found in this concept.' Lord Kinross, in his biography of Atatürk, says that Winston Churchill was to appreciate the truth of this prophetic statement many years later.

Every household was to contribute a set of linen, a pair of shoes and a pair of socks to the forces. All arms and ammunition, 40 per cent of all foodstuffs, 20 per cent of riding and draught animals, carts drawn by both oxen and horses, were commandeered from the people against ultimate compensation. Women played an important role, driving ox-carts carrying ammunition and artillery shells over long distances. In every sancak National Taxation Committees undertook the organisation of this huge war effort. There was, indeed, very little time left.

On 23 August 1921, the two armies clashed on a front approximately 100 kilometres wide. The Greek army was superior in every aspect, with the exception of its cavalry and the number of its officers. The accompanying table gives an idea of the situation. These figures show that the Greeks had three times the number of machine guns and 59% more cannon than the Turks. They had 840 trucks while the Turks had none, and they had nine times the two Turkish aircraft, illustrating the qualitative difference between the two armies. Most striking is the number of soldiers. Although the Greek population was approximately less than half that of Turkey, and although the Ottoman Empire had been able during the World War to muster 2.5 million soldiers (about half of this number from Anatolia and the Balkans), now, as the enemy drew nearer and nearer to the capital, Ankara, the Turks, with their very existence at stake, had fewer men in the field than the Greeks.

	Officers	*Privates*	*Rifles*	*Machine-guns*	*Cannon*
Turks	5,401	96,326	54,572	825	169
Greeks	3,780	120,000	75,900	2,768	286
	Animals	*Carts*	*Trucks*	*Aircraft*	
Turks	32,137	1,284	–	2	–
Greeks	3,800	–	840	18	–

Atatürk did what he had had to do at Gallipoli when his back was against the wall. He ordered his soldiers to fight to the death—in the circumstances there was no other way to victory. His order of the day was: 'There is no line of defence, there is only a surface of defence. That surface is the whole of our motherland. Our motherland cannot be abandoned until every inch of its earth has been watered with the blood of its citizens. For this reason every unit, large and small, will continue to fight, stopping at its first foothold and re-establishing a front against the enemy. Units observing a neighbouring unit forced into retreat are to fight on independently, regardless. Each in its own position is compelled to persevere and resist until the end.' After a pitched battle lasting 22 days and nights, the Greeks gave in and fell back (13 September 1921).

Let us return to the question of why Turkey, despite its higher population, was able to muster fewer men than the Greeks. This, too, seems to have been a product of the Civil War, which had just petered out. It may be said that, although the war had physically ended, the psychological trauma of countrymen fighting against each other was still fresh. In addition, there had been very little time for the TGNA and Mustafa Kemal to establish a consensus for total war against the Greeks, and therefore the manpower of Anatolia could be mobilised only to this extent. These views are likewise expressed by Atatürk in his *Speech.* Let us also note that there was a surplus of serving officers present. This once again underscores the critical role played by the 'educated', i.e. the intelligentsia, in the continuance and advancement of the Turkish nation.

The Greeks had approached to within 50 km. of Ankara and were able to retreat in a more or less orderly fashion. If the Turkish army had been less exhausted and had had more resources it might have mounted a large-scale follow-up operation, turning the Greek retreat into a rout. However, this did not occur. Moreover, as a result of their July offensive, the Greeks had reached the Eskişehir-Afyon line, thus gaining a vast amount of territory. Constantine, returning from the front, his confidence bolstered by these acquisitions, was met in İzmir with victory celebrations. His arrival was celebrated in Piraeus and Athens with festivities, and hymns of thanksgiving were sung in the churches. But the Greek assumption that they had achieved victory was an illusion. Constantine's battle-cry had been 'To Ankara!'

Despite their occupation of new territories and the great sacrifices made by their army, the Greeks had not achieved this goal. Therefore, Sakarya stands as a Turkish victory, in acknowledgment of which the TGNA honoured Mustafa Kemal with the title *Gazi* (the Victorious) and the military rank of Marshal.

A strengthened international position was the fruit of victory. The French emissary Franklin-Bouillon had arrived in Ankara at the beginning of June with the intention of making a Franco-Turkish agreement. However, he had then been extremely unenthusiastic when it came to confirming the principles of the National Pact. Immediately after the victory of Sakarya, however, a treaty conforming to those principles was signed—the Ankara Agreement of 20 October 1921. In accordance with this treaty, France recognised Turkey's existing southern borders with Syria with the exception of Hatay (Alexandretta and Antioch) where a special regime was to be established to safeguard the interests of the Turkish population. Thus a separate peace was made with France in the south, whereby the French evacuated all regions under their occupation and undertook to procure arms for Turkey. Relations with Italy had been peaceful for some time, so that Britain had become largely isolated in its policy of encouraging the Greek invasion of Anatolia. The Ankara Agreement effectively split the Franco-British alliance. Even the British came to an agreement with the TGNA government over the bilateral exchange of prisoners of war (23 October 1921). Thus Rauf, Fethi and many other Turkish political figures and officers were able to return to Turkey. It should be noted that the Treaty of Kars, between Turkey and the three short-lived Caucasian independent states, also took place during this period (13 October 1921).

20

THE GREAT VICTORY AND THE
ABOLITION OF THE SULTANATE

Peace initiatives

After the victory of Sakarya friend and foe alike were obliged to recognise that the TGNA government and the democratic-nationalist movement were forces to be reckoned with in Turkey. Mustafa Kemal's standing as the movement's leader was also enhanced by the victory, although there were some, including members of the TGNA, who still wished to see Enver at the helm of the nationalist movement. There had been intimations that Enver was preparing to enter Anatolia at the head of troops gathered with Soviet support in the event of Ankara falling to the enemy. The time was now ripe to ensure that the Greeks withdrew from Anatolia and Eastern Thrace and to make peace in accordance with the principles of the National Pact or, at the very least, adhering as far as possible to its basic concepts.

A year-long quest for peace followed in the wake of Sakarya. During this period there was almost no action on the Turco-Greek front, but as time passed this hiatus began to create tension. The Greeks probably sensed that they would not be able to hold out in the long run, or perhaps had even realised that their days in Anatolia were numbered. The Turkish army had shown itself to be a formidable fighting force and was daily growing stronger; the agreements made by the Italian and French governments with the TGNA government were clear evidence of this. It was also necessary for the Greeks to maintain an army of occupation in a large area of Anatolia at great sacrifice and expense, and to be prepared for action at a moment's notice.

The lengthening lull in hostilities also induced mounting anxiety among some members of the TGNA. Their patience was exhausted

170

and demands were heard for either war or peace. Only Mustafa Kemal and his colleagues were able to maintain an attitude of studied calm. Patiently and with unremitting effort, they were laying the foundations of a decisive victory while not giving up their search for an honourable peace without war. The TGNA decided to send its Minister of Foreign Affairs, Yusuf Kemal (Tengirşenk), to Europe to initiate peace talks. Because it was felt that support from the İstanbul government would strengthen their position with the Allies, Yusuf Kemal was sent first to İstanbul before leaving for Europe. In other words, the TGNA was in search of the same kind of support that Tevfik Pasha had given them during the London Conference. Yusuf Kemal arrived in İstanbul on 15 February 1922. Grand Vizier Tevfik and Foreign Minister İzzet Pasha received Yusuf Kemal's proposal favourably, but told him that nothing could be done without Vahdettin's approval. He was granted an audience with the Sultan and presented his case. Vahdettin listened throughout with eyes shut, and when Yusuf Kemal had finished, there was a long silence. Vahdettin said not a word, still with his eyes shut; it was as though he had fallen asleep. Finally a confused Yusuf asked to be excused and removed himself from the Sultan's presence, and then had to set off for Rome with no assurance of Ottoman support. On arriving there he found that İzzet Pasha, the Ottoman Foreign Minister, had arrived before him, and wherever he went and whatever contacts he made his actions were duplicated by İzzet. In Paris and in London the same scene was re-enacted. It cannot be known whether the results would have been more favourable if Vahdettin had not so assiduously disassociated himself from the TGNA government in the eyes of the world, but clearly the Sultan's tactics hindered the peace process, frustrating any attempts at fruitful dialogue.

At the end of March the Entente powers made their own peace proposal. Their armistice plan of 22 March 1922 specified a three-month cease-fire period between Turkey and Greece, which was to be automatically renewed at the end of each period. In the interim, neither side was to increase its armed forces' fighting capacity in any way and both were to be supervised by the Entente to ensure that these conditions were met. The Greeks accepted the armistice as written, but the Turks objected to the conditions on limitations of forces and to Entente supervision. The Turkish counter-proposal specified that Turkey would accede to an armistice only if the Greeks evacuated Anatolia within a period of four months. On 26 March the Allied powers' peace plan was communicated to the Turks. The Sèvres Treaty had again been taken as the basis on which certain changes had been made; the Aegean region and Tekirdağ (Rodosto) were left to Turkey, with the rest of Eastern Thrace allotted to Greece. The business of establishing an Armenian state was left to the League of Nations. The Turkish army was allowed a force of 85,000 soldiers. The Capitulations were to be revised, and financial obligations reduced. The TGNA rejected this plan too, insisting that any viable peace treaty must accord with the principles of the National Pact and demanding that a peace conference be held in İzmit.

Summer came with no resolution of this impasse in view. Tension was continuing to mount in Greece. At last the Greeks found a solution, which they thought would end their dilemma; they would participate in the occupation of İstanbul, thereby forcing the Turks to toe the line and become more amenable to accepting peace conditions. They readied some of their troops and officially applied to the Allies on 29 July. Left to the British, the decision would probably have been to welcome Greek participation in the occupation, but Italy and France were against it and as a result the Greek proposal was rejected (31 July). On 30 July the Greek High Commissioner Sterghiades announced that a Greek state of 'Ionia' had been established in İzmir. Both the Entente and the Ankara and İstanbul administrations protested openly at this announcement. Lloyd George must have shared his Greek friends' disappointment, since he spoke spontaneously in the House of Commons on 4 August enumerating Turkish sins such as closing the Straits to the Entente during the Great War, and the sacrifices made by Greece on behalf of the Allied powers and the trouble caused by the Turks to the Greeks.

Towards the end of July, a month before the Great Turkish Offensive, Fethi (Okyar) was sent to Europe to argue the case of the Ankara government, and was able to meet French ministers in Paris, but could not make contact with any British ministers, even with the Foreign Secretary Lord Curzon, and returned home empty-handed. Documented in British archives is the fact that during this period

Vahdettin was in secret contact with the British. At an interview on 6 April 1922 with their High Commissioner Sir Horace Rumbold and his head dragoman Ryan, Vahdettin is reported to have said: 'Do you intend to make the peace with a legal government or a revolutionary organisation? We are prepared to make the peace under conditions unacceptable to Ankara.' Thus Vahdettin attempted to 'underbid' the National Pact. He cited the Maritza river as an acceptable new frontier and said that he was willing to sign a separate agreement with Britain. At a second meeting with Rumbold three weeks before the Great Offensive, Vahdettin claimed that the TGNA government had come into being as a result of the Greek occupation and that if the occupation were to end it would lose its *raison d'être* and become redundant. However, it was of the first importance that the territories evacuated by Greek forces should be handed over to the İstanbul and not the Ankara government. In addition, Britain had to supply the İstanbul government with money, arms and naval support. Vahdettin's conduct throughout these secret meetings will be further evaluated below where the question of treason is discussed.

It has already been mentioned that the continued ambiguity of affairs after Sakarya had caused growing tension not only on the Greek side but also among the Turks. Obviously the shape of events obliged Mustafa Kemal to plan and prepare for the new offensive in total secrecy. At the same time some TGNA Deputies, unaware of these plans, feared that he intended to use his extraordinary powers as commander-in-chief to create a dictatorship. Probably influenced by those who were of this opinion, a majority of the Representative Assembly voted at a sitting on 5 May against a continuation of Mustafa Kemal's authority while he was absent due to illness. The following day Mustafa Kemal came to the Assembly and declared that this vote had deprived the army of a commander-in-chief, posing a grave danger to the country. He said: 'I have not left my post, and cannot and will not do so.' In the face of his adamant stand the TGNA reassigned him full authority.

The great offensive and victory

Secret preparations for the offensive may be summarised as collecting men and material from the east and the south, calling up new recruits, organising arms and ammunition deliveries from the Soviets, France and other sources, including matériel smuggled from arms and ammunition depots in İstanbul. In a country largely lacking roads and railways, a great part of this equipment had to be transported over long distances by ox-cart, loaded on pack animals or even carried on people's backs. In addition, because the Greeks occupied the main junctions at Afyon and Eskişehir, use of the existing railways was almost impossible. In mid-June 1922 Mustafa Kemal gave orders for the offensive. Secretly at night, the Turkish army made its way to a point south of Afyon. There a battle of annihilation was to be fought, meaning that the Greek army, was to be completely deprived of its fighting capacity. If the Turks failed in this aim and the Greeks, though defeated, were to fall back and regroup, it would become almost impossible to save Eastern Thrace because, although Greek units could easily retreat to Eastern Thrace, Turkish units would be prevented from crossing the Straits by the Entente which controlled them. At the peace conference the answer to Turkish demands on Thrace would be, 'You defeated the Greeks in Anatolia, but they still hold Thrace with a large armed force intact.'

On 17 August Mustafa Kemal left Ankara for the western front headquarters, then in Akşehir but moved to Şuhut a week later. The attack began on the morning of 26 August. The Greek army, pushed back and besieged on all sides, was dealt the death blow at the battle of Dumlupınar. To keep the routed Greek army from regrouping, the commander-in-chief Mustafa Kemal ordered a swift, three-pronged advance to İzmir. His order of the day was 'Armies, your first objective is the Mediterranean.* Forward!'

Speed was essential, both to achieve the main objective of the battle (annihilation) and to stop the Greeks from burning and pillaging the towns and villages in their path; because they had ravaged Anatolia during their occupation, the worst was expected. After the Sakarya victory, a commission of inquiry, the 'Tetkik-i Mezalim' comprising Halide Edip Adıvar, Yakup Kadri Karaosmanoğlu and Yusuf Akçura, carried out an investigation which confirmed the reality of this mistreatment. The British historian Arnold Toynbee corroborated their findings through his direct observations of the

* The Aegean sea did not at that time have a separate name in Turkish.

situation in Karamürsel. The worst was that native Greeks had been recruited into the Greek army or otherwise been made party to these offences. As a result, on the defeat of the Greek forces, they saw no alternative to fleeing the country which was their home; they burned and pillaged because they had lost all hope of returning, and did not dare to face their neighbours. They had been infected by the germ of ethnic hostility.

The Turkish victory, of which Mustafa Kemal was the architect, was so overwhelming that the Greek commander-in-chief Tricoupis and the whole of his staff were captured. He and another Greek general were brought before Mustafa Kemal who treated them with courtesy. The battle was discussed. Despite all the atrocities suffered by the Turkish people, his treatment of the defeated generals was humane and statesmanlike. On entering İzmir he refused to walk on the Greek flag unrolled in his path. The Turkish army freed İzmir on 9 September and Bursa on September 10. Unfortunately, like number of other places, İzmir was set on fire. Turcophobes have claimed that the Turks were responsible for the fire in İzmir, whereas the European superintendent of the fire brigade, in his report, attributed it to certain Armenians. The disordered remnants of the Greek army together with much of the Greek population fled from İzmir, Çeşme and Bandırma by ship.

Atatürk's victory message to the nation was as follows:

To the great and noble Turkish nation:
Our victorious armies liberated the city of İzmir on the morning of 9 September 1922 and Bursa on the evening of 9 September. The Mediterranean resounds with our soldiers' songs of victory.

The commanders and general staff of an insolent enemy striving for an Asian empire, who dared come to the battlefield, have been for days the prisoners of the Turkish Grand National Assembly government.

General Tricoupis, the enemy commander-in-chief, after many days and nights of desperate battle and having tried every means of deliverance, has at last surrendered with his retinue of generals, his general staff and the remnants of the army he commanded. If the King of Greece is not among the prisoners of war today, it is because the tendency of crowned heads is to participate in their peoples' pleasure but, on days of disaster in the field of battle, to think only of holding on to their palaces.

Now all that is left of the great Greek armies, armour-plated with the steel of Western factories, are wretched groups of soldiers abandoned by their leaders in the mountains of Anatolia; multitudes now horrified at the murders they have committed, and the weary and helpless wounded who have been left to find shelter under trees by the wayside.

Approximately two thirds of the enemy's war equipment has been abandoned in our lands. In addition to those who are prisoners of war, it is difficult to determine how much higher than 100,000 is the number of enemy casualties. I am happy to inform the nation that the official estimate of our casualties is limited to 10,000, three-quarters of whom have only light wounds.

Great Turkish Nation, our armies showed their power and capability and an excellence sufficient to strike terror in our enemies and inspire confidence in our friends. Our nation's armies demolished a great enemy army in fourteen days, and pursued them relentlessly over 400 km. They won back all of the invaded territories of Anatolia. This great victory is your work alone, because the people who, driven by greed for political aggrandisement, were almost pleased to surrender Izmir to the enemy had no relation to the nation. As for the Greek forces that invaded Bursa, they succeeded only by the unification of their goals and operations with those of the Empire's military organisation. The liberation of our country began when the nation, represented by its elected government, asserted unconditional control over its own future and only from armies born of the nation's conscience have positive and categorical results been achieved.

Great and noble Turkish nation, with my congratulations on the liberation of Anatolia, I present to you the salutations of your army from the horizons of İzmir, Bursa and the Mediterranean.

President of the Grand National Assembly of Turkey
Commander-in-Chief Mustafa Kemal

In this address Atatürk used the example of the Greek King to attack all systems of monarchy, including the Ottoman Sultanate. The declaration defends democracy: victory belongs to the nation alone. Those people who handed İzmir to the enemy 'almost with pleasure' had no relation to the nation. The Greeks succeeded in invading Bursa because they were in league with the imperial Ottoman army. Liberation could only begin with the establishment of the people's unconditional sovereignty over their own destiny and was achieved by an army born of the common will. With this declaration Atatürk was opening the way to a Republic.

As the Turkish army approached Chanakkale, British units stationed there prepared for war, and the Italians and French, aware of British intentions, withdrew to Gallipoli, the European side of the

Dardanelles (September 19). The British announced that they would fire on Turkish soldiers entering a neutral zone outside their lines. Lloyd George, frustrated by the Greek defeat and determined to ensure free passage through the Straits, was set on involving his country and the forces of the British dominions (Canada, South Africa, Australia and New Zealand) in a war against Turkey. He ordered that hostilities be engaged the moment the Turks set foot in the neutral zone. Turkish soldiers did indeed enter the zone, but they approached British lines with a peaceful rather than a warlike demeanour (24 September). Under these circumstances the British commander General Marden refrained from giving an order to fire.

While Britain clamoured to secure free passage through the Straits, and Lloyd George wanted a 'personal' war with the Turks, and the Greeks were in possession of Eastern Thrace, Turkey intended to continue its military operation to liberate Eastern Thrace with no loss of time. France intervened in the crisis at this critical moment, undertaking the role of mediator. Pellé, its High Commissioner in İstanbul, travelled to İzmir with Franklin-Bouillon to confer with Mustafa Kemal. On 24 September the Soviet government warned the Allies in a diplomatic note that if the Great Powers were to become involved in a Greco-Turkish war, this would lead to serious repercussions in Europe. On 23 September the other Allied powers proposed first an armistice and later a peace conference. As time went on, Lloyd George became increasingly isolated.

The armistice of Mudanya

The Mudanya conference convened on 3 October with İsmet Pasha as the Turkish delegate. On the other side of the conference table were the representatives of Britain, France and Italy, but a Greek delegate should surely have been present since no action had been taken to invalidate the Armistice of Mudros, and the war had been fought between Turkey and Greece. This strange state of affairs shows to what a degree Greece had become a satellite of the Allied powers and lately of Britain in particular. These facts need to be emphasised because some Turkish writers such as the novelist Kemal Tahir and the economist İdris Küçükömer have argued that the War of Liberation had not been of an anti–imperialist character but was solely as a war between Turkey and Greece.

The Greek representative, General Simopoulos, waited on board a ship anchored off Mudanya for the results of the deliberations; they were not to his liking, and he refused to add his signature to the armistice for three days after all the others had signed. The nine days of the conference were a battle of nerves. Turkey's aim was to gain immediate control over Eastern Thrace so that it could enter the future peace conference with the question of Eastern Thrace non-negotiable. This would make Turkey better able to stand firm on other issues. Although a large proportion of the Greek army had been destroyed, the Allies at Mudanya struggled to deny Turkey this advantage. İsmet Pasha, using all his powers of persuasion, defended Turkish policy with patience and persistence. Lloyd George was on the watch for a final opportunity to find a pretext for war, and ordered that if an agreement were not reached by a certain time and date the commander of the Allied occupation forces in İstanbul, Lieutenant-General Sir Charles Harington, should initiate hostilities against Turkey. However, the military were not as enthusiastic as Lloyd George for war, and the British people as a whole were exhausted with it. Although the deadline passed, General Harington, as General Marden had done at Chanakkale, ignored these orders. Greece had become a British puppet to such a degree that he was able to give an affirmative answer to İsmet Pasha's question whether the armistice would still be valid if Greece refused to sign.

According to the Mudanya armistice, the cease-fire was to take effect on the night of 14/15 October, the Greeks were to evacuate Eastern Thrace, and to prevent them from doing harm as they did so they were to hand over the evacuated territories not to the Turks but to the Allied authorities. The Allies would then hand over these territories to the TGNA forces and evacuate Eastern Thrace themselves within thirty days. The total number of Turkish soldiers present was not to exceed 8,000. Refet, responsible for the handover of Eastern Thrace, arrived in İstanbul on 19 October amidst scenes of joyous celebration. That same day, the British coalition government was forced to resign, thus bringing to an end Lloyd George's extraordinary political career. Certainly he was an enemy of the Turks but it is uncertain to what extent he can be considered a real friend of Greece. Between 31 October and 26 November the process of handing over Thrace to the Turks was completed. Meanwhile, the already dwindling power of the Palace and its government was fading to extinction, but the Allied powers' invitation to the Lausanne Peace conference was nonetheless extended to both the İstanbul and the Ankara governments. The TGNA was outraged when the İstanbul government in the person of Tevfik Pasha, emboldened by this invitation, proposed that a joint policy be established for the conference.

Abolition of the Sultanate

The extent and perfection of Atatürk's victory secured Turkey's independence and the integrity of its borders with the Treaty of Lausanne. In domestic affairs that same victory guaranteed the impregnability of the Atatürk revolution with regard to the feudal system. The shock of the Treaty of Sèvres had made clear the overwhelming need for revolution, and victory had given the architect of the revolution sufficient power and authority to achieve it. Atatürk was a master of political timing. Taking advantage of the storm of outrage created by the dual invitation, he put an end to the Sultanate at a stroke. He had not mentioned publicly any plan to establish a republic and spoke in defence of the Caliphate. However, when the TGNA Joint Committee was set to continue its interminable discussion of whether or not the Caliphate could exist without the Sultanate, Atatürk took the stand and stated that sovereignty could only exist if backed by strength and power. Thus the Ottomans had formerly been sovereign, but the nation had now taken sovereignty into its own hands. He felt the need to add: 'In my opinion, it will be appropriate for members of the Assembly and everyone else to accept this matter as a natural course of events. If the reverse should be the case, the truth will still win out, though perchance some heads may roll.' The Hodja Efendi (doctor of divinity) who was head of the committee, brought the meeting to an end saying they had 'indeed been enlightened'. On 1 November 1922 a decision was taken (with only a single 'no' vote from Ziya Hurşit) to end the rule of the Ottoman Sultanate after some 600 years. The Ottoman line was to continue its authority as the Caliphate, but the TGNA would decide which members of the dynasty would be the Caliph. The Tevfik Pasha government resigned.

Time passed with no further clarification of Vahdettin's position. On 10 November he attended the traditional ceremony of Friday prayers. Finally, fifteen days after the abolition of the sultanate, he informed General Harington in a letter that he was seeking refuge with the British. On 17 November he left Turkey with his family and close circle on board the British battleship *Malaya*. On the following day the TGNA formally deposed Vahdettin and elected his heir apparent, Abdülmecit Efendi, to the Caliphate.

Was Vahdettin guilty of treason? First, there was his action in completely forgoing Turkish independence in his peace proposal to the British of 30 March 1919. He was trying to reclaim imperial lands in return for concessions, which may be said to conform to the traditional Ottoman policy of trading economic rights for land. This was merely in accordance with his highly traditional mentality.

Secondly, he incited and did his utmost to prolong the Civil War. For a reigning absolute monarch to take up the sword against democracy and continue the struggle to the bitter end has its own justification. However, to instigate civil war during an enemy invasion drastically makes his action much more serious.

Thirdly, when one after another his loyalists had been defeated and he too had given up the fight and removed Damat Ferit from the Vizierate, he still secretly strove to come to an agreement with the British; in doing so he conspired to undermine the National Pact. Having lost all his cards in the Civil War, he should have bowed to the inevitable, but instead, even according to his own values and in the vocabulary of the Sultanate, he betrayed vediat-ullah, his sacred trust, and put a knife in the back of the *ümmet-i Muhammet* (supporters of Mohammed) by leaving them at the mercy of a non-Muslim administration. This was treason by his own understanding.

Fourthly, his taking refuge with the British was what most disturbed his supporters, who at one time claimed in mitigation that he had been abducted by the British at gunpoint. Of course, Vahdettin could have stood his ground and remained, but his liberty and possibly even his life were in imminent danger. But he has to be blamed for running to the British because at that time Britain, allied to Greece, was his country's principal enemy. He could have sought refuge in Italy or France (in fact he lived in the Italian town of San Remo until his death in 1926). Some of his supporters applaud him for fleeing with only his own personal property, instead of taking with him the total contents of the Ottoman treasury. This is a strange line of thought. Aside from the question of whether he had the opportunity to pack up that amount of loot, it is no praise to say he had the chance but didn't use it, because normally only positive actions receive praise; refraining from a dishonourable act is not usually considered praiseworthy.

21

THE TREATY OF LAUSANNE: TURKEY DECLARED A REPUBLIC

The Lausanne Conference

The Peace Conference began on 20 November 1922 in Lausanne with İsmet Pasha (İsmet İnönü) as Turkish representative. The Prime Minister, Rauf (Orbay) had proposed himself as his country's representative, but Kemal thought İsmet Pasha, in the light of his success at the Mudanya conference, best suited to the task. To strengthen İsmet Pasha's position the TGNA had appointed him Minister of Foreign Affairs.

The two sides involved in this diplomatic confrontation were divided not only by conflicting interests but also by their totally divergent outlooks. The Allied powers viewed Turkey as one of the defeated Central Powers and therefore wanted to impose a treaty similar to Sèvres. The British Foreign Secretary, Lord Curzon, was still determined to enhance his country's hegemony in the Near East at Turkey's expense. However, the Turks saw themselves as victors of their war of independence and the equals of all others at the conference, and were thus determined that their country should be regarded as an independent sovereign state. They sought validation of the National Pact and entry to the community of nations with a standing equal to that of any Western country. The Allied powers had not yet fully understood that they were confronted not by the old Ottoman regime, which was prepared to make concessions to preserve its territory, but by a new nation which would stand on principle.

From the beginning of the conference, instead of a conventionally-worded opening speech, İsmet İnönü straight away set out the main points of Turkey's case, stating that his people had suffered and

182

striven in order to become a free and independent nation according to the principles of the National Pact. In the following months, with inexhaustible patience, he refused to retreat from his commitment to these basic concepts and tried unremittingly to hammer them into the heads of the other delegates. With the conference apparently nowhere near a conclusion, Lord Curzon presented İsmet with a draft treaty reflecting his own conception of what the peace terms should be, and stated unconditionally that he would quit the conference if, by a deadline of 4 February, İsmet did not accept the proposed terms. Some delegates tried to mediate, but İsmet rejected the draft as unacceptable. When the deadline arrived Curzon boarded his train and departed, whereupon, after two and a half months of deliberation, the conference broke up without any result.

The interval of stalemate lasted for approximately three months. During this time, Turkey took military precautions to pre-empt any resumption of hostilities. In addition, the Turks also endeavoured to encourage an atmosphere conducive to their proposals being positively received.

The channel of communication chosen by the Turks for rapprochement with the British was the National Import and Export Corporation of Turkey, which had been founded ten days after the liberation of İzmir and among whose founders were fifty-four deputies of the TGNA. On 15 June 1923 this company came to a comprehensive agreement with a British company, the Corporation for the Development of Turkey. Although the United States had retreated from involvement in European affairs and not participated in the Lausanne negotiations, its influence was nevertheless felt all over the world. Therefore the Turks decided that an effort should be made to include America in their efforts to conciliate or 'sweeten' the opposition. In past years, during the Second Constitutional Period, an American finance group headed by Admiral Chester had proposed a ninety-nine-year agreement for a railway concession in Anatolia. Its terms had specified that the American group was to construct and manage a 2,000-km. railway and in return be allowed mining rights within an area of 20 km. on each side of the railway (a total area of 8,000 square km.). On 9 April the TGNA passed a bill allowing this concession. However, the deal was not concluded, probably because American enthusiasm for it had depended on Turkey gaining control of Mosul and its oil rights.

The İzmir Economic Congress

This began (17 February–4 March 1923) two weeks after the suspension of the Lausanne Conference. Industrialists, merchants, artisans, workers and farmers were represented and Kâzım Karabekir was its chairman. Atatürk's opening speech set out the concept that military victories were given a long life by economic victories, that for hundreds of years the Turkish people had followed Sultans to war with no positive outcome for themselves, whereas in the new Turkish state the economy would be of primary concern. He also proclaimed his rejection of an adventurist foreign policy. Already in 1921, speaking before the TGNA, Atatürk had outlined his conception of a soundly based foreign policy, namely that it should be proportionate with a country's strength. The Ottoman Empire had taken up Islamism but had not had the power to implement it, and therefore had become mired in situations from which it could not extricate itself. The same had been true of Pan-Turkism.

The most important measure decided on at the İzmir Congress was the abolition of tithes. An attempt was also made to determine the principles on which the development of the newly-emerging Turkish economy should be based. Another important function of this congress was to intimate to the West that, despite a policy of Turkish-Soviet cooperation and friendship, Turkey had no intention of straying from the capitalist path.

The Treaty of Lausanne

After a period of diplomatic negotiations, the Lausanne conference was reconvened on 23 April 1923, and a further three months were to pass before compromises acceptable to both sides were reached and the treaty was finally signed on 24 July 1923. The matters addressed fall under five main headings:

Boundaries and land rights. The Treaty of Lausanne ratified Turkey's borders with Syria and the Caucasian states of Azerbaijan, Georgia and Armenia. These had been previously determined by the provisions of the Franklin-Bouillon agreement signed with France for the former and by the Treaty of Kars signed with the Soviets for the latter. With the Armistice of Mudanya it had been agreed that

Turkey should have Eastern Thrace. As for Turkey's claims to Western Thrace and certain Aegean islands, the former were rejected, and of the latter three islands—Imbros, Tenedos and Tavshan—were left to Turkey. The rest of the Aegean islands were ceded to Italy or Greece, which accepted the demilitarisation of Lesbos, Ikaria, Chios and Samos. The fate of Mosul, which had been claimed by Turkey in the National Pact, was left undecided, to be settled later by the League of Nations.

The Capitulations. İsmet Pasha had strict instructions from the government not to give way over this matter under any circumstances. After a long and hard struggle, the High Contracting Parties accepted 'the complete abolition of the Capitulations in Turkey in every respect'.

Economic and financial questions. Proportional shares of the Ottoman debt were allocated to the countries which had become heirs to Ottoman lands, and were to be paid in instalments. Bond-holders were to have no control or supervisory rights over these payments. Turkey's last bonds were liquidated in 1954. Standing concessions (operational rights) accorded before 1914 were to be honoured by Turkey. A concession was made in respect of customs duties, which were to be frozen for five years at rates determined in 1916. Only in 1929 did Turkey gain full control over its own customs policies.

The Straits. Passage through the Straits was organised in a way that would ensure the utmost freedom of passage. Even if Turkey were to engage in war, neutral ships and aircraft were to be allowed through. In addition, adjacent areas on both sides of the Straits were to be demilitarised. Application of the provisions relating to the Straits was to be supervised by an international commission. These articles were clearly a severe limitation upon Turkish sovereignty.

Years later, when war again appeared imminent in Europe, Turkey applied for a re-evaluation of the Straits Question and finally, with the Montreux Convention in 1936, Turkish rights of sovereignty and independence were recognised, the International Straits Commission was abolished, and Turkey regained full control over the Straits, a situation which has prevailed ever since.

Problems related to Greece. These may be examined under three main headings.

(1) Population exchange. A decision was made to exchange the Greek minority in Turkey with the Turkish minority in Greece. Despite the obviously tragic consequences of forced migration, the conference reasoned that, given the degree of enmity between them, these two ethnic entities could not live in peace with their neighbours of the majority population.

Turkey had good reasons for supporting such a move. First, the population exchange would remove the many Greeks of western Anatolia and Thrace who had joined the Greek army during Turkey's War of Independence, thereby aligning themselves against the Ottoman-Turkish state of which they were citizens. Secondly, the Greeks of the Black Sea region had been in a state of revolt from December 1920 to the beginning of 1923, and might well rebel again or constitute an excuse for a renewed Greek invasion. In Greece the Turkish minority posed the same problems. Though neither pleasant nor humane, the exchange was intended to reduce current tension between the two countries and thus lay the foundation for better relations in the future.

During the War of Independence there were of course many Greeks who did not consort with the enemy, including notably those of central Anatolia who even cut themselves off from the Greek Patriarchate in Phanar (Fener), İstanbul, and established a Turkish Orthodox Church. However, after the population exchange its head, Pope Eftim, was left without a flock.

The total forced to emigrate were 1.3 million Greeks from Turkey and half a million Turks from Greece. Only two groups were exempt: the Turks of Western Thrace and the Greeks in İstanbul. The newcomers were given the landed property or real estate of those who had left, according to their standing. Farmers were allocated farmland, shopkeepers shops, and so on.

As a touching and interesting aside to this affair, Turkish was the mother tongue of the Greeks of central Anatolia. Many of them spoke no Greek at all, and used Greek characters in writing—the result being known as *Karamanlika*. This gave rise to a distinctive literature. A controversy blew up when a novel entitled *Seyreyle*

Dünyayi (Behold the World), written by Evangelinos Misailides and first published in 1871, was republished in Turkey in Turkish script. The first Turkish novel is reputed to be *Taaşşuk-u Talat ve Fitnat* (Talat and Fitnat falling in love) by Şemsettin Sami, published in 1872. When Misailidis' novel was reprinted, there was heated dispute in Turkish literary circles as to whether or not it was the first Turkish novel.

Those Greeks whose native language was Turkish had serious problems adjusting to life in Greece. Similarly, many Turks from Janina and Crete who spoke Greek as their mother tongue knew very little Turkish and suffered the same problem adjusting to their new life in Turkey. Indeed it seems that religious affiliation and not language had determined who was to leave and who was to stay, raising the question of religion's share in ethnicity.

(2) Demands for war reparations. Despite its efforts the Turkish delegation was awarded no reparations for the damage done in Anatolia by the Greek army, the main argument being that Greece lacked funds because of the debt it had accumulated during its war of invasion. Towards the end of the conference the Entente and Greece proposed the cession of the Karaağaç area of Edirne in lieu of reparations. İsmet was inclined to accept, but the question of reparations became a subject of acrimonious dispute between İsmet and Prime Minister Rauf and his cabinet against the proposal, and the signing of the treaty was delayed. In the end through Atatürk's intervention the Entente's proposal was accepted and the treaty could be concluded.

(3) The Greek Patriarchate of Fener (Phanar). Turkey wanted the Patriarchate relocated to some other country, but this was not accepted.

On 24 July 1923 the Treaty of Lausanne was signed with due ceremony. Thus it was internationally accepted that the dependent Ottoman state had ended and a new and independent Turkey had been established in its stead. Simultaneously, in the words of Kemal Atatürk, the death sentence passed on Turkey by the Treaty of Sèvres was rendered null and void. The process of evicting Turks from Europe, which had started with the Treaty of Carlowitz (1699), was brought to a halt at Eastern Thrace along with the danger that the same process might be extended to include the Turks of Anatolia.

Although Lord Curzon had told İsmet Pasha during the conference that even if the Turks rejected his proposals they would be kept in his back pocket only until such time as he would take them out again one by one, the Atatürk revolution was not only to secure their disappearance for a long time from the international agenda but also to prevent a resurrection of Sèvres.

It has been argued in some quarters that Lausanne was a disaster for Turkey. The loss of Mosul and of Western Thrace, the retention of so few Aegean islands and the demilitarisation of the Straits have been and still are cited as evidence of this. However, these arguments have no serious basis. The Lausanne Conference was a great and historic confrontation between countries whose power was clearly defined and its deliberations extended over five and a half months, eight if the interval of stalemate during which related diplomatic manoeuvres took place is taken into consideration. When negotiations come to a standstill one side has to make concessions when the alternative is a continued state of war, with or without the resumption of hostilities. Participants in a peace conference may later make statements to the effect that they were badly treated, but in general substantiating such claims is impossible because every transaction has a complex and interconnected structure. By objectively comparing the treaties of Sèvres and Lausanne, any objective person may easily and sufficiently determine whether the latter was a victory or a disaster for Turkey.

Establishment of the Republic

After peace was made, Atatürk was at last free to advance along the path of revolution. Paradoxically, the TGNA itself had now become one of the greatest impediments to revolutionary progress. Although the TGNA had successfully sustained the national struggle in the past and a great majority of its members still supported Mustafa Kemal, the opposition, called the 'second group', was undeniably conservative or even reactionary and, having discerned Atatürk's intention of realising revolutionary reforms, it lay in wait for an opportunity to dislodge him from his position of power. It was also doubtful whether the great majority would continue to support him when it came to revolution, i.e. restructuring the foundations of the political and social system as a secular republic. Even Rauf, one of Mustafa Kemal's closest allies in the struggle for independence, had described opposition to the Caliphate as ingratitude. A matter concerning elections brought these dissenters into the open.

On 2 December 1922 three deputies of the Assembly proposed a seemingly innocuous law stipulating that to be elected to Parliament candidates must have either been born within Turkey's present-day borders or resided in their constituencies for five consecutive years. If passed, this law would have made Mustafa Kemal ineligible as a parliamentary candidate, effectively ending his political career. Consequently, in a sharply-worded speech he denounced its underlying motives and from then on started putting discretion aside, openly declaring some of his revolutionary aims. During a tour of Western Anatolia that lasted over a month, at a press conference in İzmit he said: 'Revolution cannot be carried through by half-measures. Revolutionary legislation must take precedence over all existing legislation. As long as we are not killed and the motivation for radical change is not erased from our consciousness, the progressive revolution that we have begun will not lose its momentum for one moment.'

On 1 April 1923 the TGNA decided to dissolve itself and to hold new elections. Some Turkish writers, in comparing the First and Second Turkish Grand National Assemblies, find the former more 'democratic' in that conservative elements were represented, thus creating a more animated environment for debate. This may to a limited extent be true, but from a wider viewpoint the later Parliament was more democratic because of its more progressive character. It is doubtful whether the representation of conservatives and reactionaries, who defended the *status quo* and the Sharia, and who were against equality (as in the case of equal rights for women) and intellectual freedom from religious dogma, may be deemed democratic.

On 8 April Atatürk declared his nine principles, which as a whole constituted his platform for the upcoming election. Having emphasised that sovereignty lay with the people, he promised among other things a 'unified' system of secular education, the abolition of tithes and a shorter period of military service. Elections were to be held in August, and during the interim period, the groundwork was laid for establishment of the People's Party, which was founded on 9 September 1923. On 27 September, in an interview with a reporter for the Viennese newspaper *Neue Freie Presse*, Atatürk revealed his intention of establishing a republic. On 2 October the Entente forces left İstanbul and on 13 October the law was passed making Ankara the capital of Turkey. On 27 October the Fethi Okyar government resigned.

Forming a new government was difficult because each new cabinet minister had to be elected separately by the Assembly, which in turn would create disunity and friction within the cabinet. If a republic were to be established, the Prime Minister would be able to select the ministers with whom he would work to avoid the possibility of a lack of cooperation. Thus the republic was established in part as a practical solution to these technical problems, just as, superficially, the abolition of the Sultanate had been accomplished to resolve the crisis caused by the dual invitation to the Lausanne Peace Conference. However, the monumental consequences and revolutionary implications of both these turning points (the abolition of the Sultanate and the declaration of the Republic) are self-evident. Although Atatürk had openly declared the revolutionary character of the policies he was about to initiate, he did not fail to take advantage of any opportunity presented by circumstance or coincidence, perhaps making such steps more easily acceptable to all.

On 29 October 1923 the necessary amendment was made to the 1921 Constitution and Turkey became a republic. Mustafa Kemal, already President of the TGNA, was unanimously elected Turkey's first President. In his acceptance speech he said, 'The Republic of Turkey will in future be rendered fortunate, successful and victorious.' Thus, after Germany, Austria and Hungary, Turkey too became a republic, but with one difference; while the former had made their choice in the dark environment of rout and defeat, Turkey did so in the bright light of victory and liberation.

In Europe the 1920s were years of progress for republican systems and democracy. However, the 1930s were years in which reactionary, racist and totalitarian dictatorships developed.

22

ABOLITION OF THE CALIPHATE, LEADING TO SECULARISM

Abolition of the Caliphate

There were many possible motives for the abolition of the Caliphate. For example, in the eleventh century the Islamic scholar El Maverdi had set out the dictum that only members of the Qureish tribe could assume the Caliphate, but this was a tribe with which the Ottoman dynasty had no hereditary link. Also the Caliphate was considered ineffective. For example, during the First World War, although the Ottoman Sultan-Caliph had declared holy war on the Entente, Sharif Hüseyin, Emir of the Hejaz, was not prevented from allying himself to the non-Muslim enemies of the Ottomans and attacking Ottoman troops.

However, the most pressing argument for the abolition of the Caliphate was that members of the Ottoman dynasty who had so recently held the Sultanate also occupied this position. The Caliphate was thus a potential rallying point and power base for anti-republicans and royalist dissidents conspiring to reinstate the Sultanate. The Act of Parliament which abolished the Caliphate stated that the remaining members of the Ottoman dynasty were to leave the country, i.e. the Caliphate was abolished primarily to achieve their exile.

Also important was the fact that this measure was a requisite of secularisation because no Caliph could be expected to endorse steps leading to the establishment of a secularist system, because, as the religious leader of the Islamic world, doing so would inevitably attract the wrath and condemnation of Muslim countries and reactionaries at home.

Furthermore, the Caliph's claim to leadership of the Islamic world could cause great many complications for the Republic of Turkey in its foreign policy. At that time, all the Muslim countries with the exception of Iran and Afghanistan were to varying degrees colonies of some major power. As a result, the Caliphate's claim to leadership implied the capacity for and the probability of becoming involved in the affairs of the imperialist Powers (Britain, France, Italy, the Netherlands and even the Soviet Union), which in turn would give these countries an excuse to intervene in Turkey's affairs. This situation was in direct contradiction to Atatürk's circumspect, nationalist and peace-oriented foreign policies that were based on scrupulous non-intervention, prohibiting Turkish involvement in the internal affairs of other countries and *vice versa*.

Very quickly events showed how the Caliphate could become a dangerous focal point of unrest. The opposition press fomented anti-revolutionary sentiment by focusing public attention on the Caliphate and Caliph Abdülmecit, who was taking care to carry out the Friday prayers with great pomp and ceremony, and who demanded a higher appropriation from the government. When the press printed a letter from the Aga Khan and Amir Ali asking the Turkish government to place the Caliphate on a level that would command the confidence and esteem of Muslims and thus impart strength and dignity to the Turkish state, it was seen as foreign intervention, giving rise to great indignation in Parliament.

Prior to the parliamentary vote Atatürk thought it expedient to make sure of the army's stand on this question. On 15–22 February 1924, during military exercises in İzmir, the corps commanders pledged their support. On 3 March 1924 the Caliphate was abolished by an act of Parliament and the remaining members of the Ottoman dynasty were sent into exile. Thus, with the abolition of the Sultanate, the declaration of the republic and the abolition of the Caliphate Atatürk's three complementory revolutionary reforms constituted a foundation for the new political system of the Turkish state.

That same day two other important laws were enacted by the TGNA. The first was the Unification of Education Act (*Tevhid-i Tedrisat*) in accordance with which all schools were placed under the jurisdiction of the Ministry of Education. After this law was pro-

mulgated, all *medreses* (religious colleges) and neighbourhood religious schools were shut down. Henceforth the only type of education
available in Turkey was secular, although a limited number of Imam-
Hatip schools and the Faculty of Divinity in İstanbul were allowed
to stay open for the clearly defined purpose of training people who
wished to pursue a career in religious works. Their standing was that
of a professional school teaching a specific trade, just like the schools
for artisans or civil servants. However, today the number of students
educated in İmam-Hatip schools far surpasses the country's needs: a
flagrant disregard of the Unification of Education Act and of the
secularist principle.

The second law enacted that day abolished both the Ministry of
Religious Affairs and the Ministry of the General Staff, creating in
place of the former a Directorate of Religious Affairs, while the
latter was put under the jurisdiction of the Ministry of Defence. The
significance of these charges is revealed by the fact that while general
directorates and their directors do not determine policy, and merely
function in accordance with policies set out by the government,
ministers participate in Cabinet meetings and thereby have a say in
determining the policies not only of their own but of all ministries,
i.e. in determining government policy in general. Hence a Minister
of Religious Affairs, for example, would have influenced Turkish
foreign and educational policy, whereas a Director of Religious
Affairs would have no influence over policy, even policy directly related to religion. The motivation behind this law was evidently the
desire to prevent religious and military circles from having any say in
government. This was a forward step for secularisation and the demilitarisation of government.

The process of secularisation

Turkey's secular system, like its new political structure, was realised
through a series of successive reforms. Following abolition of the
Caliphate and the simultaneous enactment of the two aforementioned laws, on 8 April 1924 the courts of the Sharia were also
abolished. These courts consisted of a sole functionary, a judge of
Islamic law called a *kadı* who may not have had the educational qual-
ifications considered necessary for such a position. On 30 November 1925 all activities of Dervish orders and visits to tombs of sultans

and sheikhs were prohibited by law. However, some orders continued their activities in secret, and although this law is still in force today mystic orders are active and flourishing.

On 17 February 1926 the new Civil Code, which, with a few very minor amendments, was an exact translation of the Swiss Civil Code and Law of Obligations, was enacted. Thus at a stroke Turkish society abandoned the Sharia and adopted a modern legal system.

The Sharia (*Şeriat*) was a legal system that had evolved in the years following the birth of Islam. Though its basic tenets are uniform, the interpretation and application of Sharia law vary from sect to sect. The Sunni Muslim doctrine, for example, has four schools of legal thought—the Hanafi, the Shafii, the Maliki and the Hanbali—each with its own interpretation of the rules of the Sharia. Sunni Turks are generally of the Hanafi School, which is considered the most liberal sect.

At the time of its development the Sharia was a legal system comprising rules applicable to the needs of the time, many of which were progressive compared to those of other legal systems of the era. However, it was in essence a medieval system. For example: the institution of slavery is permitted; women who have committed adultery are to be buried to their waists and stoned to death; the hand of a thief is to be cut off; men may marry four women and may divorce their wives with the words 'You are divorced', a right not given to women; men inherit a full share compared to a woman's half share; the evidence of one male witness is equal to that of two females; beating is acceptable as an instrument of moral education and a man may beat his headstrong wife for not doing his bidding. Under certain circumstances, according to this conception, a beating is an educational tool. So the stick used by teachers to beat their students and the application of bastinado (beating the soles of the feet with a stick) were considered pedagogical tools and methods just like blackboards and chalk.

Nonetheless, a maxim of Islamic canonical law is 'judgments change with the passage of time.' Thus in classical Ottoman times (after 1450) it is highly unlikely that a thief who had not committed an additional act of violence would have his hand cut off, and there are only two cases of execution by stoning in Ottoman history. In the nineteenth century the Ottoman state began to apply European commercial law and penal codes. But even the Second Constitutional Government did not have the power to revise the Islamic civil code in civil matters, which constituted a stronghold of the Sharia. In 1917 the CUP government passed the Family Law Ordinance, which veered towards secularism, but it was repealed very soon after the Unionists fell from power. However, the Unionists did achieve the total abolition of slavery.

The greatest achievement of the Civil Code of the Republic was its establishment of equal rights in almost all areas for men and women. In contrast the Sharia viewed women as inferior beings, as did all medieval legal systems. In the Europe of the Middle Ages the question of whether or not women even possessed a soul was apparently a matter of theological debate, and if a woman was more eloquent or more intelligent than her peers, she might be accused of witchcraft and, if convicted, burned alive.

On 10 April 1928 the article of the Constitution stating that the religion of the Republic of Turkey was Islam was rescinded, and nine years later, on 5 January 1937, two years before the death of Mustafa Kemal, secularism, one of the six principles of the Republican People's Party, became a provision of the Turkish constitution. Secularism had first been adopted by the Republican People's Party at its 1927 general congress and in 1931 the decision was taken that secularism should become one of its six basic principles. Although a commission for reform of Islamic practice was formed in 1928, Atatürk never acknowledged or took up the results of its work: the acceptance of secularism as a concept compatible with Islam must have been sufficient for him.

The nature of Turkish secularism

Along with the establishment of the republic, secularism is one of the two cornerstones of the Atatürk Revolution. It is a separation of religion from social affairs so that no religion, sect, creed or mystic order can affect social affairs in any way, or demand privileges for itself. Furthermore the law is applied without reference to any particular religion or sect.

Likewise, the state takes an impartial view of all religions and sects and does not involve itself in religious affairs, although in certain circumstances it may be required to intervene, for example, if a religious sect should order its followers to engage in human sacrifice or to commit suicide. In the United States Christian Scientists believe the Bible and prayer are a cure for all the earth's ills and therefore find it unnecessary and even sinful to refer to a doctor. Consequently, many adherents die of simple complaints for which medicine has found a cure. If a child is suffering from appendicitis and its family refuses to consult a doctor, the state, even a secular one, may have to intervene.

Although it was intervention on the part of the state, the establishment of a Directorate of Religious Affairs for Sunni Muslims in Turkey created two advantages. One, it can oversee the practices of Sunni Islam, the religious belief of the majority of the population, and is therefore more or less able to prevent any violation of secularism. Two, it can ensure that in villages or neighbourhoods struggles will not break out between groups and sects to gain control of the neighbourhood mosque. Such quarrels could escalate indefinitely and whichever groups or sects were unable to take over a mosque would then initiate campaigns to obtain the resources to construct their own. Germany provides an example of such a situation. In Turkey, however, because such matters come under the auspices of the Directorate of Religious Affairs, mosques are impartial places of worship for all and every Sunni sect or group. Of course, the Directorate must also take care that its treatment of affairs is even-handed in relation to other sects or religions.

Some pro-Sharia groups perceive secularism as an evil perpetrated upon Islam by Atatürk. But the Sharia is a restrictive chain binding Islam to the Middle Ages and to underdeveloped countries. The breaking of this chain in Turkey has given Islam the opportunity to become a religion of the contemporary world and of advanced nations. The existence of the Sharia was for Turkey (and can be for some other Muslim countries) an impediment to development and survival. If those defenders of the Sharia who wish to shut women up in their homes could ban them from the workplace, it would mean half of Turkey's population would not be participating in the race for development, and it could be argued that Muslim countries in this situation have little or no hope of taking a place among advanced and civilised societies. Another negative factor is that ostracism of women from participation in social life disadvantages them culturally, which is detrimental to the whole of society. Our most important vehicle of culture is language and the most basic step of education is the act of a mother teaching her child to speak. In a male-dominated society children learn how to express themselves in their mother-tongue from their mothers, rather than from their fathers. The child, male or female, of a mother who has a vocabulary of, say, 500 words will be at a disadvantage compared to the child of a mother with a larger vocabulary. From the logical development of this most basic of arguments, it may be concluded that barring women from social life will have negative repercussions on the cultural standards of the whole of society, including that of the male half.

A further benefit proceeds from secularism because it ensures the impartiality of the state in relation to all religions and religious groups, and thereby promotes domestic peace and well-being. As such it can be a vehicle for alleviating traditional tension between Alevi and Sunni Muslims. In 1978 in Kahramanmaraş one group of Muslim Turkish citizens attacked another, brutally killing them. While some wanted to characterise this incident as a conflict between rightists and leftists, almost all the rightists involved in the events turned out to be Sunni and almost all the leftists Alevi, suggesting that this was clash between the two religious communities. The fact that such an incident happened at all demonstrates that the state had not been sufficiently impartial or secular. There were, unfortunately, recurrences, and in 1995 one of the worst incidents took place in İstanbul.

In some circles it is argued, 'There may be a secular state but there are no secular Muslims.' This is of course a fallacy. Any person who accepts secularism is secularist and may also be a Muslim, Christian or other believer. Thanks to the Revolution Turkey now has a great many secular Muslims, i.e. Muslims who accept secularism, many of whom continue to carry out their religious duties diligently. As the revolution of enlightenment spreads, the number of secularists may be expected to increase and Turkey's place in the forefront of civilisation will be dependent upon this development. Like other world religions Islam is spread over a large geographical area. It has many sects and mystic orders, each with its own characteristics. Hence to recognise and respect the beliefs, practices and rights of others in peace and brotherhood is a necessity of the unity of Islam. Therefore, secularist Islam must be viewed as any other sect or order and accepted as a new type of Islam.

23

REVOLUTION AND ATTEMPTS
AT COUNTER-REVOLUTION

The Constitution of 1924

The 1921 Constitution had been conceived during the days of the Civil War and the War of Independence to cope with the practical realities and exigencies of those times, but Turkey's political structure had not yet been fully defined. After the Sultanate and Caliphate had been abolished and the republic established the need arose for a more comprehensive constitution, hence the creation of the 1924 Constitution, which was to a certain extent a continuation of the 1921 concept of unified legislative and executive power.

The National Assembly was given not only the power to reject the government and to dismiss a minister from office at any given time, but also exclusive power to dissolve itself before completion of its full four-year term. Basic rights and liberties were granted, subject to further pertinent legislation, but social rights such as the right to strike were not taken in hand. Nor was provision made for a supreme or constitutional court to determine whether specific laws complied with the Constitution. Interestingly provisions in the draft law for a seven-year presidential term, for the power of the president to dissolve the National Assembly and for the president to be the commander-in-chief of the armed forces were voted down by the Assembly. As a result, after every general election (every four years), the TGNA elected a new president and reserved for itself the power of commander-in-chief. Had Atatürk insisted, the presidency would very probably have been empowered as specified in the original draft, from which one may conclude that he did not press the point. The Constitution became law on 20 April 1924.

198

The Progressive Republican Party

The new Constitution opened the way for the emergence of the multi-party system and those who disapproved of the way things were going seized the opportunity. With the exception of Atatürk, those people who had at one time been at the helm of the Amasya Military Organisation—Kâzım Karabekir, Rauf, Refet and Ali Fuat—now became the leaders of the opposition. While Rauf and Refet were conservatives, Karabekir and Ali Fuat, though not so conservative, still had misgivings about Atatürk's radical policies. Possibly all four missed the days when in the Amasya Military Organisation and the War of Independence they had been of consequence. Immediately after the signing of the Treaty of Lausanne Rauf had resigned from the Cabinet, frustrated at not having been elected Turkish delegate to Lausanne and offended that his views had had no effect on negotiations for Greek reparations. After the final victory of Turkish arms Karabekir and Ali Fuat had been appointed Inspectors of the First and Second Armies respectively and, as in the case of other corps commanders, had also been elected to Parliament.

Karabekir, on 26 October, and Ali Fuat, on 30 October, resigned from their military posts to take their places in the National Assembly. Atatürk, realising that a counter-movement was developing, decided to separate the military from political affairs. Towards this end he personally asked the seven army corps' commanders to resign from the National Assembly. While five acceded to his request, two chose to resign from the army instead and remained as Deputies, though one later had a change of heart and returned to the armed forces. Having been refused their positions as Deputies by the TGNA on the grounds that they had not formally handed over their commands, Karabekir and Ali Fuat were compelled to return to their posts to fulfil their military obligations.

On 17 November 1924 the Progressive Republican Party was founded (the People's Party had added the word 'Republican' to its title, becoming the RPP, on 10 November, and the Progressive Party followed suit). Karabekir was elected the party's President with Adnan Adıvar and Rauf Vice-Presidents and Ali Fuat General Secretary. It had the support of about thirty Deputies. The fact that their programme included the formulation 'respect for religious opinions and beliefs' ('*efkâr ve itikadat-i diniyeye hürmetkârdır*') might not in

itself have been that important, but in the absence of any other conservative party, and in view of the fact that this party was to the right
of the RPP, the Progressive Party would quite likely become a
magnet for conservatives and reactionaries of all kinds, and with its
first branch being established in Urfa, a conservative stronghold, the
likelihood increased.

The Sheikh Sait revolt

The Sheikh Sait revolt began on 13 February 1925 in Piran, a village
in the eastern Anatolian province of Bingöl and quickly spread to
the district of Lice (Lidje). Rebels then took the city of Elazığ while
the rebellion spread to the Muş-Varto district, and on 7 March the
insurgents attacked Diyarbakır. The leader of the revolt, Sheikh Sait,
as a landlord, headman of his clan and a member of the Nakshibendi
religious order, also had influence over other clans. This uprising, in
the name of the Sharia and the Caliphate, was initially perceived by
the Fethi Okyar government as a simple lapse of security which
could be easily quelled. However, the gravity of the situation became
apparent when the rebels defeated army units sent against them. In
the face of this increasingly serious threat the Fethi Okyar government resigned to be replaced by the İsmet Pasha government (3
March 1925), which demanded and was given extraordinary powers
by the National Assembly which enacted the Law for the Maintenance of Order (Takrir-i Sükûn Kanunu). Courts of Independence were
established and oppositional newspapers were shut down, and on
31 May 1925, after an extensive military operation, the revolt was finally suppressed. Rebel leaders were tried and executed, and in the
aftermath on 3 June the Progressive Republican Party was shut down.

The Sheikh Sait Rebellion, springing as it did from issues related
to religion, appears to have been a counter-revolutionary, feudal
movement. Because the revolt arose among the Kurds and the
Kurdish-nationalist movement was initiated during the post-Mudros
period when the Kurdish Advancement Society had first been
organised, it was not surprising that nationalist elements were implicated in the rebellion. Indeed the court determined that a leader
of the Kurdish Advancement Society, Seyyit Abdülkadir, was one of
the conspirators and condemned him to death. However, the fact
that some Kurdish nationalists took part in or were leaders of this

revolt is not in itself sufficient reason to conclude it was a Kurdish national movement. Nationalism presupposes a common awareness of the concept of modern democratic citizenship and in a social fabric dominated by tribalism the ideology or question of nationalism does not arise. A parallel may be seen in the Sharif Hüseyin uprising which occurred in the Hejaz. That was not a nationalist but a tribal revolt, and judging by the slogans employed by the leaders of both revolts they drew upon religious and feudal rather than nationalist themes.

According to Mete Tunçay, the Law for the Maintenance of Order forced the Atatürk era into the mould of a single-party system. However, although this was an important turning point, the single-party mould was not a foregone conclusion as early as 1925. At the very least, the 1930 experiment with the Free Republican Party is evidence that throughout the 1920s Atatürk still harboured the hope and intention that the Republican revolution should develop a multi-party system.

It has also been suggested that the British had a hand in the rebellion, though this was not proved at the trial and, in any event, in situations such as this conclusive evidence is seldom to be found. However, it is certain that at the time Turkey was contending with Britain for control of Mosul and thus found itself in a difficult position due to the revolt. Hence the fact that Mosul and its oil reserves were of great importance to Britain must be taken into consideration.

Four days after the rebellion, on 17 February 1925, tithes were abolished by the TGNA, a measure previously proposed and accepted in principle at the İzmir Economic Conference and one of the tenets of the RPP. It has been argued that this was a misguided policy, because at the time it had been a major source of much needed government income. Although this may be technically and financially correct, the measure still got rid of the more or less tyrannical tax-farming system. Of course, if the government had replaced the tax-farming system with its own tax-collecting system, employing government officials instead of tax-farmers, the financial drawback might have been overcome, but at that time and for a long while after it is doubtful that the government had reached the level of organisation needed to institute a new system of collecting taxes in kind. As a result, no matter what the financial consequences were the abolition of tithes and the tax-farming system must be hailed as a liberating action, freeing the farmer-villager from hundreds of years of oppression.

The Hat Reform—abolition of the fez

On 23 August 1925 Atatürk, on a tour of the country, arrived in Kastamonu wearing a hat. Although those around him had conformed to his wish and were also wearing hats, they were not at all comfortable with this new manner of dress; some of them, in order to refrain from calling it a hat, the headgear of non-Muslims, described it as a sun-shade cap—a '*şems siperli serpuş*'. Atatürk, however, in a speech made in İnebolu (a city in the Black Sea region) made it crystal clear, saying: 'This headgear is called a hat.' On 25 November the 'Hat Law' was enacted whereby the fez was prohibited and all civil servants were to wear hats. From that time on, the fez disappeared and city people wore hats and villagers wore caps.

The Hat Reform is not easily understood by those who are unaware of its historical connotations. The symbolism of the hat arose from the conventions of the Ottoman Empire according to which headgear was worn to identify one's station: one's religion, profession and social status. All minions of the Sultan, minority groups, religious personages, Janissaries or other branches of the military etc. could be identified in the street by their headgear. When people died their headgear would be placed at the head of their coffins, and those families that had the means would have an effigy of it carved as a headstone for their loved one's resting place.

The hat was an item worn only by non-Muslims, and when Mahmut II decreed that his civil servants and soldiers must wear the fez, which was similar to what Greeks wore, he was attacked as the 'infidel Sultan'. Now Atatürk was taking a similar but even bolder step. Some people have belittled this innovation, calling it 'wardrobe reform', saying that the subject of one's sartorial inclinations is superficial and artificial, that what is important for society is a contemporary outlook and the establishment of modern institutions. However, Atatürk, in a speech made in Kastamonu on 24 August, said, 'Civilisation is a fire so strong that it burns to ashes those who ignore it.' He wanted to Westernise Turkey, not just in its institutions and mentality but also in its appearance. This was not simply imitation or artifice but another precaution to fend off recurrence of the calamity posed at Sèvres; an easily recognisable signal to the European public, 'We are a people such as you. Therefore, our country cannot and will not ever become a colony.' As such it was an extremely practical and effective way of communicating this message, because while the foreign public at large may be oblivious to another country's advances, the casting aside of a national symbol cannot be easily overlooked.

The period between the two World Wars was one during which imperialism was rampant, regardless of the League of Nations. In the Old World at the end of the Great War there were only a few under-developed non-European countries that had managed to more or less retain their independence: Ethiopia, Turkey, Iran, Afghanistan, China and Thailand. Of these, Afghanistan—serving as a buffer zone between Russian and British imperialism—and Thailand—performing the same function between British and French expansionism—had managed to retain a certain degree of independence. Of the other four, three were crushed under the boot of imperialism, either between the two World Wars or during the Second World War: in 1931 China was invaded by Japan; in 1935–6 Ethiopia became a colony of Italy; and in 1941 the Soviet Union and Britain came to an agreement whereby they invaded Iran, one from the north and the other from the south.

Turkey alone remained independent in great part because it had successfully conveyed the message, 'We are Europeans and not a country to be colonized.' The Hat Reform played an important role in communicating this message. In 1934 a statement of imperialist aims released by Mussolini caused disquiet in Turkey, whereupon both the Italian Under-Secretary for Foreign Affairs and Mussolini himself informed the Turkish Ambassador that the statement in question had not been intended for Turkey as Turkey was a European country.

Of course the Hat Reform also conveyed a clear message to the Turkish public that Turkey *would be* a European country and that it was making the passage from the medieval to the modern age. There were those who rebelled against it, for example in Sivas, Erzurum, Rize and Maraş. It even became a symbol of anti-modernism for the secret society organised by İskilipli Atıf Hoca, who was condemned to death by the Court of Independence for his counter-revolutionary activities.

Assassination attempts against Atatürk

Apart from the aforementioned consequences of the Civil Code another significant event of 1926 was an attempt to assassinate Atatürk. Earlier, during the War of Independence, the British had plotted to have him killed, engaging an Indian assassin named Mustafa Sagir, but in 1921 their plot was discovered and Sagir was executed. At a later date Manok Manukyan was employed to kill Atatürk by Armenian terrorists resident in Greece, but in 1925 he too was caught and executed. The 1926 attempt was organised by three members of the National Assembly—Ziya Hurşit of Lazistan, Şükrü of İzmit and Arif of Eskişehir—whose plan was to attack his car with bombs and handguns on 15 June as he passed through the Kemeraltı district of İzmir. The assassins were to flee to the island of Chios in a motorboat belonging to Şevki of Crete, but when Atatürk's visit was postponed to the following day he reported the plot to the authorities.

Many people were implicated, including some former members of the old CUP. Evidently, though he had no part in organising the plot, even the Unionist Cavit Bey knew it was to take place. Very probably these old guard Unionists, despite being of a democratic-nationalist bent, thought the revolution had gone too far, too fast. Or possibly they were discontented at being left on the sidelines. The Court of Independence presided over by Ali Çetinkaya ordered a comprehensive investigation. In addition to the Unionists, the leaders of the Progressive Party were also arrested, although Prime Minister İsmet İnönü tried to prevent the latter arrests and as a result himself came close to being detained. Eighteen people were executed, among whom were Cavit Bey and Doctor Nazım.

In all, five assassination attempts were uncovered, the fourth being that of Hacı Sami and his fellow conspirators coming from the island of Samos who were caught in 1927 and the fifth, thought to be the work of Ethem the Circassian, resulting in a gang of five being rounded up near the Syrian border (21 October 1935). These events illustrated to what lengths the enemies of Turkey and its revolution were willing to go to destroy Atatürk, and it is probably because of these security problems that after 19 May 1919 he did not visit any foreign country and only went to İstanbul as late as 1927.

In 1927 Atatürk wrote a detailed history comprising his view of events from the day he stepped off the ship at the port of Samsun on 19 May 1919 to the present. He may have felt that a turning point had been reached and that an assessment was needed of all that had gone before. Supported by a great deal of documentary evidence and written in a very short period of time, this record is known as his *Speech*, because that year, for six hours a day over six days of October, he read it out at the opening of the Second Congress of the Republican People's Party. It is a primary historical source documenting the period from 1919 to 1926. In closing Atatürk addressed Turkey's youth and entrusted the Republic to them. The word 'youth' may be understood in both a literal and a symbolic sense, denoting revolutionism. As may be remembered, throughout the nineteenth century, all revolutionary movements inspired by the French Revolution were prefixed by the adjective 'young'. One of the best-known was 'Young Italy', headed by Mazzini. There were also, of course, two generations of 'Young Turks', that of Namık Kemal and that of the CUP era.

24

THE CULTURAL REVOLUTION COMES
TO THE FORE

Alphabet reform

As stated Atatürk's *Speech* marked a turning point for the Republic. By 1927 the political system had been established and the foundations of secularism laid and reinforced. Without disassociating himself from domestic politics and foreign affairs, Atatürk then focused his attention on cultural matters and to a lesser extent on the economy.

The first important step in the Cultural Revolution was the introduction of Turkish-Roman characters in place of Arabic script, a bold and, from a certain point of view, astonishing move.

Shortly after 730 CE, as the Turks were developing written characters and were beginning to use them in their literary works, they adopted Islam. During the process of conversion they abandoned their alphabet and instead began to use Arabic script. Abandoning Arabic characters after approximately a thousand years may seem strange, but closer study reveals this to be a rational and logical development.

There were a number of factors which made this reform viable. One was the little the Ottomans had done to increase literacy among the Turks. In 1918, despite the educational reforms of the Second Constitutional Period, the rate of Turkish literacy was not much higher than 5%. By 1927 it had increased to only 10.7%. Had it reached, for example, 20% or 25% Atatürk might not have conceived of this as being a feasible reform.

The transition was further rendered possible because the impressive and extensive array of books in Arabic script which filled Ottoman libraries contained to a large extent an accumulation of medieval knowledge, which was undoubtedly of historical value but had little relevance to the world of the twentieth century. In the nineteenth century the Ottomans had made some effort to have Western works translated, but owing to the complexities of the Ottoman language, laden with Arabic and Persian words, the translations were obscure and so not easily understood by a great many readers. Changing the alphabet was an excellent way of ridding the Turkish language of Arabic and Persian expressions because written in the Turkish-Roman alphabet, they became awkward and had little hope of survival. As a result of the more recent changes in the Turkish language and its enrichment with Turkish vocabulary and modes of expression many contemporary Turks, even university graduates, have difficulty in understanding Atatürk's *Speech*, just as many English speakers today find it difficult to understand the language of Shakespeare. Atatürk and his associates' may have wanted to cut the ties binding Turkey to that very medievalism embodied in the accumulation of knowledge contained in Ottoman libraries, following the example of Tarık bin Ziyad who burnt his boats before advancing to conquer Spain.

Also, linguistically the Arabic alphabet was not at all suited to the Turkish language because Arabic is very rich in consonants but poor in vowels, whereas Turkish is more or less the reverse. For example, in Arabic there are two variations (in pronunciation and character) of the letter T, three of H, four of Z, three of S and two of K, whereas in Turkish each of these has only one form. On the other hand, Arabic has only three vowels—A, U and I—while Turkish has eight. Consequently vowels are hardly ever used in written Arabic (with the exception of the long 'A' sound and vowels written in Koranic scripture), which is not a great obstacle to comprehension, but causes a problem when deciphering the Turkish language written in Arabic characters. For instance, if the letters 'gl' were written in Arabic script in reference to a Turkish word, the reader would have to decide whether gal, gel, gıl, gil, gol, göl, gul or gül was being referred to, whereas in Arabic the word or syllable would be much easier to identify, there being only three options, gil, gul and gal.

The matter of nationalism may also have been influential in deciding that Turkey should have its own distinctive alphabet. (This may very well be the reason why the Chinese people refuse to consider modifying their written characters despite the difficulties of learning to write them.) Of course it might have been possible to create a Turkish version of Arabic script, without totally rejecting it, but in this context the decision to integrate with Europe was apparently influential and in 1929 courses in Arabic and Persian were dropped from the high school curriculum.

Preparatory work for the alphabet reform began in early 1928. On 8 January the Minister of Justice, Mahmut Esat (Bozkurt), made a speech on the subject of the Roman alphabet at the Ankara Turkish Hearth and on 21 May the TGNA passed a law for the use of international numbers. This was merely the first step. Atatürk chose to begin his campaign for alphabet reform in İstanbul, arriving there on 4 June and applying himself with great enthusiasm to the project. He then made İstanbul his departure point for tours of the country with stops at Tekirdağ, Bursa, Chanakkale, Gelibolu, Sinop, Samsun, Amasya, Tokat, Sivas, Şarkışla and Kayseri until his return to Ankara on 21 September. On the evening of 9 August, at Sarayburnu Park near the Topkapı Palace in İstanbul, he explained the implications of the alphabet reform to the public and in the Dolmabahçe palace workshops in which Atatürk took part were held to discuss the new alphabet. Finally on 1 November the TGNA passed the law concerning the new alphabet. From 1 December on newspapers and periodicals, and from January 1929 all books, were to be printed in Turkish-Roman characters. On 1 January 1929 national schools were opened for adults to learn the new written language and by 1936 2.5 million people had received diplomas from them. The alphabet reform had been quickly realised.

An experiment in multi-party politics

In 1929 Atatürk co-wrote with his adopted daughter, the historian Afet İnan, a book entitled *Civil Knowledge*, which became the textbook of secondary school civics courses. Although the book was first published under İnan's name, she herself later added photocopies of Atatürk's handwritten manuscript to a 1969 reprint, confirming that a major portion had been his contribution.

In this work Atatürk described democracy as a rising tide which, being the best of all political systems, would inevitably gain ground throughout the world. He further stated that the republican system was the most developed form of democracy and that it was superior to constitutional monarchy. This documented opinion is relevant today, because Atatürk is criticised for not having made democracy one of the six principles of the Republican People's Party. However, one of those principles being republicanism, and this, allied to the aforementioned views, verifies that these criticisms are unfounded.

Despite the unfavourable socio-political conditions of the time, in 1930 Atatürk decided that a political system with more than one party should be established, but taking precautions to ensure that the new party would not provide an opportunity for counter-revolution. He made Fethi Okyar (a personal friend who at the time was Turkish Ambassador to France) responsible for founding an opposition party.

In August of that year correspondence between Atatürk and Fethi Okyar furnished the latter with documentary proof, in effect a contract, that Atatürk would fully support this undertaking. As reassurance Atatürk asked his sister, Makbule, and some Republican People's Party deputies to join the new Free Republican Party (the FRP, also called the Free Party) which was founded on 12 August 1930. He also pledged his impartiality towards the two parties. Ahmet Ağaoğlu, a proponent of classical liberalism and a dedicated individualist, was the second most influential person in the FRP.

Atatürk's aim was to create an environment conducive to debate of economic issues without in any way jeopardising the revolution. This aim was underlined at the opening of the Ankara-Sivas Railway on 30 August 1930 when İsmet İnönü spoke about the moderate étatism of the RPP in reference to Free Republican Party criticism of the government railway construction programme.

In October 1929 the crash on the New York Stock Exchange caused the US economy to enter a phase of great depression which spread to Europe, spiralling into an era of world depression, unemployment and poverty. This had serious repercussions for the Turkish economy in general and its agricultural sector in particular, along with major decreases in Turkish exports. Because impoverished and desperate people would clearly be more easily influenced by reactionary propaganda, it has been suggested that Atatürk supported the multi-party system as a means of finding a remedy for economic depression. While this may have been a factor, it seems that his true motive was democratisation. Indeed Atatürk must have taken his decision for this initiative *before* August 1930, very probably in 1929.

The FRP experiment soon met with disaster. Reactionaries and those badly affected by the plight of the economy flocked to its banner, but no one listened to Fethi Okyar's speeches in defence of the principles of the revolution, and his visit to İzmir culminated in wild demonstrations and bloody confrontations. The officials of the Republican People's Party were intimidated by the developments and on 17 November 1930 Fethi and his FRP supporters, realising where events might lead, terminated party activities. The Party had been active for only three months. A month later Fethi Okyar's worst fears were realised. Just as the Progressive Party had met its end with the Sheikh Sait rebellion, the FRP also met its end with a reactionary incident. Although the Free Republican Party had already been deactivated, it seems it was implicated in a violent incident that occurred in Menemen.

On 23 December 1930 some members of the Nakshibendi order, led by Dervish Mehmet, travelled from Manisa to Menemen where, on their arrival, they began to assemble the people around a green flag taken from a mosque. Reserve officer Fehmi Kubilay, on arriving at the scene, tried to intervene but was shot dead by reactionaries who then cut off his head, stuck it on a pole and displayed it to the crowd. Two watchmen were also killed. Repression followed and martial law was declared. A military court was established, which condemned twenty-eight people to death.

These incidents, following the founding of both the Progressive Republican Party and the Free Republican Party, showed the multi-party system could not work until the Revolution was better established. In any event the 1930s were years when democracy was under threat, a situation that was to prevail until the end of the Second World War when Europe, with the help of its allies, freed itself from fascist dictatorship. Turkey, throughout this time, was also influenced by these events.

People's Houses and Rooms

In 1931 Atatürk was active in founding cultural centres called People's Rooms and Houses. The effects of the Menemen Incident were to a certain extent a catalyst in this, channelling his attention towards cultural affairs. The medieval brutality of displaying Kubilay's severed head must have made a deep impression, causing Atatürk to take up cultural development as a remedy to reaction. On 10 April 1931, at an extraordinary general congress, the Turkish Hearth Society decided to dissolve itself. Doubtless, the government and/or Atatürk was behind this decision as the Hearths, though founded as cultural centres, were becoming hotbeds of reaction. Handed over to the Republican People's Party, they were reopened on 19 February 1932 and renamed People's Houses and Rooms. By 1950 478 People's Houses and 4,322 Rooms had been established. The People's Houses had nine departments of educational, social and/or cultural activity: (1) language, literature and history; (2) fine arts; (3) theatre; (4) sports activities; (5) social welfare; (6) educational courses for the people; (7) publications and libraries; (8) village welfare; (9) museums and exhibitions. Taking into consideration Turkey's lack of libraries and musical and theatrical facilities in schools and also the great need for cultural facilities for adults, the importance of these institutions is self-evident.

Historical studies

History was another one area of culture on which Atatürk focused his attention, but notwithstanding the fact that he had adopted or supported the development of certain views of history and was even the author of certain minor works, his experiments in historical analysis should be evaluated in the light of his political preoccupations.

Because history is one of the most effective ideological weapons in the arsenal of imperialism it was natural for Turkey, having experienced the shock of Sèvres and overcome the threat at Lausanne, to give it serious attention. One of the foremost historians of the early Republic, Enver Ziya Karal, has dubbed the historiography of this period 'defence historiography'. Western imperialists had attempted to create a Greek Eastern Thrace, a Greek İzmir-Manisa-Ayvalık area and an Armenian Eastern Anatolia, but in so doing had based their case on historic rights regardless of the majority of the Turkish population. One response focused attention on the history of Anatolia prior to the Greeks and Armenians, arguing that the Hittites were of Turkish origin and embracing and emphasising their history as part of Turkish history, and thus establishing a moral deed of right to the region.

Turkey also took up the study of physical anthropology in answer to the racist theories based on physical characteristics, such as the shape of people's skulls, which were prevalent in some European countries at the time. To counter the contention that the Turks were not a civilised people, the history of Central Asia was analysed and a theory developed from the premise that Central Asia, the birthplace of the Turks, was the cradle of civilisation from which the majority of the world's peoples had emerged. In the process many wholly or partly imaginary theories were manufactured. However, at the time, such theories were popular in certain parts of Europe and this Turkish trend was merely an offshoot. Atatürk also attached great importance to psychology, realising that hundreds of years of Turkish defeat had created a national inferiority complex that might impede the rebirth and development of the new Turkish nation. Accordingly he put as much emphasis on nurturing 'pride' in past accomplishments and on creating a sense of 'self-confidence' or 'trust' in the future as he did on working hard in the cause of development. He perhaps thought that a certain amount of fantasy was a necessary balm for national depression and wanted to create a myth along the lines of the Arthurian Legends, even if it should last for only a short period of time.

If contemporary Turkish historiography has reached a higher level than that which preceded it, this is in great part due to Atatürk's encouragement. As with many other intellectual fields, the discipline of history in Ottoman times was greatly limited in reach, interest having been confined to only Ottoman history and Islamic history, the latter being concentrated on the birth of Islam and the era of the four Arabian caliphs following Mohammed. Other subjects such as world history, the history of Europe and Turkish history before Ottoman times were almost totally neglected and the Ottoman methodological focus was on wars and dynasties. Certainly during the Second Constitutional Period a start was made to atone for this neglect, but it is thanks to Atatürk that this small beginning was transformed into a concentrated effort to produce a body of work. As part of this effort, on 15 April 1931 the Turkish Society for Historical Studies, later the Turkish Historical Society,

was founded, and on 8 July 1932 the first Turkish Historical Congress convened, with the second in 1937.

Language reform

The Ottoman language, used by the literate upper classes, included
innumerable Arabic and Persian words and phrases. Some samples
of Divan—Ottoman court poetry and prose—are so full of Arabic
and Persian expressions that it is difficult to find a word of Turkish.
Although their language was essentially a written one, the Ottomans
were not concerned that the majority of the population was illiter-
ate, and hence there were no facilities for the majority of Turks to
learn to read and write, let alone to comprehend the intricacies of
the Ottoman language and literature. Consequently, the people
spoke only Turkish. The educated few were of course familiar with
the Ottoman language, but as a rule no women, not even of the upper
classes, were educated. As a result the female half of the population
had no knowledge of Ottoman and were left with no alternative
other than to converse among themselves and with their male relatives in Turkish. Hence the illiteracy of the great majority of society,
including the whole of the female population, kept the Turkish
language alive, though not as a language of culture or literature.

With the development of journalism in the mid-nineteenth century, a more easily comprehensible, more Turkish, Ottoman language began to evolve. During the 1897 Ottoman-Greek war Mehmet
Emin (Yurdakul), using only Turkish words, wrote patriotic poetry
which can be easily understood even today. Although advances were
also made during the Second Constitutional Period (Ziya Gökalp's
articles for the *Young Writers* periodical of Salonika are an example of
the less ornate vocabulary employed during this period), examples
such as Atatürk's *Speech* written in 1927 are not easily understood
today. The liberation of Turkish from Ottoman (Persian and Arabic)
expressions was initiated as a major undertaking in the 1930s and is
an ongoing process. The Turkish Society for Language Studies was
founded on 12 July 1932 and was later renamed the Turkish Language Society. Its first general congress was held on 26 September 1932,
and soon after its foundation the call to prayer began to be made in
Turkish instead of Arabic. Atatürk too joined in the business of transforming the language and for a time even wrote his communiqués

and speeches using vocabulary so wholly Turkish that even now many people are not familiar with all the words he used.

Much has been said and written about language reform and the 'extremes' to which it has been taken. Although Turkish words readily understood by the public at large, when used in place of obscure or unknown Ottoman expressions, seldom encounter criticism, the use of some newly derived Turkish words instead of their better-known Ottoman synonyms (such as *okul* in place of the Ottoman word *mektep*, meaning school, *betik* for the Ottoman word *kitap*, meaning book and *dinlence* as a synonym for *tatil*, vacation) does arouse criticism from conservatives. Their arguments range from the contention that this renders grandparents and parents unable to communicate with their children and grandchildren to the claim that this is a communist plot to divide the generations and weaken Turkish society.

From time to time language policy fluctuates as governments are influenced by one or other of the aforementioned arguments. For example, the language of the 1924 Constitution was revised in 1945 to accord with what was then accepted as standard Turkish, after which the Constitution was called the '*Anayasa*'. In 1952, during the Democratic Party era, a return was made to the 1924 wording whereupon the '*Anayasa*' reverted to its Ottoman title, the '*Teşkilat-i Esasiye Kanunu*'. During certain administrations the state-controlled TRT (Turkish Radio and Television) has tried to discourage the use of certain Turkish words. Although the majority of administrations have been indifferent or even opposed to reforming the Turkish language, the process has continued primarily through the efforts of the literati. Prior to the 12 September 1980 coup the Turkish Language Society was a major contributor to this reform.

Reasons for this language reform are numerous. First, it evolved from a democratic concept of bridging the cultural gap between government and the people, the elite and the common man, although of course it may be contended that manufacturing new Turkish words to be used in place of familiar Arabic or Persian equivalents is not essentially democratic. Another motive is the wish to create a precise and more readily comprehensible language. Hence the reform involves finding Turkish synonyms not only for Arabic and Persian vocabulary but also for words and concepts of Western origin:

bilgisayar for *kompüter* (computer), *ilginç* for *enteresan* (interesting). Thereby it is hoped that Turkish will become a richer and more aesthetic language that will generate literary, philosophical and scientific works. A third motive is nationalism. Many Turks object to the presence of foreign words in their language, be they Arabic, Persian, French or English, a view which is in general characteristic of leftist nationalists or Kemalists. Rightist nationalists are generally either indifferent or even opposed to language reform. A fourth motive is the desire to liberate Turkish from yet another tie with Eastern, medieval culture, by liberating it from the Ottoman language. Very probably conservative antagonism has its source in this motive.

Atatürk gave great importance to historical and linguistic studies. It is striking that he established both the History and Linguistic Societies as independent associations and not as government institutions, making it impossible for the government to interfere in their work. He also bequeathed the income from his personal fortune to these two institutions and both societies have proven worthy of his trust and have undertaken a great many projects, including publishing many works through which they have gained international respect. It is therefore extremely unfortunate that those responsible for the 12 September 1980 military coup transformed these societies into state institutions and reallocated Atatürk's bequest to state departments, acts that may be construed as violations of institutional rights and of Atatürk's trust. The objectives of the government in question in nationalising these societies was evidently to inhibit the language reformation process and to replace Kemalist ideology with its own official ideology (that of the 'Turkish-Islamic synthesis') manufactured and supported by its own institutions. Nevertheless, they have not been that successful.

In the Atatürk era, so that Turkey should not be lacking in any cultural area, many projects were initiated for the development of theatre and Western music. On 1 November 1924 the School of Music Teachers (Musiki Muallim Mektebi) opened in Ankara. Talented young musicians were sent to Europe for further education, and in 1936 the Ankara State Conservatory was founded under the auspices of the famous German and Hungarian composers Hindemith and Bartok. Carl Ebert came from Germany to found theatre and opera departments and in 1940–1 graduates of the Conservatory began to stage plays and operas. In his speech at the

1941 graduation ceremony the Minister of Education Hasan Ali Yucel saluted a new phase of Turkish humanism born of the State Conservatory. The School of Ballet was opened in 1949.

Universities

In 1827 the first Western-style school of higher education of the Ottoman era, the İstanbul School of Medicine, was founded. Institutions of higher learning had been seen first and foremost as professional schools. In time the idea arose that there was need for the disciplines of higher learning to be organised into universities, which would be centres of basic sciences and research, but various initiatives in this direction soon petered out, only to be taken up again in 1900 when the Darülfünun was founded in İstanbul. The Darülfünun was Turkey's sole university until the İstanbul Technical University was founded in 1944. (Before 1946, many separate faculties had been founded in Ankara but they were not merged into a university until 1946.) Because the Darülfünun was in many ways considered inadequate a Swiss expert in education, Albert Malche, was called upon to make a study to rectify the situation. Malche's report reflected his critical views of the situation. After 30 January 1933, when the Nazi party came to power, Germany began to purge from its universities, with no thought for their worth or stature, those academics (Jews, leftists, democrats etc.) deemed unsuitable by its totalitarian racist ideology. Turkey took advantage of the opportunity this situation presented.

On 31 May 1933 a law was passed closing down the Darülfünun and founding the University of İstanbul. Only fifty-nine Turkish academics out of 151 were kept on, though many of those who lost their jobs found work in government offices. Meanwhile academics purged from German universities were invited to join the staff; 142 of them accepted. They were specialists in a variety of disciplines, professors of zoology, Sumerian culture, law, philosophy, economics, physics, medicine etc. Many were world-renowned scientists. At a stroke one of the world's most prestigious Teutonic universities was established in Turkey. Almost all the Germans stayed on until 1945, and a few even longer. Most of them learned Turkish and were soon able to teach with no need for translators. Without doubt theirs was a great contribution to the development of higher learning in modern Turkey.

25

ECONOMIC AND POLITICAL DEVELOPMENTS

Ideology and periodicals

Atatürk's reaction to the failure of the Free Republican Party experiment was twofold. On the one hand he concentrated on honing the single-party system with measures such as closing down the Turkish Hearths, establishing the Houses and Rooms of the People under the jurisdiction of the RPP and terminating the activities of the Masonic Lodges (1935). At the third General Congress of the RPP he was declared Permanent General Chairman. On the other hand he actively encouraged the development of a pluralist voice in the world of letters in the realisation that it could not as yet be maintained in the political arena.

Kadro was one of the periodicals published during this period (from January 1932 to January 1935). Its founders included Şevket Süreyya Aydemir, İsmail Hüsrev Tökin, Yakup Kadri Karaosmanoğlu, Burhan Belge and Vedat Nedim Tör, three of whom (Tökin, Aydemir and Tör) had been Communists earlier in their careers. Aydemir, with Vala Nurettin and Nazım Hikmet, later a renowned leftist poet, had studied Marxist doctrine at a university in Moscow at the time of the War of Independence, and on his return to Turkey had worked for a Communist periodical *Aydınlık* (Light), for which he was sentenced to a term in prison. He later took advantage of a political amnesty and entered the civil service.

The aim of *Kadro* was to serve as a platform for the development of a Kemalist ideology based on the premise that the world's fundamental socio-political conflict was not between the working classes and the capitalist class, as advanced by Marxism, but rather between affluent, developed countries and underdeveloped ones, because developed countries could give a share of the spoils from the exploitation of their colonies to their own working classes. National independence movements were the only solution to this conflict between imperialist powers and their colonies. Turkey's war of independence and Kemalism constituted the model on which these movements could be based. *Kadro* also upheld a thesis of étatism, arguing that although class conflict had not yet fully emerged in Turkey, it was sure to do so with the development of capitalism, but that Kemalism could prevent it from gaining a foothold by its application of étatist policies.

Another periodical, published from June 1932 to May 1934, was *Kooperatif* owned by Ahmet Hamdi Başar. In the 1920s Başar had tried to organise a Muslim businessmen's union in İstanbul, but his original and unorthodox views on Turkey's social structure and developmental strategies made him unpopular with one administration after another. He later became one of the founders of the Democrat Party (Demokrat Parti), but was unable to gain acceptance there either. His periodical, *Kooperatif,* took up the cause of the agricultural community and advocated the establishment of cooperatives. Its main argument was that villagers, who were Turkey's largest consumer group, should not have to pay the price for the advancement of industry by being burdened with the low quality but expensive products of a domestic industry protected from foreign competition by high import tariffs.

A third periodical, *Intellectual Movements* (Fikir Hareketlei), was published from October 1933 to 1940 by Hüseyin Cahit Yalçın. Siding with liberal democracy and focusing on Europe, it endeavoured to reflect the ideological struggles predominant in the world at that time between liberal democracy, socialism, communism and fascism (National Socialism in Germany). As Turkey was also affected by these struggles columnists of the three aforementioned periodicals and the liberal Ahmet Ağaoğlu, writing columns for the daily newspapers, violently attacked each other's views. Many people in Turkey, particularly the youth, were swept up in these currents and as a result the idea arose that Kemalism should be promoted as an ideology in itself; and at its third congress (10 May 1931) the RPP adopted the six principles.

Recep Peker, who became general secretary of the RPP in 1931, came under the influence of fascist ideology during a visit to Italy in

1932. Hasan Riza Soyak, Atatürk's secretary, relates in his memoirs that on his return Recep Peker even proposed changing the RPP programme and regulations to bring them in line with fascist doctrine. His report, having been submitted to İnonü, was then set before Atatürk who greeted it with contempt and rejected it.

After years of working in the rank and file of the RPP, Hıfzı Oğuz Bekata began to address the younger generation through his periodical *Era* (*Çığır*), established in 1933. From the outset its subject-matter was inspired by totalitarian principles and as a result argued the need for an RPP youth organisation. Although the RPP at its 1935 congress finally accepted the idea in principle, the project was never implemented.

Although the RPP, under the influence of the ideological struggle raging in Europe, sometimes tended towards totalitarian principles, either out of a sense of self-preservation or owing to some facet that was seen as attractive, it never fell under their sway. Atatürk himself was evidently the major obstacle to any such development, as the closing of *Kadro* in 1935 illustrates. *Kadro*, having taken a stand against individualism and becoming increasingly anti-democratic, paradoxically defended this stand in the name of Kemalism. Displeased, Atatürk asked its owner, Yakup Kadri Karaosmanoğlu, to shut down. (Karaosmanoğlu, a renowned novelist, was later appointed Turkish Ambassador to Albania.) Along with its totalitarian ideology, the fact that it cited the Turkish War of Independence as a model for colonies may also have been objectionable to Atatürk who tended to caution in foreign policy.

An event that suggested a move from authoritarianism towards totalitarianism occurred following Atatürk's dismissal of Recep Peker from the position of General Secretary of the RPP on15 June 1936. After this date the Minister of the Interior automatically assumed the role of Secretary General of the RPP and governors became the heads of RPP branches in their provinces, a move reminiscent of Germany, where the Nazi party engulfed the government. However, as RPP historian and parliamentarian Fahir Giritlioğlu argues, the state was not being transformed into a totalitarian party, but on the contrary the party was being incorporated into the bureaucracy and was thereby being drained of power. In totalitarian states the party organisation infiltrates and dominates both the state apparatus and the civil and social structures, whereas during the Atatürk period the opposite was true; the RPP organisation was so weak in some regions as to be practically non-existent. Another indication of the gulf between Kemalist and fascist ideology lies in the importance given to women's rights. The ideal woman of fascist ideology was first and foremost a mother and homemaker, whereas the Turkish Republic took particular pride in its graduate women, triumphantly proclaiming the advent of the country's first professional women in all the newspapers: its first female lawyer (1927), judge (1930), municipal council member, dentist and doctor (1926), pilot, diplomat (1932) and member of parliament (1935). In fact, in the 1935 elections, eighteen women were elected to parliament, in just one year after Turkish women had been enfranchised and given the right to be elected, a status far from being realised in a number of European countries, including some with long-standing democratic traditions. Thanks to its policies Turkey today probably has a larger proportion of professional women in the workplace than a great many developed countries.

İsmet İnönü, who had been Prime Minister for a year from 1923 to 1924 and then continuously from 1925 to 1937, finally had to resign from the position on 25 October 1937. As during that period Turkey had been struggling to survive in the face of the imperialist threat, it had seemed natural that İnönü, the victorious commander of the First and Second Battles of İnönü, and the architect of the Mudanya Armistice and the Peace of Lausanne, should be vested with power in the political administration of the Republic. Since historian Şevket Süreyya Aydemir has called Atatürk the 'unique' man, it followed that İnönü was the 'second' man. That these two powerful men were able to work harmoniously for so many years to create a new Turkey may be taken as an indication of the extraordinary rapport which existed between them. Of course they were not without their differences of opinion and friction did arise over major issues of foreign and economic policy (İnönü was more étatist than Atatürk). But long years of working together perhaps caused their relationship to deteriorate and Atatürk's incipient illness, making him more irritable than in the past, may have exacerbated the situation. Indeed the first symptoms of Atatürk's cirrhosis emerged in 1936. Finally in 1937 they parted ways and Celal Bayar became Prime

Minister, a year before Atatürk's death. By 1938 Atatürk's capacity to take an interest in affairs of state had diminished and he evidently concentrated most of his rapidly draining energy on the question of Hatay.

Foreign policy in the Atatürk era

Even though it was not until 1931 that Atatürk first summarised his attitude towards foreign affairs with the words 'Peace at home, peace in the world', his foreign policies had always been consistent with this line of thought. Until full independence had been achieved Turkey had been obliged by circumstance to adopt 'active' foreign policies, but they became wholly peace-oriented thereafter. For example, Turkish relations with Britain, which had deteriorated greatly owing to the question of Mosul from 1926 onwards, began to improve, culminating in King Edward VIII's unofficial visit in 1936.

In spite of the USSR's communist regime, Turkey maintained an atmosphere of close friendship which was reinforced by the 1921 Moscow and the 1925 Friendship and Non-Aggression Treaties. In 1932, when Turkey became a member of the League of Nations, the USSR was assured that this would not affect Turkey's policy of friendship. In any event, the USSR itself soon adopted a positive attitude towards the League, becoming a member in 1934.

In the period between the two world wars fear of Italian expansionism was prevalent in the Mediterranean region. This drew Turkey and the other Balkan nations, including Greece, into close relations with one another. In 1930 Venizelos paid an official visit to Ankara for talks with Atatürk and in 1934 the Balkan Entente was signed by Turkey, Romania, Greece and Yugoslavia in Athens. Bulgaria abstained because of its dissatisfaction with the Treaty of Neuilly, but still continued to have cordial relations with Turkey.

As war clouds massed on the horizon, the unfairness of the demilitarisation of the Straits became increasingly apparent and their security became an issue of primary importance. In 1936 Turkey officially requested a reassessment of the Straits regime laid down at Lausanne. That year a conference was held in the Swiss town of Montreux, resulting in a treaty whereby Turkish sovereignty and Turkey's right to defend the Straits was ratified and the International Straits Commission abolished.

222 Economic and Political Developments

The Treaty of Ankara had not given the province of Hatay (Antioch and Alexandretta) to Turkey, even though it fell within Turkish frontiers drawn by the National Pact and the majority of its population was Turkish. A special regime separate from that of Syria had been established to safeguard Turkish rights. In 1936, when France undertook to end its mandate over Syria and Lebanon in three years, the question of Hatay again arose. Turkey applied to the League of Nations, requesting that Hatay be allowed to determine its own future. As a result of the Council's deliberations, on 2 September 1938 a referendum was held and Hatay was established as an independent state. Tayfur Sökmen was elected President and Abdurrahman Melek became Prime Minister. On 23 June 1939, with a treaty between Turkey and France, the annexation of Hatay by Turkey was agreed.

Economic policy in the Atatürk era

The new Republic was faced with an economy not only ravaged by war but also agriculturally and industrially backward. From the outset of the Atatürk era, even before étatism had become the dominant principle of economic development, the state consistently played an important role in encouraging and supporting the private sector, an example of which was the Law for the Encouragement of Industry enacted by the TGNA on 28 May 1927. With the Treaty of Lausanne, customs duties had been frozen until 1929, which limited the scope of government protection afforded to domestic products. However, low interest credit was made available to the private sector by the Bank of Business (İş Bankası), founded on 26 August 1924 with money that had been provided by Indian Muslims in support of the War of Independence. In 1925 the Turkish Bank of Industry and Mining (Türkiye Sanayi ve Maadin Bankası) was founded to organise state-owned enterprises such as factories and mines inherited from the Ottomans, and the same year a law was enacted for the founding of sugar-processing factories. During this period and before étatism was officially adopted as a government policy, many textile factories, presumably supported by the state, were also founded by the private sector. After 1929 the state ensured more effective protection for domestic industry, be it state- or private sector-owned, by increasing customs rates on imports.

A second major characteristic of this era was the policy of nationalisation of foreign investments. At that time the people of Turkey were still suffering from the after effects of the Treaty of Sèvres, with its threat to their independence still fresh in their minds. Even after the Treaty of Lausanne Western imperialist aims were still considered a primary threat and the administrators of the Republic were keenly aware that foreign investment could become a bridgehead for expansionism. As a result foreign enterprises providing municipal services such as railways, docks, waterworks, electric and gas installations were nationalised at every opportunity, a strategy facilitated by worldwide economic depression.

A third characteristic of this era was the precedence given to railway construction, to which the state apportioned a major share of its extremely limited resources. In 1923 there were 3,350 km of railway lines and by 1939 another 3,000 km had been added. The Ankara-Kayseri-Sivas-Erzurum line, the Samsun-Sivas line, the Zonguldak-Ankara line, the Sivas-Malatya-Fevzipaşa line, the Malatya-Diyarbakır line, the Balıkesir-Kütahya line and the Kayseri-Ulukışla line were all constructed during this period. Since the Second World War Turkey has concentrated solely on motorway construction. Consequently its railways have almost become obsolete, but during the Atatürk era railways were a priority because coal for steam engines was a domestic resource. Giving priority to motorway construction would have created an increased demand for petrol that in turn would have created an import-dependent economy, a great drawback particularly in wartime. In addition, if Anatolia were to be invaded inhibiting enemy progress would be more easily achieved by damaging the railways rather than the motorways. In the period leading up to the Second World War these were considerations of primary importance to the Atatürk administration, and when war broke out it became apparent just how pertinent they had been. Of course these measures were conceived as precautions against not only a state of war in general but also a specific imperialist attack against Turkey.

A fourth economic characteristic of this era was that all enterprises were undertaken using a minimum of foreign credit, i.e. financed to the greatest extent by domestic capital. Also the value of Turkish currency was stable throughout this period because steps such as deficit spending were not resorted to and, as a result, inflation was almost non-existent. Nowadays the people of Turkey are familiar with inflation and have become accustomed to its negative economic and social consequences. Anxiety over retaining hard-won independence and keeping the door closed to foreign intervention were the considerations underlying the policy of depending on domestic capital instead of foreign credit, which was used to a limited extent only when truly necessary.

The economist Korkut Boratav distinguishes three sub-periods:

(1) *1923–9.* This period was both import friendly and a time when private enterprise was encouraged. The economy was open to imports because customs duties, which had been frozen till 1929 by the Treaty of Lausanne, did not give effective protection to domestic production.

(2) *1930–2.* This was a transitional period during which protectionist measures were introduced to support the private sector, and domestic products replaced imports in the Turkish market. Industrialisation was based on private enterprise, but thanks to customs independence, domestically produced goods were protected from foreign competition. Owing to these developments, a trend towards import substitution began. However, worldwide economic depression prevented Turkish industry, dependent as it was on the private sector, from making any real progress and as a result étatism, a planned economy inspired by the Soviet example, came to the fore.

(3) *1933–9.* Turkey embarked on its first five-year plan. Industry flourished and numerous factories were founded: textile factories in Malatya, Kayseri, Ereğli, Nazilli and Bursa; a synthetic silk factory in Gemlik; glass and leather factories in İstanbul; paper in İzmit; iron and steel in Karabük; a sugar-processing plant in Eskişehir; and an aeroplane factory in Kayseri. Sümerbank, founded in 1933, was the leading institution of industrialisation. In 1935 the Institute of Mining (Maden Tetkik Arama) and the Hittite Bank (Etibank) were founded to finance and develop the mining sector. However, in 1936 just as a second five-year industrial plan was being developed; the Second World War intervened, preventing it from being implemented. (During the war the Turkish army expanded from 120,000 to 1.5 million soldiers.) From 1930 to 1939 the growth-rate of

Turkish industry averaged 11.6 per cent, an extremely high degree of growth. In 1929 industry's share of the Gross National Product was 11 per cent, reaching 18 per cent in 1939. This development was achieved with minimum resort to foreign credit and with no trade deficit. Thus the foundations of industry in Turkey were laid.

26

EVALUATION OF ATATÜRK
AND HIS REVOLUTION

Seldom in the history of any country has one person changed both the historic current of that country and the lives of his fellow countrymen to the extent that Mustafa Kemal Atatürk did in Turkey. He was both soldier and statesman, the leader of Turkey's military and political War of Independence against the Entente Powers and of its Civil War waged against the monarchy, both of which were successful. Under his leadership Turkey was not only pulled back from a process of disintegration and annihilation, it also gained acceptance at Lausanne as an independent state with the same legal status as the countries of Europe. He put an end to the archaic Ottoman Empire and erected in its place a modern Turkish Republic, and in constructing this modern society became the architect of revolutionary reforms, creating a new alphabet, a new university and a new legal system, and affecting the fine arts, religion and relations between the sexes. Consequently the Turkish people cannot help but have feelings towards him that also to a certain extent impede an objective evaluation of his achievements. With more than half a century having passed since his death, the distance of time might now facilitate an objective evaluation to challenge the adverse criticism of Atatürk that in recent years has been on the rise.

This criticism derives from two sources; on the one hand there are the pro-Sharia groups and on the other the proponents of 'civil society' and the 'second republicans'. The latter hold Atatürk responsible for the most repressive measures of the 12 September 1980 military coup, simply because actions were undertaken in the name of Kemalism, while blatantly disregarding the fact that the policies were in direct conflict with Kemalist principles. They then proceed to condemn the earlier military coups of 27 May 1960 and 12 March 1971 on the same principle. Believing that they are the true defenders of democracy, these groups have somehow managed to establish a common front with the pro-Sharia groups. The verbal and mental acrobatics employed by this common front to equate the works of Atatürk with those of the perpetrators of the September coup is possible only by denying the revolutionary character of the Kemalist movement and reducing it to the status of an ordinary military coup.

The first step towards reaching a true understanding of the Atatürk movement is to determine what needs it was addressing. Realising that the Kemalist Revolution was not a series of arbitrary measures taken by an extraordinarily powerful military leader is vital. Had this been the case, the reforms would not have withstood the passage of time and would have been rejected soon after his death. However, after half a century Atatürk's revolution still stands, suggesting it was an expression of and had its source in motives acknowledged by the Turkish people and supported by the common will, implying that it can perhaps also be called the Turkish Revolution.

The need for such a revolution has already been dealt with. Post-Sèvres the Turkish people came to the horrific realisation that after their eviction from Rumelia the inexorable process of their eviction from İstanbul and Anatolia would begin. If the Turks had been satisfied with their victory of 1922 and the Treaty of Lausanne that process would most certainly have been revived at the first opportunity. Indeed Lord Curzon had specifically warned İsmet Pasha that this would be so. To prevent this and to be considered a part of Europe, it was necessary to become European.

Having determined the need for revolution, it remains to determine its nature, not merely by an explanation of the six principles or arrows (also the symbol of the RPP), which are the general means employed, but by analysing three aspects of the Revolution's character.

The philosophical character of the Revolution

On a philosophical level the Kemalist Revolution was one of enlightenment; an educational undertaking to bring about a cultural and intellectual passage leading the nation out of the medieval and into the modern age. It was modelled on and inspired by the Enlightenment of eighteenth-century Europe which was based on the Renaissance and humanism, both of which were rooted in Graeco-Roman culture. That the Kemalist Revolution was one of enlightenment is best and most comprehensively explained in Suat Sinanoğlu's work *Turkish Humanism* (1980) in which humanism is defined as 'unlimited intellectual freedom', i.e. the human intellect is not to be confined by any dogma or supernatural concept. Conservatives' concerns regarding loss of national identity and becoming a carbon copy of foreign values are baseless in this context because a carbon copy of foreign values will not find acceptance in an intellectually liberated society. Such a society will evolve its own identity and character. Humanism upholds positive values such as love of mankind, nature, art and country. Atatürk himself was both humanist and statesman, as proved by his actions: even during the most critical period of the War of Liberation he refrained from having a holy war declared; he treated the defeated enemy commander Tricoupis, who had been taken prisoner, with deference; he refused to walk on the Greek flag; and he openly stated his respect and sympathy for the Anzac soldiers fallen at Gallipoli. At a time when totalitarianism was prevalent in a large part of Europe, and despite the fact that many people in his circle were under its influence, Atatürk totally rejected the ideology, inviting to Turkey liberals, Jews and leftist academics who had been purged from Germany.

Kemalism as a development model

The development policy of the Revolution may be described as integral, i.e. wholesale development in every field. Importing technology, machines, equipment, instruments and factories is not sufficient for such development, because the underlying force creating this technology is Western science, without an understanding of which any technological gains would be baseless and insubstantial. Thus scientific knowledge is necessary in order to have a complete grasp of technology.

At its highest level science borders on philosophy. Therefore Turkey had also to assimilate Western philosophy, the humanities of which it is a part, and the social sciences. However, for philosophy to thrive, its relation to art and culture should not be overlooked. Thus technological, scientific, philosophical, cultural and artistic development are inseparably connected and individuals and institutions should not be restrained by social, political or religious dogma, because for them to be productive, freedom of thought, together with respect for science, culture and art as well as for those who expend effort in these areas is essential.

According to Atatürk's integral view of development, the founding of the University of İstanbul was as important an event as the construction of the Sivas-Erzurum railway; the founding of the Conservatory and the creation of the new alphabet were just as important as the construction of the Nazilli textile or Eskişehir sugar factories. If anything, for Atatürk cultural affairs were probably of relatively more consequence.

Integral development can be better understood by comparing it with its opposite, materialistic development. Certain oil-rich Arab sheikhdoms can be used as a reference point. Thanks to their petrodollars, these countries are able to import state-of-the-art technology, cars, planes, computers and indeed, whole factories while sea water is processed for drinking and agriculture is made to flourish in the desert. However, although these countries enjoy the benefits of twentieth-century technology, their social and cultural systems still languish, more or less, in the first millennium. Imported technology and other scientific paraphernalia have not been enough to bring them, as nations, into the modern age or brought about the establishment of modern societies.

After 1950, though of course not to the same degree of these Arab statelets, Turkey also abandoned integral development to a certain extent and was precipitated towards materialistic development. Thereafter motorway-dam-factory construction projects were given priority, and as a result cultural and social development became secondary considerations.

The ideology of Atatürk: his Six Principles

Of the six arrows of Atatürk and his Republican People's Party—secularism, republicanism, nationalism, étatism, revolutionism and populism—the first two have already been treated at length and it has been determined that republicanism was not limited in the mind of Atatürk to a formal system of government, but was rather the ideal form of democracy. Indeed, at a time when totalitarian trends were on the rise in Europe Atatürk rejected fascism, held fast to his democratic principles, and Turkey thus was relatively more democratic than the average European state. For this reason 142 German fellows rejected by German universities preferred the security of Turkey. There is no reason to suppose that the cream of this scientific community should be so unaware and desperate as to quit one dictatorship for another.

Since then democracy in Turkey has advanced even further, but not as far as the democracies of Europe. Consequently Europeans, and many Turks too, are critical of Turkey's democracy and find it lacking.

Nationalism. The ideal of this nationalism is peaceful co-existence. It renounces aggression and territorial expansion and its philosophy was summarised by Atatürk as, 'Peace at home, peace in the world.'

It also bears no relation to racism. In his declaration, 'Happy is he who says I am Turkish', Atatürk used the word 'says' rather than 'is' to clarify the point that all citizens of the Republic of Turkey are Turkish, be they of Greek, Circassian, Kurdish, Armenian, Jewish or Arab origin.

Kemalist nationalism is not of the right nor is it conservative. It is a nationalism that does not concentrate on gaining regional power or power over the Islamic world, unlike right-wing nationalists who generally tend to limit their ambitions to regional affairs and to put the emphasis on economic, political and military objectives. According to the Kemalist view of nationalism, Turkey should be able to compete on equal terms with the world's most civilised countries, as much in the humanities, art and literature, human rights and science as in military and economic affairs.

Revolutionism. Kemalist Revolution is a means of spreading enlightenment to the whole of Turkey and to all of its people through effective policies for the realisation of integral development. This is a long-term goal not yet reached but to be achieved sooner rather than later. Until that time comes revolutionism will remain on Turkey's agenda and entails pursuing the goals of the Revolution with enthusiasm and perseverance.

Populism. As an ideology which safeguards the people, promoting policies for the welfare of all, populism should not be confused with crowd pleasing or vote hunting in order to win an election. The concept of 'the people' may be interpreted as encompassing all classes and groups of society, but it primarily refers to the underprivileged, peasants, workers and all lower income categories. Populism aims at raising their standards on every level and achieving both material and cultural social justice.

Up till 1945 the Atatürk Revolution advanced under the advantageous circumstances of a single-party system. In such circumstances it is of course much easier to implement projects that may not be popular in their initial stages but which are later seen to be of long-term benefit. It must be acknowledged that to espouse the cause of populism while resisting vote-hunting is not an easy option in a multi-party system, yet once the revolution has become widespread and enjoys popular support, it can still make progress in such an atmosphere. However, in Turkey it still requires the presence, even if not in power, of a strong party to defend its reforms which, moreover, all parties should uphold in principle.

Etatism (direct intervention by the state in the economy). Etatism is a policy that was developed through experience. In the 1920s the newly emerging Turkish capitalist class was unable to make much industrial progress on its own and in addition the economy was debilitated by the 1929 world economic depression. Etatism was adopted to alleviate this situation and thanks to the resulting policies a substantial foundation of industry was laid during the Atatürk era and throughout the years to come. Furthermore its beneficial effects were felt through the provision of housing, schools and a social and cultural environment for workers employed in government enterprises, i.e. the functions of a social state were thereby established, and up till 1980 étatism fulfilled their major requirements.

State enterprises had great success not only in Turkey but also in the developed capitalist countries of Europe, for example, the Renault automobile company in France. In the 1980s, a worldwide campaign to denationalise began, gaining momentum from the collapse of the Soviet system. Not only in ex-communist but also in capitalist countries, efforts have been and still are being made to privatise state enterprises.

As for Turkey, although its capitalist class has made great progress, it is not yet as strong as those of developed countries. Therefore étatism still retains its function.

Contrary to popular opinion, state enterprise need not be unproductive and unprofitable and it is within the power of government to render state managed enterprises productive. If the government allows its state enterprises to become unnecessarily indebted, if necessary investments are not made, if more personnel than required are employed or if sufficiently qualified managers are not employed, then motivation is clearly lacking for making these enterprises profitable and productive. Today, if the state monopoly Tekel is able to supply each and every grocery store with *rakı* but is incapable of supplying them with sufficient beer and matches, there must be an underlying motive. That motive is the government's desire that beer and matches produced by the private sector should be sold. *Rakı*, however, is produced solely by Tekel, so it is properly produced and distributed.

Another factor in favour of state enterprise concerns the fact that no matter how much the electorate believes the state enterprises are unprofitable, public surveys show there is also an awareness that they create employment. Hence, there is little likelihood that the Turkish electorate will vote for a party that promises a programme of widespread privatisation. This might well strengthen the vote-catching potential of radical parties, which would benefit through protest votes, a situation not at all beneficial for Turkish democracy. At the very least, until Turkey's economic development is on a par with that of Europe, étatism must needs remain on the agenda as it seems difficult to reconcile a policy of all-embracing privatisation with the multi-party system.

Part IV

İSMET İNÖNÜ AND HIS MULTI-PARTY SYSTEM

27

PRE-WAR AND WAR YEARS; THE İNÖNÜ ERA

The İnönü presidency

On 10 November 1938 Mustafa Kemal Atatürk, a great figure of world history and the greatest of Turkish history, died. Approximately a year earlier he had appointed Celal Bayar as Prime Minister, ending the Atatürk-İnönü administration that had prevailed since 1925 with Atatürk as President and İnönü as Prime Minister. Had İnönü still been Prime Minister there would have been no question as to who should succeed Atatürk as President, but, owing to the cooling of their relations, there was doubt in some minds. During the terminal phase of Atatürk's illness two cabinet members, Minister of the Interior Şükrü Kaya and Foreign Affairs Minister Tevfik Rüştü Aras, who were against İnönü becoming President, held talks with the President of the TGNA, and Abdülhalik Renda, and the chief of staff Fevzi Çakmak, and Celal Bayar as to whether one of them would consider putting himself up as a candidate. However, İnönü was so dominant a force in the bureaucracy, the RPP and, as a result, the TGNA, that none of the three potential candidates took the proposals seriously. Furthermore, Fevzi Çakmak, expressing the point of view of the Armed Forces, openly stated that the next President

233

of the Republic should be İnönü. Thus, on 11 November 1938 the TGNA elected İnönü as the second President of the Turkish Republic.

İnönü reconfirmed Celal Bayar as Prime Minister but Şükrü Kaya and Tevfik Rüştü Aras were conspicuously absent from the new government. Less than a year later, however, Celal Bayar was pressured into resigning following investigations into the affairs of his intimates, and on 25 January 1939 Refik Saydam became the new Prime Minister.

From the beginning of his presidency İnönü indicated that he stood for a more pluralistic and a more democratic approach to government than that of the Atatürk era. At the opening of the RPP Congress in Kastamonu on 6 December 1938 and at the University of İstanbul on 2 March 1939 İnönü spoke of transforming the RPP into an institution that would embrace each and every citizen of the republic, and of ways in which policies for a populist administration could be realised.

In May 1939, at the fifth general congress of the RPP, a decision was taken to establish an 'Independent Group' within the TGNA, headed by Ali Nihat Tarlan and consisting of twenty-one Deputies selected by the RPP congress, to undertake supervision of government policy. Its establishment was facilitated by the fact that since 1931 there had already been independent Deputies in Parliament. In addition, the procedure since 1936 of the Minister of the Interior automatically being made General Secretary was abandoned in order to regenerate the party.

On the eve of the 1939 elections party delegates were invited to Ankara to give their views before the candidates for Parliament were determined. The fact that people such as Kâzım Karabekir, Fethi Okyar and Hüseyin Cahit Yalçın, who had distanced themselves from the RPP during the Atatürk era, were included in the RPP list of candidates and were subsequently elected to Parliament was a sign of a more relaxed atmosphere.

Nevertheless, at an extraordinary RPP congress convoked on 26 December 1938 Atatürk was posthumously awarded the title 'Eternal Leader' and İnönü was given the titles 'National Leader' and 'Permanent General Chairman'. Since these titles could not have been bestowed without İnönü's approval, a certain disparity between words and deeds is evident. A further inconsistency, at odds with declared policy, became apparent when the Independent Group proved to be ineffective in carrying out its supervisory function. The threat of war may well have be the reason behind these inconsistencies. As the nation faced the ordeal of the Second World War, the gap in authority created by Atatürk's death meant a firm hand at the helm of state should have been deemed necessary.

The Second World War

Italy and Germany had both been pursuing policies of aggression for some years. In 1935–6 Italy moved against and colonised Abyssinia (later Ethiopia). In 1936 Germany reoccupied the Rhineland, which had been demilitarised by the Treaty of Versailles. In 1938 it annexed Austria after effecting its internal collapse and immediately began demanding territory from Czechoslovakia. Britain and France held a conference with Italy and Germany in Munich to maintain the peace and, as a final concession, accepted that the Sudetenland in Czechoslovakia should be ceded to Germany (29 September 1938). However, only six months later the Germans occupied the whole of Czechoslovakia.

On 31 March Britain and France took a definite stand, clearly defining their position of putting a stop to rampant German expansionism by guaranteeing the integrity of Poland's borders. On 7 April 1939 Italy invaded and occupied Albania. This was a development of great relevance for Turkey, precipitating a rapprochement between Turkey, Britain and France. Turkish relations with Britain, already much improved, were reinforced with a declaration of mutual assistance, on 12 May 1939, followed by a Turco-French declaration (23 June 1939). These declarations culminated in a treaty of mutual assistance between these three states, in case of war in the Mediterranean, signed on 19 October 1939.

In the meantime, at a series of meetings in Moscow British and French representatives were trying to build an alliance with the USSR. However, these were half-hearted attempts made by low-level British and French representatives, who did not have the authority to smooth the way for Soviet demands. This made Stalin even more wary of the West and confirmed his suspicions that the West would prefer the Soviets and Germans to fight each other. Consequently, on 23 August 1939, when Hitler offered Stalin a non-aggression pact along with a share of Polish territory, Stalin accepted and the world, astounded, was treated to the spectacle of the Nazis and Communists signing a pact. This turn of events made Turkey extremely uneasy, because it had a steadfast policy to maintain good relations with the Soviet Union.

The invasion of Poland by Germany on 1 September 1939 was the last straw and two days later Britain and France issued declarations of war against Germany. Thus the Second World War began and on 17 September the Soviets occupied eastern Poland.

Although war was declared in September 1939, there was no military action on the Franco-German front until Germany attacked France on 10 May 1940. In recent years, France had been suffering from a lack of consensus. While one portion of the French left, the Socialists, hoped to establish socialism by democratic methods, another group, the Communists, intended to bring about a revolution. To a large segment of the French right, however, a socialist regime, no matter how it should come about, was anathema. As a result, many groups on the right felt more of an affinity with fascism, some even considering Hitler less of a threat than the French left. This situation impinged on events when France, after declaring war, instead of containing her French fascists, embarked on a campaign against the French Communist Party, which was declared illegal. When the German blitzkrieg against France began, the French army was quickly defeated and the French government, influenced by the pro-Hitler leanings of the right, sued for peace, even though the option of continuing the fight remained.

Meanwhile, with Italy declaring war on France and Britain, the question of Turkey entering the war came to the fore. Turkey declared its neutrality (14 June 1940) based on the argument that entry into the war would conflict with its treaty with the USSR, a position İnönü was to uphold till very nearly the end of the war. As Bulgaria was a German ally, Turkey was in the difficult position of having a virtual frontier with Germany. The situation was exacerbated when, in the spring of 1941, Germany invaded Yugoslavia and Greece. Turkey was from then on in direct confrontation with Nazi Germany. The question then was whether Hitler would attack Turkey in order to reach Middle Eastern oil.

However, Hitler was deluded enough to prepare an attack on his true objective, the Soviet Union. Four days before the German offensive on Russia began, the Turco-German Friendship and Non-Aggression Pact was signed. It was specifically stated that this should in no way infringe upon Turkey's treaty relations with Britain and France. Despite the divided views of politicians and the press, some siding with Britain, some with Germany, throughout these dangerous times, Turkey managed to maintain a delicately balanced policy of neutrality.

Throughout 1941 and 1942 Germany invaded far into Soviet territory with devastating effect. The Soviets lost an estimated 20 million people, roughly the population of a medium-sized country, but they refused to yield. They received large amounts of aid from Britain and also from the United States. Eventually Germany's might began to wane. Soviet counter-offensives began in November 1942 and brought about the German army's surrender at Stalingrad in January 1943. That same year the Allies began to get the upper hand in the North African theatre of war and landed in Italy.

At this juncture the Allies, with Britain taking the lead, began to pressure Turkey to enter the war. On 30 January 1943 the British Prime Minister Winston Churchill came secretly to Turkey for talks, meeting İnönü at Adana. At the end of the year İnönü was summoned to Cairo for a meeting with Roosevelt and Churchill and was confronted by the argument that Turkey should enter the war in accordance with the 1939 mutual assistance pact. Churchill insisted on Turkish support for a new front to be opened in the Balkans (in this way he hoped to prevent the Red Army from obtaining a foothold in Eastern Europe). İnönü's counter-arguments were based on the weak state of the Turkish army's arms and equipment. Although the Allies had provided a certain amount of aid, it was not sufficient for such a great undertaking; it would have been virtually impossible for Turkey, with its unmechanised army wielding few modern weapons, to pursue an offensive war against Germany.

Although the Germans were in retreat and German cities were being bombarded every night into rubble, they continued to fight effectively and with great tenacity. For example, towards the end of the war, they succeeded in unleashing their new inventions, the V-1 pilotless plane and V-2 rocket, on London and southern England.

The new Allied front opened in France rather than in the Balkans with the D-Day landing in Normandy on 6 June 1944. Turkey had already stopped its shipments of chrome to Germany in April and severed all relations on 2 August 1944.

Before the war was finally over the Allies agreed to establish the United Nations, a new organisation to replace the League of Nations, to keep the peace. For this purpose, an international conference was convened in San Francisco. The condition for membership was to have declared war on Germany and Japan, which Turkey had done on 23 February 1945, when there was no question of having to actively participate. In any event, Germany surrendered unconditionally on 7/8 May 1945. It is said that up to the very end Hitler had retained hopes of joining with the Western allies in an attack on the Soviet Union as the bastion of Communism. A short while after the War relations between the Soviet Union and the West were to turn sour, but by that time the Third Reich and its dream of European domination had been annihilated.

Turkey and İnönü have been criticised for not participating in World War Two. According to its international treaties, when hostilities began between Germany and the Soviets Turkey should have entered the war. However, the inferior state of the Turkish army's equipment and weapons and its lack of modern technology would certainly have made this a pointless gesture. İnönü very probably feared that defeat by Germany would have disastrous consequences. Although this would have been a common defeat, certain territories in Thrace might have been occupied by Germany, in which case Turkey and the Revolution itself would have been in jeopardy. To liberate occupied Turkish territory it might have become necessary to call in the Soviets, whose expansionist aims towards Turkey were apparent. In the face of these imponderables İnönü, with good reason, strove for neutrality for as long as possible and stood out against any kind of adventurism.

Economic policy

On 18 January 1940 the Refik Saydam government, established after the resignation of Celal Bayar as Prime Minister, enacted the National Protection Law to keep the economy and market prices under control. Thus a war economy was initiated. With the sudden death of Refik Saydam in 1942, Şükrü Saraçoğlu became Prime Minister (9 July 1942) and Behçet Uz became Minister of Commerce.

Up till that time prices had been kept more or less under control, but with impediments to increased production and imports, many products became unavailable and as a result a black market developed. To try to put an end to the black market the new government performed a *volte-face* by freeing market prices. The Provisions Undersecretariat created by law and its related institutions were abolished. Prices soared and the general rate of inflation for 1942 reached 90 per cent and for 1943 75 per cent. The situation of farmers, merchants and industrialists took a turn for the better, but low-income city-dwellers found themselves in desperate straits. The Turkish people were not accustomed to inflation and there was great public agitation. As a result it was decided to tax the extraordinary wealth accumulated due to the war.

The Capital Tax, enacted in November 1942, was a one-off tax levied on the capital, but not the income, of the bourgeoisie. Those who were unable to find within one month the amounts determined by the tax commissions were first collected in camps and then sent to Aşkale in Erzurum to complete sentences of forced labour such as rock-breaking. This was a dark episode in the progress of the Turkish Republic. In the first place, forcing people to pay their debts by performing physical labour was an archaic concept. Secondly, racial and religious discrimination resulted in non-Muslims and, to a lesser extent, Sabatayists (Jews who had converted to Islam) being apportioned higher taxes than Muslims. Almost all the 1,400 people sent to Aşkale were non-Muslims. Thirdly, the period permitted for payment was too short to allow the selling of property in order to raise funds. Consequently property values fell as people scrambled to sell. Following considerable criticism of this drastic measure from abroad, the law was repealed at the beginning of 1944.

In June 1943 the Agricultural Products Tax Law, also conceived as an extraordinary measure for wartime conditions, was passed. Farmers were to pay in kind or in cash 10 per cent of their produce. This taxation was similar to that of the tithe system, but was paid directly to the state, not to an intermediary. This law too was repealed in 1946.

Village Institutes

The Ottomans had not interested themselves to any great extent in public works in Anatolia. As a result there was no infrastructure, let alone roads. It was a scene of thousands of small, isolated villages, dotted over the generally rough and mountainous terrain where villagers had eked out an existence for hundreds of years under primitive conditions.

By 1940, although progressive measures such as education and public works had been implemented in the towns of Turkey, the rural areas of Anatolia had, in general, yet to enjoy the benefits of the Republican era. The lifestyles, level of technology and mentality of rural inhabitants remained that of the medieval or perhaps an even more primitive age. 81 per cent of the population of Turkey lived in villages, meaning that a very large proportion of the population existed at this very low level. According to the 1935 census, only 23.3 per cent of the male and 8.2 per cent of the female population were literate, and of 40,000 villages (later determined more accurately to be 60,000) 31,000 had no schools. The village schools that did exist were mostly three-year schools offering the most basic curricula. Because the Republic was poor and villages were spread over huge expanses of rough or mountainous terrain, roads, schools and electricity could not yet be provided, and even if schools had been built, teachers from the towns would not happily have endured the hardships of village life. In the Atatürk era a solution to this problem was found within the existing organisation of the armed forces; those villagers capable of reaching the rank of sergeant or corporal were retrained as village teachers.

The Village Institute experiment went even further, creating a formidable organisation that would affect education in the four corners of Anatolia in as short a time as possible. With the Village Institute Law promulgated on 17 April 1940, Village Institutes were opened in eleven districts determined by the Ministry of Agriculture. Three teacher training schools which had opened in 1937–8 were also transformed into Village Institutes, and students for the institutes were selected from among the graduates of five-year village schools. These students followed a five-year curriculum consisting of cultural-theoretical and applied technical-agricultural courses. In applied technical-agricultural courses, students learned bricklaying, construction and carpentry by constructing buildings for the Institute, and new methods of animal husbandry and agriculture by working in the Institute's vegetable plots and fields. Boys and girls learned and worked together.

Graduates were appointed to schools in their own districts. The appointment of a teacher was notified to the relevant village three years in advance so that the village could build a school and housing for the appointee. The state allocated 60 Turkish liras capital to each teacher, and a plot of land and agricultural tools to be used for applied courses in agriculture, and so the teachers could grow their own food. During the first six years teachers' salaries were fixed at 20 Turkish liras. In 1942 a three-year Institute of Higher Learning was opened in the village of Hasanoğlan near Ankara, and by 1948 the number of Institutes had risen to twenty-one. By 1954 twenty-five thousand teachers had been trained by the Institutes. In a short period of time, during a world war, and under conditions of great deprivation, Turkey was able to educate 25,000 teachers in and for its villages. This great achievement was the result of cooperation between İsmet İnönü, Hasan Âli Yücel (Minister of Education) and İsmail Hakkı Tonguç (General Director of Primary Education).

It was also of great consequence that villages thus came into contact with modernity. The graduates of the Institute knew something of carpentry and construction work, had some knowledge of healthcare and were able to solve the problems villagers had when confronted with the administration. Furthermore, because they were people of that region, they were able to comprehend the problems and the mentality of the villagers with whom they could easily communicate, and had few problems of adaptation. Graduates of the Village Institutes included novelists of renown such as Fakir Baykurt, Mahmut Makal and Talip Apaydın. If today the Atatürk Revolution has established roots and Turkey has achieved a degree of progress, the important part played by the Village Institutes cannot be denied.

28

İNÖNÜ ESTABLISHES THE MULTI-PARTY SYSTEM

The international environment

The end of the Second World War not only marked the downfall of German aspirations for hegemony over Europe and those of Japan in the Far East, but also spelled defeat for their ideologies of fascism and racism. Henceforth, the ideologies of democratic-capitalism and communism were to compete against each other in the global arena.

In 1939 Turkey had sided with the Western bourgeois democracies. At that time, the Soviet Union, allied to Germany, had evinced expansionist aims towards Turkey, but when the Soviet Union was attacked by Germany it became an ally of the Western democracies. However, it did not renounce its expansionist policies. Indeed under Stalin it harboured the aim of reasserting its domination over territories that had been part of Tsarist Russia before the First World War, which meant acquiring territory from Turkey, Finland, Poland, Czechoslovakia and Romania and the annexation of Latvia, Estonia and Lithuania. The Turkish territories the Soviets had their eyes on were those that Russia had gained through 1878 Treaty of Berlin and that the Ottomans had re-acquired with the 1918 Treaty of Brest-Litovsk. However, despite Stalin re-acquiring all the other territories in question, those of Turkey remained elusive.

On 19 March 1945 the Soviet Union declared that it would not renew its 1925 Friendship and Non-Aggression Pact with Turkey but would negotiate a new one. Turkey agreed to this, whereupon the Soviet intention of common defence of the Straits became apparent. When the Soviets made an official demand, Turkey rejected it unconditionally. Meanwhile, in Georgia professors were issuing statements to the effect that the Anatolian regions of Kars and Ardahan should be handed back, and in Bulgaria the question of 'rectifying' frontiers with Turkey became an issue. Soviet relations with the West had not yet gone into decline, so in order to undermine Turkey's standing in the eyes of the West Stalin focused attention on the subjects of Turkey's late entry into the war and its selling of chrome to Germany. For as long as the West did not break its close wartime ties with the Soviet Union, Turkey endured a period of international isolation, but in time cordial relations with the West, particularly with the United States, resumed. The arrival of the battleship *Missouri* in İstanbul was symbolic of this rapprochement. Earlier, on 12 March 1947 President Truman had declared to Congress that he had initiated a policy of aid (later to be called the Truman Doctrine) in order to protect Turkey and Greece from the Soviet threat. That same year a Turkish–US military aid agreement was concluded, to be followed in 1948 by an economic aid agreement within the framework of the Marshall Plan whereby US aid was provided to prevent Europe from sliding towards Communism. In 1949 Turkey became a member of the Council of Europe.

Transition to the multi-party system

In this environment İnönü decided to initiate the transition to a multi-party system and having done so, whether in power or opposition, with patience and perseverance, and sometimes even in defiance of the inclinations of his own party, he resolutely strove for the establishment of the system.

İnönü's commitment to this decision was primarily motivated by his understanding of integral development. To keep up with Europe, where the multi-party system was the dominant one, Turkey had to adopt it too. This would, of course, also be advantageous for Turkish foreign policy because a Turkey that had adopted Western values could more naturally rely on Western support against the Soviet threat. There was, however, one other consideration. While the systems of political democracy in Europe were generally inclusive of socialist and even communist parties, in Turkey the system was closed to the left. Not only were socialist and communist parties prohibited but a deliberate and exaggerated enmity towards communism and socialism was adopted, giving rise to prohibition and penalisation of all socialist leanings and ideologies. Articles 141 and

142 of the Turkish Penal Code brought extreme penalties such as seven and a half to fifteen years' imprisonment against those responsible for 'communist propaganda', penalties the courts did not hesitate to apply. The ostensible reason for this was that in 1945 the Soviet Union had forwarded demands concerning the Straits, Kars and Ardahan. Since then Turkey has achieved significant increase in its security thanks to the Truman Doctrine, its membership of the Council of Europe and, a short while later, its membership of NATO. Moreover, after the death of Stalin in 1953 the Soviet Union presented Turkey with a diplomatic note stating that it relinquished its demands on the disputed territories and was ready to sign a friendship pact. Nevertheless, the same atmosphere prevailed until the 1960s and may even be said to exist in part today.

For many years the poems of Nazım Hikmet, one of Turkey's greatest poets, completely disappeared from public view owing to his being a Communist and having fled to the Soviet Union. People did not even have the courage to acknowledge they owned a copy of his works. Even today his poems are not included in school textbooks, whereas those of Rıza Tevfik, one of the co-signatories of the Sèvres Treaty, are, as indeed they should be. Also 'Russian salad' was absurdly known in Turkey as 'American salad', which must have been a surprise to visiting Americans. Although this unhealthy atmosphere was influenced to a degree by the McCarthyism of the United States (1949–53), it was more pronounced and lasted longer in Turkey.

Some of this antipathy to the left may also have come from those who, having not sincerely or only partially assimilated the Atatürk Revolution and its 'unlimited intellectual freedom', knowingly or in many cases unwittingly, masked their thoughts and feelings with an extreme anti-Communist stance, exemplified by the accusation brought against the Village Institutes of nurturing communism.

For whatever reason, this limitation to political and intellectual freedom rendered Turkish democracy lacking in comparison to the West European form. This in turn reduced international respect for Turkey. In contrast, during the Atatürk era, the Turkish political system was not less but more advanced than the European norm and Turkey had accordingly been held in respect.

The first steps towards a multi-party system were prefaced by İnönü's propitious announcement made on 19 May 1945, on the occasion of the Youth and Sports Festival, that 'government by the people' would be promoted. In the environment conducive to the development of democracy which prevailed in Europe at the end of the war some RPP members, dissatisfied with the prevalent single-party system, had already begun to agitate for reform of the political system. Four Deputies of the Assembly who were of this per-suasion—Celal Bayar, Adnan Menderes, Fuat Köprülü and Refik Koraltan—presented the RPP group with the 'Motion of the Four' (*Dörtlü Takrir*) on 7 June 1945. In this motion they particularly emphasised the need to create an environment conducive to free discussion within the party.

At that time a draft of the Land Reform Law (Çiftçiyi Topraklan-dırma Kanunu) drawn up by İnönü and Agriculture Minister Şevket Raşit Hatiboğlu was on the parliamentary agenda. According to Article 17 of this law, in order to provide land for peasants with little or none, the government was authorised to expropriate the lands of the great land-owners. All lands with the exception of those under 50 *dönüms* (fifty thousand square meters) could be expropriated, if necessary. According to Article 21, compensation was to be determ-ined in accordance with declared land-tax evaluations rather than market values. This particular article caused much agitation among land-owning Deputies. Adnan Menderes, one of the great land-owners from the province of Aydın in Western Anatolia, was at the head of the anti-law faction as the draft was being discussed in the Assembly. İnönü, however, was adamant. Atatürk, in his later spee-ches at successive openings of Parliament, had stressed the need to provide land for landless peasants, but no material steps had been taken or were then possible. Now İnönü had taken up this cause in earnest. Possibly he was not motivated solely by the idea of social benefit for the peasants but also hoped to gain their political support in the multi-party environment. If this is true, he was greatly mista-ken, as the land-owners dominated the shaping of public opinion in rural areas. Although the Land Reform Law was passed by the TGNA on 11 June 1945, not only was its main architect, Hatipoğlu, unable to regain a seat in any succeeding cabinet, but in the second Hasan Saka government of 1948 Cavit Oral, a great landowner from Adana and an adversary of the Land Reform Law, was made Min-ister of Agriculture. Needless to say, the above-mentioned Article 17 was never implemented and distribution of land to the peasants was limited to a portion of Treasury lands.

Founding of the Democrat Party

Although the Democrat Party was not born purely as a result of opposition to the Land Reform Law, it did play an important part in the founding of the party and in its gaining widespread support.

On 12 June İnönü ensured that the RPP Group rejected the Motion of the Four. His wish was that the malcontents within the RPP should split off and found a new party. There were three benefits he hoped to gain from this. First, it would ensure the establishment of a multi-party system; second, it would rid the RPP of unwanted oppositional elements; and third, there would be no danger of this split creating a counter-revolutionary party. However, Bayar and his colleagues were far from enthusiastic about breaking off from the RPP, seeing the founding of a new party as a venture into the unknown. It was preferable to stay in the RPP and try to dominate it. They were well aware of what had happened to the Free Party, despite Atatürk's many assurances, and Bayar did not want to follow in the unfortunate footsteps of the FRP founder Fethi Okyar.

After the Motion of the Four had been rejected, Adnan Menderes and Fuat Köprülü began to write oppositional articles for the *Vatan* newspaper arguing in favour of democratisation. The RPP, evaluating this as a breach of party discipline, expelled them from the party (21 September). The way in which Celal Bayar chose to show support for his two colleagues indicates that he was not yet convinced about the soundness of founding a new party. He resigned from the Assembly (28 September), rather than the Party, though this gesture resulted in the considerable loss of his salary as a Deputy.

Nonetheless, İnönü obdurately continued to argue for the establishment of a new party. On 1 November 1945 in his opening speech before the Assembly he stated outright that the country was in need of an opposition party, disregarding the fact that the National Development Party (Milli Kalkınma Partisi) had already been founded by businessman Nuri Demirağ. (Because Demirağ was a conservative, İnönü deliberately ignored the existence of this party.) Eventually Bayar was won over and on 1 December he announced that his group would found a party and on 3 December he resigned from the

RPP. The following day he accepted İnönü's invitation to have a private talk over dinner.

4 December 1945 was also the day of the 'Tan Incident'. The *Tan* newspaper, published by Zekeriya Sertel, was known for its support of the socialist left. At the time Sertel was about to begin publication of a new periodical, *Views (Görüşler)*. Its advent had been advertised and it was known that Adnan Menderes and Fuat Köprülü were to be among its writers. That day some people described as 'youths' chanting anti-Communist and anti-Russian slogans attacked and then demolished the *Tan* publishing house and also bookstores selling leftist works. The fact that the police did nothing to intervene gave rise to accusations that the RPP had instigated or even organised this uncivilised and unlawful business. The DP was perhaps being warned to keep its distance from the left.

Indeed it was apparent that the RPP wanted a complete void on its left. Three leftist parties were shut down in 1946: the Social Democrat Party in March and later in December, the Turkish Socialist Party (Chairman Esat Adil Müstecaplıoğlu) and the Turkish Socialist Workers' and Peasants' Party (Chairman Şefik Hüsnü Deymer). That Recep Peker during his term as Prime Minister spoke of rendering the Village Institutes 'more national' was an indication of how pervasive the anti-left atmosphere had become.

In 1947 a witches' cauldron of accusations against the leftist academics Niyazi Berkes, Pertev Naili Boratav, Muzaffer Şerif and Behice Boran was being brewed in the faculties of Linguistics, History and Geography of Ankara University, beginning with student demonstrations and eventually growing to encompass the university administration, the TGNA and the courts. Three of these distinguished academics were forced to leave the university. Boran did not leave the country but Berkes went to Canada and Boratav to France, and both were successful in their new academic lives. Thus the Turkey that had welcomed German professors fleeing from the injustice of fascism was now devouring its own intellectuals.

The Democrat Party was founded on 7 January 1946 with Bayar becoming its first Chairman. Attracting people who for a variety of reasons were dissatisfied it soon gained extensive support. As may be inferred from its name, the primary aim of the DP was to ensure democratisation. The RPP administration, in answer to criticism of the electoral system, initiated the single-stage election process for the first time in Turkish political history. It also gave jurisdiction over the press to the courts, putting an end to the government's power to shut down newspapers, and the universities were made autonomous. To gain the support of peasants and workers the RPP abolished the Agricultural Products Tax (Toprak Mahsülleri Vergisi) and enacted laws to establish a Ministry of Labour and social security for workers. İnönü's title of 'Permanent General Chairman' was rescinded and it was accepted that class-based parties and trade unions could be founded. The RPP also cunningly moved the 1947 elections forward to 1946, leaving the opposition little time to organise.

The election held on 21 July 1946 was single stage but not under the control of the courts. An open ballot system was employed and the votes were counted in secret. The majority system was employed, i.e. even if a party was ahead by only one vote in a province, it would win all the parliamentary seats of that district. The DP was able to muster only 273 candidates for 465 parliamentary seats of which it won only 66. It was evident to all that the election had not been conducted fairly. As a result, DP-RPP relations soured and this was inevitably reflected in the atmosphere of the Assembly.

After the 1946 elections

In the new administration İnönü made Recep Peker Prime Minister in place of Şükrü Saraçoğlu. The Peker Administration's devaluation of the Turkish lira, known as the '7 September Decisions', created a great sensation because at that time any change in the value of currency was an extraordinary event. The US dollar rose from 1.40 TL to 2.80 TL. When Prime Minister Recep Peker, angered by Menderes during a parliamentary session, said that the latter's criticisms were 'the emanation of a psychotic mentality' and accused Celal Bayar of inciting the people to rebellion, the DP parliamentary group as a whole walked out in protest. İnönü intervened and after an İnönü-Bayar tête-à-tête, a calmer atmosphere prevailed.

The DP had its first General Congress in January 1947, resulting in a formal statement, the Liberty Pact (Hürriyet Misakı), according to which, if certain political demands of the Democrat Party were not accepted, the DP Deputies would boycott the National Assembly. The DP demands were, in summary, that laws conflicting with the Constitution should be repealed, that an election law ensuring fair elections should be enacted, and that the president of the state should not, at one and the same time, be the president of a political party (as was the case with İnönü). Yet, no matter how fiery the DP opposition, it met with an equally harsh and intractable response from Recep Peker who called the DP threat to quit the Assembly 'communist tactics'. İnönü was well aware that this did not augur well for the multi-party system. In the role of mediator, after numerous interviews with Bayar and Peker, he circulated the '12 July Declaration' in an attempt to reconcile the two sides. Although the Declaration did effect a thaw in relations, Peker refused to modify his acrimonious manner. In fact, he had not come to terms with the multi-party system. Consequently, İnönü began a counter-campaign to rid the RPP of Peker's negative influence, resulting in a group of young Deputies headed by Nihat Erim voting against Peker in the RPP group (the 35's Movement). For a few days Peker and his supporters gave the impression that they intended to defy İnönü, but in the end Peker resigned and the Hasan Saka government was formed (9 September 1947).

The ongoing conflict in the RPP between those for conciliation and those for inflexibility was even more pronounced within the DP. Supporters of aggressive tactics dominated the DP group and blamed party administrators for yielding too much. When in March 1948 this tension peaked some Deputies and their supporters were expelled. These people initially created an Independent Democrats' Group in the Assembly and on 20 July 1948 founded the Nation Party (Millet Partisi). Among its founders were Marshal Fevzi Çakmak, Hikmet Bayur, Kenan Öner, Osman Bölükbaşı and Sadık Aldoğan. Fevzi Çakmak became the party chairman. The Nation Party accused the Democrat Party of being a false opposition in collusion with the administration. However, this split within the DP did not give rise to any significant decrease in grassroots support, as was proven by the results of the 1950 election. Nonetheless, up till the 1950 elections the DP's position was weakened by the loss of half its parliamentary seats.

The Günaltay government

Prime Minister Hasan Saka differed from Recep Peker in not condoning aggressive tactics. However, he lacked the will to bring the cause of democratisation to fruition, a case in point being the new election law enacted in 1948, which did not include control of the judiciary over elections. Consequently the DP boycotted local elections and by-elections. On 15 January 1949 Hasan Saka resigned and Şemsettin Günaltay became Prime Minister in his stead.

Günaltay was a historian who had been involved in the Islamist current during the Second Constitutional Period. During the vote of confidence, he promised to establish a sound democracy. In practice, however, his first acts were in the realm of religion. Ten-month courses had already been established in 1948 for the training of imam–hatips (religious functionaries who lead the people in prayer in mosques). Later, in 1951, the DP government was to transform these courses into training-schools of religion with a curriculum equal to a secondary school diploma. Furthermore, the Günaltay government, in line with a decision previously taken by the RPP group, made religion a primary school elective subject. Parallel to this, a Faculty of Theology was founded as part of Ankara University. In 1956 religion was made a regular subject in middle school education, though children whose parents did not want them to attend were exempted. In 1967 religion was made a *lycée* subject and in 1974 obligatory 'Moral Instruction' courses were added to the middle and lycée curricula. Although these practices differed from those of the Atatürk era, they did not infringe on secularism.

However, what did infringe on secularism were the constitutional amendments of the 12 September 1980 military administration, which made all religious instruction obligatory. Thus an inappropriate imposition was laid on parents who did not wish their children to attend courses in religion or who belonged to a different faith. Although these classes in religion are proffered as 'religious culture', it is evident that they are transformed in many cases into courses of religious indoctrination, according to the interpretation of the teacher in any individual classroom. Also contrary to secularism is the huge number of imam–hatip schools.

On 20 June 1949 the Democrat Party held its second General Congress at which the DP, spurred on by the Nation Party's accusations of their being a compromised opposition, came out with a declaration called the National Assurance Oath (Milli Teminat Andı) according to which, if any vote-tampering should occur, the people would have the right to defend themselves through legal channels, but whichever government should be responsible would attract 'the enmity of the nation'. Use of the word 'enmity' (*husumet*) resulted in RPP ridicule, and the nicknaming of the declaration the 'National Enmity Oath', notwithstanding which a new draft election law was put before the TGNA in February 1950. For the first time in Turkish political history there would be judicial control of elections. Backed by the DP vote, it became law. However, the one crucial disadvantage of this law was that it specified the employment of the simple majority ('first past the post') system rather than a proportional electoral one. Ironically, the majority system was to work to the detriment of the RPP in the following three elections, all of which took place in the 1950s.

In the elections held on 14 May 1950 the DP received 55% and the RPP 41% of the vote. Obviously the RPP had lost the election, but it had not been completely routed and retained a large proportion of votes. However, the majority system transformed this defeat into a debacle because the DP won 85% of the seats (408 Deputies) while the RPP won only 15% (69 Deputies). The DP heralded this success as the beginning of a new era. This was indeed a watershed in Turkish political life. Following the revolutionary era with its one-party system which had ended in 1945, with Turkey's second general election the reins of government were being handed over to an opposition party without upheaval. This was as much an achievement of İsmet İnönü and the RPP as it was a victory for the DP.

An evaluation of İsmet İnönü

Whether in power or in opposition, İnönü successfully defended and upheld the principles of the Kemalist Revolution. Furthermore, he made contributions of great consequence to the Revolution, specifically the establishment of the Village Institutes and the multi-party system. It may even be argued that the Village Institutes made the revolution of Kemal Atatürk an irreversible process.

Democratisation of the system was a truly courageous step taken in accordance with the Kemalist concept of integral development, i.e. that Turkey should strive to measure up to universal ideals. İnönü, in or out of power, worked ceaselessly and with great patience throughout the years to preserve and safeguard the system, just as one would nurture a delicate flower in parched soil. In the aftermath of the 27 May 1960 coup, which felled his political rivals, he did everything in his power to bring about a return to the multi-party system as soon as possible. He also foiled two attempted military coups instigated by Talat Aydemir. Nevertheless, how successful the multi-party system has been in Turkey, and the extent to which it has served democracy (equality and freedom) is a subject still being debated.

However, the İnönü period did have its negative moments: the racist aspect of the Capital Tax which infringed upon basic human rights; the fact that Nazım Hikmet languished in jail for so many years; the *Tan* Incident; the purge in the faculties of Linguistics, History and Geography of Ankara University; the emasculation of the Village Institutes; and the fact that the multi-party system was established without a socialist left. These were major defects for which İnönü was undoubtedly politically responsible. Perhaps, and very probably, İnönü had not wished these episodes to take place and was even troubled by them, but his hold on power was not sufficient to prevent them. Although İnönü was indeed a great statesman and was the 'National Chief' of his era, he was not as forceful and powerful as Atatürk and possessed neither the latter's political influence, nor his extraordinary strength of character.

29

THE DEMOCRAT PARTY ERA

The Democrat Party's first successes and the first
repressive measures

The DP era began in a spirit of optimism and with great expectations. Celal Bayar, elected President of the Turkish Republic by the TGNA, resigned from the leadership of the DP, handing this duty over to Prime Minister Adnan Menderes. Refik Koraltan was elected President of the TGNA and Fuat Köprülü became Minister of Foreign Affairs.

While the Democrat Party was still in opposition, it had promised the right to strike as part of its platform of democratisation. However, shortly after coming to power those promises were forgotten and instead the DP concentrated all its resources on economic development. In any event, in those years conditions were favourable for the further development of the Turkish economy. The Korean war had broken out in 1950, causing prices of raw materials and agricultural produce to rise in world markets. Meanwhile in Turkey agricultural output had greatly increased owing to the marked rise in the number of tractors and other agricultural machinery in use (number of tractors in use: 1924: 220; 1930: 2000; 1948: 1,756; 1950: 9,905; 1956: 43,727). Arable land was extended from 9.5 million hectares in 1948 to 14.6 million hectares in 1956, an increase of approximately 50 per cent, and after the Second World War, encouraged by the United States, extensive motorway construction was initiated, giving rural regions access to markets that had previously been out of reach.

Turkey's entry into the North Atlantic Treaty Organisation on 18 February 1952 was an important achievement in foreign affairs. Turkey had sent its soldiers to fight in the Korean War as a contri-

253

bution to the United Nations effort and had thereby overcome the objections of Britain and certain other countries to Turkey's membership. This development, coming after the Truman Doctrine, the Marshall Plan and membership of the Council of Europe, confirmed Turkey's place in the Western alliance and put an end to its period of isolation. Events were developing along very positive lines for Turkey and the DP administration.

Notwithstanding this positive trend, there was a sense of unease and vexation emanating from the DP and more specifically from Menderes and Bayar. Possibly they felt their position was insecure, although the 1954 elections resulted in an even greater victory for the DP than those held in 1950. For this reason, some historians have concluded that Bayar and Menderes suffered from 'İnönü phobia', i.e. fear of İnönü's prestige.

On 8 August 1951 the People's Houses and Rooms were nationalised by the TGNA. Till then they had been an organisation of the RPP, which during the one-party era had not been a drawback, but in a multi-party system, as a cultural organisation providing a public service, they could not remain the organ of any one party. For whatever reasons, the RPP had neglected to attach the People's Houses organisation to the Ministry of Education—with the proviso that it should continue in its previous function—during its own administration. However, the DP, in undertaking its nationalisation, now omitted that all-important proviso, and as a result these centres of culture (478 People's Houses and 4,322 People's Rooms) were allotted to the Treasury as though they were merely material assets. The organisation's educational and cultural function was ignored and negated and consequently, the process of the enlightenment of the people received a grievous blow. Even today, no equivalent organisation has been founded to fill its place. Considering that a great majority of Turkish schools still lack cultural facilities such as libraries, auditoriums etc., the gravity of this blow becomes more apparent. Unfortunately the DP administration seems to have been motivated more by its desire to weaken the power of the RPP than by a commitment to Turkish enlightenment. Furthermore, the DP administration completed the process of undermining the Village Institutes, initiated by the RPP towards the end of its administration, by transforming them all in February 1954 into primary school teacher training colleges.

In 1953 the DP initiated another measure to the detriment of the RPP by enacting a law confiscating all the RPP's property as 'illegal acquisition' and allocating it to the Treasury (14 December 1953). This action was aimed at limiting the activities of the main opposition party, but it seems the DP was averse not only to the RPP but to opposition of any kind, as it also had the Nation Party shut down on the grounds that it was anti-revolutionary and anti-Kemalist (8 July 1953).

As the 1954 elections drew near, the government passed a law imposing heavy penalties on journalists who openly criticised the administration. Those brought to trial were deprived of the right to prove the accuracy of their writings, an injustice that provoked defiance within the ranks of the DP itself. Nineteen DP deputies participated in the movement for 'the right of proof', but it was treated as a joke by Menderes and achieved no results, and the Nineteen either resigned from the DP or were expelled. Among the Nineteen, who towards the end of 1955 formed the Freedom Party (Hürriyet Partisi), were such persons of note as Turan Güneş, Ekrem Alican, Fevzi Lütfü Karaosmanoğlu and Ekrem Hayrı Üstündağ.

In the 2 May 1954 elections the Democrat Party received 57% and the Republican People's Party 36%, reducing the RPP's share of seats in the Assembly to thirty-one. Things then went from bad to worse. Investments were made and credit distributed without any overall plan, in the most part to gain political advantage for the DP. This in turn gave rise to inflation and a foreign currency bottleneck resulting in goods shortages. The government refused to consider and was even contemptuous of proposals for a planned economy. Furthermore, Turkey's application for a $300 million credit was rejected by the United States.

In 1955 the DP invoked the National Protection Law (Milli Korunma Kanunu) instituting police and judicial measures, price controls and rationing. All government officials and employees after completing twenty-five years of public service could be relieved of their duties 'when necessary' and then retired. Thereby university staff and judges were threatened with job loss and many were purged. Heavy prison sentences and fines were brought against dissident journalists and the press, and in the summer of 1955 RPP General Secretary Kasım Gülek, on a tour of the Black Sea region, was arrested in Sinop, hauled off to İstanbul and jailed for a day. And in 1956 Gülek's visit to shop-owners in Rize was accounted by the court to be an anti-government demonstration for which he was given a six month term in prison.

The question of Cyprus

From 1954 onwards Cyprus found itself on the Turkish political agenda. Greece had been suing for control of Cyprus, then a British crown colony, and Turkey decided to make its own claims. Greek Cypriots staged demonstrations in favour of *Enosis* (Union with Greece) and bloody terrorist acts followed. In 1955 Britain held a conference in London to review the situation.

Then, on 6 September 1955 an İstanbul newspaper reported the bombing of Atatürk's house in Salonika. That evening throughout İstanbul thousands of Greek houses, businesses, churches and ceme-teries were attacked, pillaged or destroyed. Because these incidents had taken place simultaneously, the suspicion arose that they had been premeditated. At first the police did not interfere, but later they were helpless to stop the violence. The incidents were finally brought to a halt at midnight by army intervention. Martial law was declared, and because the outbreak was construed as a communist plot many leftists were arrested and were only able to prove their innocence after being held in prison for many months. Much later, after the 27 May 1960 coup, the Yassıada High Court concluded that ex-President Celal Bayar, ex-Prime Minister Adnan Menderes, ex-Minister of the Interior Namık Gedik and ex-Foreign Minister Fatin Rüştü Zorlu were responsible. Apparently Zorlu, at the time attending the Cyprus Conference in London, ignited the 6–7 September incidents with his message to Ankara: to show 'how far we will go in insisting on our rights…orders to be given for vigorous action to those concerned will be extremely useful.' The Yassıada court came to the conclusion that the DP organisation had been utilised to activate these incidents because they had broken out simultaneously in many different districts of İstanbul and İzmir. In Salonika Greek authorities arrested some Turks who were found guilty by a Greek court of the bomb throwing. One of these was later made a provincial governor in Turkey. It would appear that the 6/7 September incident, similar to the *Tan* incident of 1945 but on a broader scale, was another unfortunate example of the use of illegal force by the state. The Democrat Party rejected a proposal for a parliamentary investigation. Only Namık Gedik resigned from his ministerial post.

Turkey had initially laid claim to the whole of Cyprus (with the slogan 'Cyprus is Turkish and will stay Turkish'), but after reassessment it was decided that this was unrealistic and a new demand arose for the island to be partitioned between Greece and Turkey (the new slogan being 'Partition or death!'). However, with an agreement concluded between Turkey, Britain and Greece in Zürich and London on 13 and 19 February 1959, Cyprus became an independent republic in 1960. The Cyprus constitution contained certain clauses, under the guarantee of all three signatories, granting special rights to the Turkish Cypriots in the government and Parliament. The three signatories—Turkey, Greece and Britain—were to have privileged status, with the right to intervene in case of infringement. Britain was to keep its air bases and Turkey and Greece were allowed to station a garrison each. A constitutional court headed by a Federal German judge was to oversee the workings of this order. Archbishop Makarios was elected President of the Republic of Cyprus and Dr Fazıl Küçük was elected Vice-President. Thus the Cyprus question was brought to what was to be a temporary rather than a permanent conclusion. A short time later the order created in Zürich and London was overturned by Greek efforts.

The 1957 elections: the Democrat Party strays from the path of democracy

In 1957 the DP again won a majority, but its total fell to 48 per cent of the vote, giving it 424 seats. The RPP obtained 41 per cent of the vote (178 seats), while the Republican National Party (headed by Osman Bölükbaşı) and the Freedom Party won four seats each.

In 1958, confronted by insoluble economic crisis, the government (having no other way to obtain foreign credit) was forced to accept the conditions set out by the International Monetary Fund and the World Bank. On 4 August 1958 these measures were implemented to stabilise the economy and as a result the US dollar rose from 2.80 to 9.00 Turkish liras. The National Protection measures were brought to an end and to rein in inflation state-owned enter-prises raised the prices of their products. The DP, which had pre-viously been considering the privatisation of state-owned enterprises, because the private sector was reluctant to take them over and/or invest their own capital in new enterprises, found itself having to expand the sphere of the public sector. In time, however, private sector industrial investment expanded. In general, industry aimed at producing goods which had heretofore been imported, thereby sat-isfying already established market demand with domestic products (import substitution). For example, when, because of foreign currency shortage, bathroom hardware, batteries and central heating equipment could no longer be imported, they began to be produced domestically.

In the autumn of 1958 the DP administration adopted a new series of repressive measures. At the time, stabilisation measures ini-tiated to cope with the economic crisis, and a major devaluation of the lira, had sent prices spiralling upwards, having a devastating effect on the public at large. In addition, despite the disadvantages of the majority system, in the 1957 elections the RPP had succeeded in winning a large number of seats in the Assembly. In the face of the continuing deterioration of the economic situation it was highly likely that the RPP would win the next election. However, Men-deres and his circle, for whatever reason, found the idea of having to surrender power totally unacceptable.

Coincidentally, two different events taking place in foreign countries also served as rationalisations for intensifying the DP's repression of the opposition. One of these was the 14 July 1958 rev-olution in Iraq. The DP administration had intended to initiate closer relations with Middle Eastern countries with the hope that in time Turkey might rise to a leading position in the region. The dif-ficulty was that Turkey had no intention of making any concessions concerning its NATO connection, its relations with the United States and its position in the Cold War. But the primary concern of Arab democratic-nationalists was the Palestinian question. As the United States and Western Europe were the foremost supporters and allies of Israel, it was impossible for Turkey to initiate closer relations with these Arab countries (headed by Nasser's Egypt since the 1952 Republican Revolution) without forgoing its alliances.

Because the other Arab nations were administered as feudal princi-palities, though for them too the Palestinian question was of great importance, protecting themselves against republican, democratic-nationalist movements, which might destroy their status quo, was of even greater consequence. Hence, they were more readily prepared to enter into relations with the West. Consequently Turkey, as part of the Western Alliance, was only able to establish the Baghdad Pact 'against communism in the Middle East' with Iran, Iraq, Pakistan and Britain as members and the United States giving outside support. On a personal level too, DP leaders had developed warm relationships with the Iraqi royal family and with Premier Nuri as-Said, and Iraqi officials tended to spend their holidays on the Bosphorus.

Then suddenly, on 14 July 1958, the Iraqi army staged a coup d'état and King Faisal and Nuri as-Said were killed. The DP gov-ernment was much disturbed by this upheaval. The Turkish army was put on alert along the borders with Iraq and Syria, and it has even been claimed that Menderes entertained the idea of military intervention in Iraq, but was dissuaded by the United States. In answer to Lebanon's and Jordan's petitions for Western support, American forces were sent to Lebanon and British forces to Jordan. Conse-quently, the İncirlik military base in Adana was utilised by the United States for the military landing in Lebanon.

In the eyes of the DP administration the Iraqi Revolution was instigated from outside, whereas according to the Turkish opposi-tion it was a rebellion against an oppressive administration. The Soviet Union officially protested against the Turkish government's foreign policy on this issue. On 5 March 1959 the United States and the remaining members of the Baghdad Pact including Turkey signed a mutual assistance agreement in accordance with which, should Turkey be attacked, the United States would come to its aid. The United States had already accepted such an obligation in relation to Turkey with the North Atlantic Treaty Alliance, but this pact encom-passed the concept of intervention in the cases of both direct and 'in-direct attack'. Hence, if an uprising or other upheaval were to occur in Turkey, America would be enabled to send in its troops at the Turkish government's request.

According to various sources the Iraqi Revolution heightened the DP administration's fears of revolution. While the bilateral

agreement concluded with the United States must have given some
reassurance to the DP leaders, it must also have increased their com-
placency and the bravado they displayed in their attitude towards the
opposition.

A second incident in foreign affairs, which may have motivated
the DP's initiation of a new series of repressive measures against the
opposition, took place in France where on 31 May 1958, in a time of
national crisis Charles de Gaulle, leader of the French resistance
against the German occupation during the Second World War, became Prime Minister. Algeria, seen by the French not as a colony but
as a region of the French homeland, had been enveloped in a bloody
insurgent war since 1954. Hundreds of thousands of people had died
and de Gaulle, as saviour of France in the Second World War, had
been charged with solving this great national problem and with
establishing the peace. Following this, with the support of the
French Assembly and the electorate he put an end to the traditional
French parliamentary system with the Constitution of the Fifth
Republic which instituted a semi-presidential system. De Gaulle,
bringing to bear his status as a charismatic war leader, became what
may be called a 'democratic dictator'. However, Menderes, inspired
by the political developments in France, very probably chose to ignore
the circumstances under which de Gaulle had come to power. There
were no such problems in Turkey and neither Menderes nor Bayar
could be considered saviours of the nation.

On 6 September 1958, speaking in Balıkesir, Menderes accused
the opposition of intending a revolution similar to that in Iraq and
made mention of the gallows awaiting those with such intentions.
On 21 September, speaking in İzmir, it was clear from his wording
that he wished to take the Gaullist system as his model. He also made
the point that should state officials meet with resistance now, a ces-
sation of democracy would result. İnönü did not leave these statements unanswered, but the intentions of the administration had
become apparent with the establishment of the Motherland Front
(Vatan Cephesi), for which Menderes had called on 12 October
1958 in Manisa in response to the Opposition's 'Hate and enmity
front'. After this Motherland Front organisations sprang up all over
the country. It was a 'Motherland front' in name only as its members
were in actual fact joining the DP. One after the other the names of

its founders and new members were read every day over the radio (then a state monopoly) and the campaign elevated political tension to new heights. The Opposition was doing everything in its power to avoid being crushed by these developments. On 24 November 1958 the Freedom Party decided to unite with the RPP. At the Fourteenth RPP Congress, convened on 12 January 1959, a document called the First Aims Declaration was accepted. The most important of the tenets contained therein were the establishment of a social state, freedom of the press, the right to strike and to found trade unions, an assembly of two houses, a constitutional court, proportional representation, university autonomy, a supreme judicial council and the impartiality of the state broadcasting system. These very concepts were later to become the basic principles of the 1961 Constitution.

The DP administration seemed to have come to a point where it could no longer bear the idea of opposition leaders circulating freely throughout the country. As early as in 1952 the DP had begun to apply pressure on opposition leaders (mainly İsmet İnönü and Kasım Gülek) to prevent them from touring the country. This pressure showed itself in coercive measures adopted by the police and gendarmerie, local administrators, public prosecutors and the courts, and also took the form of hostile behaviour on the part of DP partisans. During İsmet İnönü's October 1952 Aegean tour attacks on his person took place in İzmir and protest demonstrations occurred in Akhisar and Manisa. İnönü was to arrive in Balıkesir on 8 October, but on that day the governor met him at the outskirts of the city saying he could take no responsibility for the incidents that would break out were İnönü to enter the city and could also offer him no protection, on which İnönü cancelled his visit. On 18 April 1954, at an open air meeting held in Mersin İnönü, attacked by DP partisans, was forced to jump for his life over a wall. Incidents such as these continued and became increasingly serious. During another of İnönü's tours of the Aegean, on 30 April 1959 the governor of Uşak went to great lengths to prevent İnönü visiting a War of Independence headquarters and, because they refused to fall in with his wishes, the director of the police and the commander of the gendarmerie were relieved from their duties that very day. That night the DP gathered supporters from certain factories who the following day stopped İnönü's car on its way to the train station. As İnönü tried to make his way through the crowd on foot, a stone hit his head. (He was aged seventy-five at the time.) Such incidents were repeated throughout his journey. In İzmir all RPP activities were obstructed and DP partisans wrecked the premises of the *Democratic İzmir* newspaper.

On 4 May in İstanbul, as İnönü was being driven from the airport towards the city, DP partisans armed with sticks and stones massed in the district of Topkapı. The Director of Traffic barred İnönü's way with his car. When İnönü's car came to a halt it was surrounded by thugs. As the Director was urging İnönü to move into his car an army major, who had been observing the situation although he was not on duty, ordered soldiers in the vicinity (who till then had been content to remain onlookers) to clear the way with their rifle butts and have the Traffic Director's car removed. The press was forbidden to report these events and newspapers came out with blank columns. Although at the Yassıada trial Menderes and Bayar were not found legally responsible, they were undoubtedly politically responsible as leaders of the DP for this and similar incidents.

Events leading to the 27 May coup

That same year (1959) RPP General Secretary Kasım Gülek was met with organised agitation in Geyikli, Chanakkale. Then in the spring of 1960 the Yeşilhisar Incident took place and when İnönü attempted to go to Kayseri, unrest erupted there too.

The DP administration, unable to intimidate the opposition into cancelling its tours, decided to take measures to rid itself of the problem in its entirety. In a declaration published on 12 April 1960 the DP group accused the RPP of 'plotting armed insurgence against the government' and certain organs of the press of supporting these plots by publishing false and distorted news reports. The declaration also stated that the DP caucus had decided to form an Investigation Commission which, within a period of three months, would find out the truth of these matters. The motion was passed in the TGNA on 18 April 1960 and on that same day in the Assembly İnönü made two speeches in which he stated that it was the RPP itself that had brought about the transition from revolution to democracy and that it was therefore out of the question for it to entertain any idea of a coup. He also warned that the new commission would be an illegal body above the TGNA, bringing an order of oppression, and that this situation would indeed bring about a revolution, which would have its source outside the RPP. His famous words were: 'It is a dangerous undertaking to deflect this democratic regime from its true course, turning it into a regime of oppression. If you persist on this path, even I will not be able to save you... When conditions demand it, revolution is the lawful right of nations.'

The Investigation Commission was formed regardless, composed of fifteen members, all from the DP ranks, and its first act was to prohibit:

(1) all party activities (although only the RPP was to be investigated);
(2) all publications relating to commission activities;
(3) all publications relating to debates in the TGNA on the subject of the workings of the commission.

The *Ulus* and *Democratic İzmir* newspapers defied the prohibition by publishing İnönü's speeches in full. Through these and other channels İnönü's words became known throughout the country. He had openly declared in the Assembly that the RPP had no intention of surrendering. He had also pointed to a way out of the crisis, free and democratic elections, but Menderes interpreted İnönü's warning that 'revolution may arise' to mean the RPP itself intended to stage a revolution, and thus persuaded the DP group to take further measures.

A law enacted on 27 April 1960 granted the Investigation Commission extraordinary powers, allowing it to suppress any published material, to close down printing offices and periodicals, to take precautions and make decisions concerning all political activities for the furtherance of the investigation and, in order for it to realise this aim, to make use of all the agencies of the state. Those who, in any way or manner, opposed the precautions or decisions of this commission would be sentenced to a period of one to three years' imprisonment, and those who leaked information regarding the workings of the investigation were to be imprisoned for terms from six months to a year. The Commission was to function as the preliminary inquiry stage in the penal process.

İnönü's response was, 'You say that you have taken necessary precautions and will implement them... All unlawful administrations that have instituted regimes of oppression have, in their own time, made this same statement. The conspirators of oppression who have embarked on this path must think that the Turkish nation does not have the self-respect equal to that of the Korean nation.' (The Korean dictator, Rhee, had been forced by students' and people's demonstrations to resign on 21 April 1960.) For this speech alone, İnönü was banned from twelve sessions of the Assembly.

On 28 April the students of the University of İstanbul organised a large demonstration. The police were unable to disperse the crowd and army units had to be called in. One student died, forty people were injured, and Rector Sıddık Sami Onar was assaulted. The government declared martial law and university classes were suspended. The prohibitions on the press caused increasingly exaggerated rumours to spread and the following day in Ankara students of the faculties of Political Science and Law held further demonstrations. When the police could not cope, army units were again called in. The administration had recourse to increasingly harsh measures. Menderes meanwhile broadcast his speeches by radio and paid a visit to the Aegean, finding reassurance in the crowds of people who came to meet him in İzmir. On 30 April Professor of Constitutional Law Ali Fuat Başgil advised Celal Bayar that the time had come for them to resign. Bayar's answer was, 'No, the time for censure is past. Now is the time for repression.'

Meanwhile, the army was also giving signals of discontent. The army commander General Cemal Gürsel, on holiday in the lead-up to his retirement, wrote a letter to the National Defence Minister Ethem Menderes, saying that the President and the government should step down. On 21 May War College students marched in protest down Atatürk Boulevard in Ankara, but the government's only reaction was to declare a holiday for the College.

Menderes was not persuaded by the efforts of the DP General Council and the DP Assembly Caucus to turn from his chosen path. Consequently, on 27 May 1960 the coup came. A junta consisting primarily of young officers and calling itself the National Unity Committee overthrew the government.

The National Unity Committee (1960–1)

The National Unity Committee (Milli Birlik Komitesi), the NUC, was composed of thirty-eight officers from all branches of the armed forces, and its President was General Cemal Gürsel, who was well-liked and respected by the military.

Members of the cabinet, Members of Parliament of the Democrat Party and many other DP members were arrested to be tried by the High Court of Justice composed of civilian judges at Yassıada, an island in the Sea of Marmara near İstanbul. Charges included corruption by government members, incitement of riots in İstanbul against Greeks during the Cyprus crisis in 1955, inciting attacks against RPP leaders, subverting the Constitution and using state utilities for partisan purposes. Many were found guilty and condemned, some to lighter, some to heavier sentences. Fourteen people were condemned to death, eleven of whom, including ex-President Celal Bayar (because of his advanced age), had their sentences commuted to life imprisonment. Death sentences against the ex-Prime Minister Adnan Menderes, the ex-Minister of Finance Hasan Polatkan and the ex-Foreign Minister Fatin Rüştü Zorlu were approved by the NUC and carried out.

The NUC wanted a new constitution promoting democracy to be drawn up and free elections to take place as soon as possible. However, within the NUC there was a group of fourteen members, headed by Alpaslan Türkeş, who were opposed to relinquishing power until certain reforms they deemed necessary had been accomplished. With a sudden internal coup on 13 November 1960 the fourteen were ousted from the NUC and sent to foreign posts.

On 6 January 1961 the Constituent Assembly began work. It was composed of the NUC and the Representative Assembly, the latter composed of members from parties other than the Democrat Party, from professional and business groups and from other non-governmental organisations. The new Constitution drawn up by the Constituent Assembly was ratified by a 9 July 1961 referendum drawing a vote of 60.4 per cent in favour. Elections took place in October employing the proportional electoral system. Although the RPP was the biggest party, it did not hold a majority of seats in the TGNA, and, up till the beginning of 1965 Turkey was governed by coalition governments with İnönü as Prime Minister.

The Democrat Party evaluated

The DP's strength lay in its ability to create activity and enthusiasm in economic development. Its defects were that in creating economic growth it lacked a development plan and consequently brought the Treasury to the verge of bankruptcy. This was very probably one of the factors that opened the way for the 27 May coup.

Other negative characteristics and policies of the DP, as pointed out above, included:

(1) its primitive or autocratic conception of democracy that did not recognise the rights of the opposition parties, and its policy of repression in general;
(2) its abolition of the People's Houses and Village Institutes, resulting in the erosion of cultural development;
(3) its attitude of being above the law, as exemplified by attempts made on İnönü's life and the 6/7 September incidents;
(4) its generally hostile relations with the opposition;
(5) its neglect of Turkish independence as seen in the series of bilateral agreements (some documented, some verbal) concluded with the United States, ensuring the latter a great latitude of action;
(6) In the sphere of religion, the RPP had already made certain concessions, but the DP took this much further, so that Menderes in particular became the great hope of the reactionaries.

In relation to point 4, DP adherents put the blame on İnönü for their ongoing strife. Certainly İnönü never ran from a fight, but since it was the party in power the onus of establishing better relations was on the leaders of the DP. For example, despite RPP-DP animosity during the 1946–50 RPP Administration, İnönü had made the effort to create an atmosphere conducive to warmer relations, which assumed material form in his 12 July Declaration. Menderes and Bayar seldom if ever, and then only on a superficial level, made any such effort. It is well known that polarisation had at that time divided the citizenry in neighbourhoods, villages, coffee houses and mosques, to such an extent that it endangered national consensus.

On the other hand, a positive aspect of the DP was its involvement of the common man in politics through its creation of local organisations, which was useful for the people's education in democracy. Even the RPP and other parties possibly experienced the positive effects of this development. However, this developing political awareness of DP grassroots supporters did not bring about any progress towards democratisation in the DP's own internal organisation, unlike the interesting and democratic development witnessed within the RPP.

When the RPP fell from power and became an opposition party many of its members, accustomed from the very first days of the Republic to being in power, vanished from public view. The party organisation fell apart at the seams, as though it had been disbanded. Such was the situation at the RPP eighth congress in June 1950. İnönü was re-elected President but his hand-picked candidate for General Secretary, Nihat Erim, was not elected. Instead the majority elected Kasım Gülek, a hand-shaking, friendly, pleasant personality. Despite the fact that İnönü, essentially a tradition-bound bureaucrat, did not much approve of this choice, Gülek had been elected by the delegates and as General Secretary, in turn, made an extraordinary effort to revive the party. Kasım Gülek remained General Secretary of the RPP till 1959, succeeding congresses refusing to give more power to the President or to central party organs. However, in 1959, when the RPP had become organisationally stronger, İnönü re-established his grip on the reins and Gülek was never again re-elected General Secretary.

Part V

MILITARY INTERVENTIONS AND THEIR AFTERMATHS

30

THE 1960s AND 1970s

The coup d'état of 27 May was equally a revolution broadening and consolidating the foundations of democracy established by Atatürk and İsmet İnönü. It brought about a reorganisation of government based on the 1961 Constitution, which retained concepts of the national pact and the earlier 1924 Constitution, such as the definition of all citizens of the Republic as Turks regardless of ethnicity or religion, and the right to vote and be elected on the basis of equality, while also establishing a new system of division of powers with checks and balances to prevent autocracy. Although a new constitution was drawn up after the 12 September 1980 coup, most of the institutions founded by the 1961 Constitution are still standing.

The 1961 Constitution established concepts and institutions such as the social state, the right to strike and collective bargaining, the pluralist approach, the Constitutional Court, the Supreme Judicial Council, the State Planning Organisation, Turkish Radio and Television and the Republican Senate. The Turkish Scientific and Technological Research Institute, the Export Development Centre and the National Productivity Centre may also be accredited to this period. The Constitutional Court is a check on the legislative system, an obstacle if not to the enactment at least to the implementation of laws passed at the whim of a temporary popular majority. The Supreme Judicial Council ensures the independence of the judiciary. The autonomy of Turkish Radio and Television (TRT) prevents radio and television from being used as vehicles of propaganda for whichever party happens to be in power. And the State Planning Organisation, though not empowered to prevent arbitrary investment, has at the very least the power to inhibit the implementation of fly-by-night schemes.

As time passed the opinion began to prevail that the upper house, the Republican Senate, was not a wholly positive creation because first, referral to the Senate greatly slowed down the legislative process, and secondly, Senate elections (for renewal of one-third of its members every two years) created a perpetual pre-election atmosphere. Hence, with the 1982 Constitution, the Republican Senate disappeared.

Though not included in the 1961 Constitution, the 27 May regime also brought in the proportional representation election system, a cornerstone of pluralism, which has been applied ever since. The institutions and principles of the 27 May 1960 revolution have been partly eroded by the counter-revolutionary coups of 12 March 1971 and 12 September 1980, but with the exception of the Senate they have not been completely eradicated.

Honour is due to İsmet İnönü and therefore to the Republican People's Party for firmly establishing the multi-party system in 1945. Turkey is also indebted to the NUC and therefore to the military for bringing about a more contemporary democracy, an honour which İnönü and the RPP also share in because the cultural and intellectual development of society necessary for such a change evolved under the influence of their 1950–60 struggle and, in a more substantial sense, their First Aims Declaration. In any event, the majority of the Constituent Assembly of 1961 was composed of members of the RPP or those who shared its views.

Another invaluable service in the name of democracy rendered by İnönü during his tenure as Prime Minister was his suppression of the two military coup attempts (22 February 1962 and 21 May 1963) undertaken by Talat Aydemir, an army officer who, unable to become a member of the National Unity Committee in 1960, later subscribed to the belief that the order which emerged from the 1961 regime was not sufficiently 'revolutionary'.

The inclination of the 27 May regime towards contemporary and pluralist democracy resulted in an important gain for Turkey as in time movements to the left of the RPP were afforded room to live and breathe. Hence in 1961 twelve trade unionists founded the Workers' Party of Turkey (Türkiye İşçi Partisi). Mehmet Ali Aybar became its leader in 1962. In their 1964 party programme the word 'socialism' could not yet be used, so the phrase 'pro-labour planned étatism' was employed. Later, however, the WPT was able to declare itself a socialist party.

In 1964, for the first time in many years, a poem by Nazım Hikmet was published, appearing in Doğan Avcıoğlu's *Yön* (Direction) magazine. Although this poem was selected because it was 'politically correct', the gesture of publishing a Communist poet's work was still progress for the freedom of the press.

On the eve of the 1965 elections, wary of losing votes to the WPT, the RPP declared itself to be 'left of centre'. This concept was gradually to evolve into 'social democracy' and 'democratic left'.

Pluralism also allowed the Islamist right gradually to establish itself and to form a political party. However, insofar as parties of this persuasion covertly or overtly uphold the system of the Sharia, for some it is a matter of dispute whether or not and to what degree their existence may be considered an advantage for democracy.

After the 27 May coup the Democrat Party was abolished by a court decision. Two parties emerged, the Justice Party (Adalet Partisi) and the New Turkey Party (Yeni Türkiye Partisi), both vying for the DP's vote potential, which was consequently divided between them in the 1961 election. Later the Justice Party (JP) under the leadership of Süleyman Demirel won over the whole of the DP's electorate and went on to win both the 1965 and the 1969 elections.

Though differing in some aspects, throughout the 1960s and 1970s the Justice Party was a continuation of the DP, mirroring its polarity with the RPP and the left in general until 1980. The NUC had a share in prolonging this polarity because of the executions of Menderes, Zorlu and Polatkan. By that time the death penalty had been or was being abandoned by contemporary society as an archaic method of punishment, awakening feelings of repugnance and pity for the condemned. In addition it served as a precedent for further political executions—of Talat Aydemir and his associate Fethi Gürcan, of Deniz Gezmiş and his associates, Hüseyin İnan and Yusuf Aslan, and the many executions which took place after the 12 September 1980 coup. Of course none of this should obscure the possible gravity of the actions for which they were being judged guilty.

The Justice Party continually took sides against the 1961 Constitution, a cornerstone of contemporary democracy in Turkey, and its campaign was to provide fuel for the 12 March 1971 and 12 September 1980 counter-revolutionary military coups.

In 1968, when university students, first in France, then in other countries throughout Europe and in the United States, rebelled against the status quo, a movement was touched off in Turkish universities too. However, while in other countries it soon faded, in Turkey it took root and was increasingly influenced by radical leftist ideology. Instead of taking legal action in the courts against this movement, the JP administration preferred to let it be understood that they favoured the activities of the radical right-wing youth organisations called 'komando' or 'ülkücü', who literally took up cudgels against the left.

At the time the parties of the left were having little success in elections. The RPP, with its slogan 'left of centre', saw its vote-share in the 1965 elections fall from 37 to 29% and the Workers' Party of Turkey gained only 3% of the vote, which translated to fifteen parliamentary seats thanks to the national balance system employed that year. In the 1969 elections both WPT and RPP results fell even further (2.6% for the former and 27% for the latter).

The 27 May 1960 coup had awakened hope in the leftist intelligentsia that a new progressive Turkey was about to be born, but after successive elections had dampened their expectations some began to abandon hope in the democratic process. Parliamentarianism was ridiculed as 'sweetie-pie democracy' and 'Filipino democracy' and talk of 'a non-parliamentary opposition' began, with some even entertaining hopes of a pro-socialist military coup. Doğan Avcıoğlu of the press and Mihri Belli, head of the National Democratic Revolution movement, were both of this persuasion, though from different standpoints.

Meanwhile the right-wing Justice Party had its own problems. It had emerged from the 1969 elections with 47% of the vote, but since then the economy had deteriorated to the point of stagnation. On 9 August 1970 the government was forced to resort to the first devaluation of the Turkish lira since 1958, causing the exchange rate of the US dollar to rise from 9 to 15 liras. Because it had become clear that the Demirel administration and the Justice Party as a whole favoured the industrial over the agricultural bourgeoisie, forty Deputies split from the JP to form the Democratic Party (Demokratik Parti) on 18 December 1970 with Ferruh Bozbeyli as the party leader. This exodus was occasioned by allegations of an 'imaginary exports' (hayali ihracat) racket concerning Demirel's nephew.

In 1970 the situation began to escalate, degenerating into violence and political instability. On 15–16 June workers brought life to a stop in İstanbul as they held demonstrations protesting against a draft law which would limit the activities of the Confederation of Revolutionary Labour Unions (DİSK—Devrimci İşçi Sendikaları Konfederasyonu). Student demonstrations were beginning to resemble 'urban guerrilla' type actions, manifested in bank robberies and anti-American acts. Universities too were the scene of major incidents. On 3 March 1971 the Turkish People's Liberation Army of Deniz Gezmiş and his fellow conspirators (university students in Ankara) abducted four American military officers. When security forces initiated a search for the missing persons in the Middle East Technical University campus, it became a battlefield of students versus security forces. Finally, the Chief of the General Staff and the Armed Forces' commanders handed the government the 12 March Memorandum (12 Mart Muhtırası), which held both the government and the Assembly responsible for the current situation in that they had failed to bring about the reforms specified by Atatürk and by the Constitution. It stated that Turkey was in need of a 'strong and trustworthy' supra-party government that could be depended on to bring about reform. In these circumstances Demirel resigned.

The 12 March 1971 coup

From these developments the general impression had formed that a left-wing coup was in the offing. However, a rumour began to circulate to the effect that a leftist coup had indeed been in preparation but that the 'top brass' had staged their own coup to block it. This rumour was substantiated by the fact that immediately after the coup took place the officers who had prepared the leftist coup—five generals, one admiral and thirty-five colonels—were relieved from duty. Nihat Erim, resigning from the RPP, formed a 'supra-party' government.

Eleven ministers became the brains trust that was to implement reform, while the government as a whole took on the task of trimming certain constitutional rights seen by Erim as 'luxuries'. Erim was in the position of having to satisfy the left while catering to the right, since the government still had to answer to and have laws passed by the National Assembly in which the Justice Party was the majority. In April the escalating terrorism of activist youth organisations of the left (called 'urban guerrillas') provided him with an excuse to tip the scales in favour of the right and martial law was declared.

Following the kidnapping of the Israeli Consul in İstanbul a curfew was established and private homes throughout the city were searched one by one. Leftist intellectuals, workers and university students were arrested and tried en masse. The brains trust wavered in the cabinet till December in expectation that some 'reforms' would be implemented, but it was becoming increasingly clear that this was a forlorn hope as long as the JP dominated the National Assembly and the conservative elements of the military (spoken of as the Cevdet Sunay-Memduh Tağmaç-Faik Türün junta) dominated the country. The brains trust resigned and Erim formed a new government.

All that remained was for the right-wing agenda to be completed, i.e. to suppress the left (later on, Ziverbey Kiosk in İstanbul, used as an interrogation centre, became known as the torture chamber), and to trim the Constitution. The resultant constitutional amendments curtailed basic rights and liberties: the autonomy of TRT was rescinded; the government was invested with the authority to issue decrees having the force of law (*kanun hükmünde kararname*); State Security Courts were formed; and the Workers' Party of Turkey and the National Order Party were shut down.

Momentous events were also taking place in the RPP. Following İnönü's announcement of the 'left of centre' policy, RPP votes in the 1965 and 1969 elections had fallen to an increasing degree. Strong criticism came from those who thought the two were connected. Bülent Ecevit, however, strenuously defended this policy and, moreover, wrote a book entitled *Left of the Centre*. At the 1966 RPP

Congress the left of centre won the day and Ecevit was elected Secretary-General. However, the RPP right wing, headed by Turhan Feyzioglu, initiated a harsh counter attack, but at the 1967 Extraordinary Fourth Congress it was defeated. Consequently forty-eight conservative RPP Deputies split off to found the Reliance Party (Güven Partisi), and the remaining right wing of the RPP undertook the struggle for party ascendancy under the leadership of Kemal Satır.

İsmet İnönü had initially looked askance at the 12 March 1971 coup, but with Nihat Erim emerging as Prime Minister he decided to support the government. This led İnönü and Ecevit to part ways, because Ecevit viewed the 12 March coup as a blow against the RPP 'left of centre', then on the verge of power, rather than against the Demirel administration. He therefore found it totally unacceptable to support this government and resigned from his position as General Secretary of the RPP in protest. İnönü thus took up a position on the right and thereafter cooperated with Kemal Satır's RPP conservative faction. However, the grassroots of the RPP sided with Ecevit.

This situation came to a head at the Extraordinary Fifth RPP Congress on 5 May 1972 when İnönü, during the vote of confidence for the Party Council debate, openly stated, 'It's either him or me'. The majority sided with Ecevit and the following day İnönü resigned from the chairmanship of the RPP after having occupied the position for thirty-three years. On 14 May Ecevit was elected Chairman. Kemal Satır and his supporters broke away and after trying to found their own party joined the Reliance Party.

In 1973 Cevdet Sunay's tenure as President was drawing to an end. The army intended Faruk Gürler, who was then Chief of General Staff, to be elected President. To this end Gürler resigned and was appointed to the Senate by Sunay. However, Ecevit and Demirel joined forces to ensure that retired Admiral Fahri Korutürk was elected rather than Gürler, signalling the end of the 12 March regime. That year parliamentary elections were held on 14 October.

The RPP emerged from the election as the biggest party with 33.3% of the votes and the Justice Party as second party with 29.8%. On the far right, the National Salvation Party (Milli Selamet Partisi), founded in place of the National Order Party, won forty-eight seats.

To general amazement, the RPP under Ecevit, recognised as the Kemalist party, formed a coalition government with the National Salvation Party, the most rightist and reputedly Islamist party (25 January 1974). The Ecevit government rescinded the prohibition on the cultivation of opium poppies (brought in by the Erim government at the behest of the United States) and granted amnesty to all who had been condemned during the 12 March administration.

In July 1974 Cyprus again became the critical issue in Turkish foreign affairs when, encouraged by the military dictatorship in Greece, whose aim was to bring about *Enosis,* the Cypriot EOKA carried out a coup in Cyprus, overthrowing the government of Archbishop Makarios. The situation of Turkish Cypriots became even more precarious. Turkey held meetings with Greek, British and US representatives, but to no avail, as no peaceful resolution to the situation could be reached. When it became apparent that the other guarantors of Cypriot independence intended to accept the coup as a *fait accompli,* and in the face of previous Greek massacres of the Turkish community, Turkey implemented its right to intervene as specified in the Zürich and London settlements.

On 20 July 1974 a Turkish expeditionary force landed in Girne (Kyrenia), overwhelming the forces of the Greek National Guard and accomplishing Turkey's First Peace Operation (Birinci Barış Harekatı). After a cease-fire had been called, a Turkish-Greek-British conference was held in Geneva with disappointing results. Thereupon the Turkish army carried out its Second Peace Operation on 14 August and took control of the northern territory which first became the Turkish Federated State of Cyprus on 13 February 1975. When negotiations with the Greek Cypriot administration failed, the independent Turkish Republic of Northern Cyprus was proclaimed on 15 November 1983. Meanwhile, in Greece the failure of Greek ambitions had led to the overthrow of the Colonels and the establishment of a civilian government under Constantine Karamanlis. Today Greece, in rejecting any viable solution to the situation, relies on Western prejudice against Turkey. Turkey, on the other hand, owing to its huge foreign debt and its weak international lobby in the United States (where minority groups pressure Congress) and in Europe, is unable to make itself heard in the international political arena. As a result, the Turkish Republic of Northern

Cyprus is to date recognised only by Turkey, whereas the separations that have occurred in the former Soviet Union, Yugoslavia and Czechoslovakia have been readily accepted by the international community.

The events in Cyprus led to two reactions. One was the campaign of assassinations organised by the Armenian ASALA terrorist organisation against Turkish diplomats. Thirty-four diplomats were murdered, ten were wounded. The perpetrators of a great proportion of those crimes were never brought to justice and the episode is an international scandal. However, in 1983, when the ASALA planted a bomb at Paris Orly Airport killing eight Turkish Airways passengers, some of whom were French citizens, not only were the perpetrators caught but, moreover, an abrupt halt was brought to ASALA terrorist activities. The second reaction to the Cyprus situation was the US arms embargo against Turkey which was continued until 26 September 1978.

In September 1974, no longer able to maintain the coalition with the National Salvation Party, Ecevit handed in his resignation, but the RPP was unable to find a suitable partner that would agree to an early election. Demirel's Justice Party, on the other hand, was unable to form a coalition of the right because the Democratic Party, vehemently opposed to Demirel as Prime Minister, refused to join with the JP. The result was a crisis lasting 213 days, throughout which government administration was undertaken by the supra-party Sadi Irmak cabinet, which had received seventeen votes of confidence. At last Demirel, adopting a policy of polarisation on the right and with the support of nine Deputies who had resigned from the Democratic Party, was able to form a coalition government calling itself the Nationalist Front. It allotted three cabinet seats to the extreme right Nationalist Movement Party (Milliyetçi Hareket Partisi) led by Alpaslan Türkeş (who had been one of the radical officers ousted by the NUC junta) despite the fact that they had only three seats in the National Assembly. This Nationalist Front was reminiscent of the Motherland Front of the Menderes era in that there was a sense that those who did not participate were under a cloud.

Indeed, after the 12 March regime came to an end in 1973 violence broke out again between left and right movements inside and outside the universities. When the armed activists of one side became dominant in a faculty they refused the other side entrance to the campus, thus preventing them from attending classes. From time to time bloody incidents took place. In many cases the university administration, the police and the judiciary refrained from interfering.

Demirel passed off these incidents with a facade of nonchalance, remarking, on demonstrations that 'the roads are not worn out by walking,' but in fact he continued to favour radical groups of the right. Violent actions against Ecevit were perpetrated such as those which took place at the Gerede RPP meeting in 1975 and at the Taksim Meeting and at Çiğli Airport in İzmir, leading up to the 1977 elections. Again in 1977 'unknown perpetrators' opened fire at a 1 May meeting of the Confederation of Revolutionary Labour Unions (DİSK) in İstanbul and in the ensuing panic thirty-four people died in the crush.

The RPP emerged from the 1977 elections as the largest party, with a higher percentage of the vote than in 1973 (41.4%). However, this was still insufficient to form a government on its own. When an RPP minority cabinet was unable to win a vote of confidence, Demirel formed the Second Nationalist Front, which lasted for only five months, after which Ecevit 'transferred' eleven Deputies from the Justice Party (each of whom was made a cabinet minister), thereby managing to form a government in January 1978 that lasted until October 1979. The Ecevit government was confronted by major economic and political problems. In October 1973 the world fuel crisis had exploded, giving rise to large increases in the price of petrol and related products. In Turkey consecutive administrations, including that of Ecevit, fearing negative reactions from the electorate, were careful not to pass these increases on to the consumer. To avoid doing so, Demirel resorted to a high interest rate method of procuring funds called a convertible deposit account (*dövize çevrilebilir mevduat*), thereby incurring a huge increase in foreign debt. The cumulative result of this policy was shortages of basic necessities such as cooking oil and calor gas.

Meanwhile, violent incidents were on the increase. On 22 December 1978, for undetermined reasons, the security forces of the state were unable to bring violent outbreaks in Kahramanmaraş under control and the incidents seemed to approach the level of civil war. One hundred and nine people died and 500 private homes and places of business were destroyed. The events were described as political conflict between right and left, but in actual fact the conflict was between Alevi and Sunni Muslims and the result of a longtime neglect of secularism. In the cities terrorist incidents were no longer confined to student or youth organisations. Many people on the left and right, prominent persons such as trade unionists, public prosecutors, professors, journalists and directors of police were attacked or murdered, in many cases by persons unknown. Some of the victims who were not of any radical persuasion, had not taken sides in the left-right struggle. A great proportion of these crimes remain unsolved or, as in the case of the renowned editor of *Milliyet*, Abdi İpekçi, the murderers somehow could not be kept behind bars.

In October 1979, when the RPP lost the interim election, Bülent Ecevit resigned as Prime Minister and Demirel formed the new government with a Justice Party minority cabinet. Because it had support from other parties of the right, it was known as the Third Nationalist Front or 'the veiled Nationalist Front'. This administration had no choice but to implement a stability programme to revive the stricken economy. Turgut Özal, who had worked for the World Bank from 1971 to 1973 and who at the time was Undersecretary to the Prime Minister and Acting Undersecretary for the State Planning Organisation, was made responsible for creating a package of measures for economic stability known as the 24 January Decisions (1980). As a result, the Turkish lira was devalued, from 47 to 70 Turkish liras to the US dollar, the prices of products of public enterprises were to be determined in a free market and the economy was set on the path of becoming export-oriented. For this economic package to work it was essential to freeze workers' wages, which was difficult to achieve within a pluralist context. However, the 12 September 1980 coup facilitated the implementation of the 24 January Decisions, particularly with regard to the restriction of wage increases. It was no surprise when, during the Bülent Ulusu Administration, installed by the 12 September coup, Turgut Özal was made Minister of State in charge of the economy and Deputy Prime Minister. He was to become Prime Minister in 1983.

Violence and terrorism continued unabated. The Chief of the General Staff, General Kenan Evren, who was to head the 12 September 1980 coup, was to complain that approximately twenty persons per day, a total of 5,241 people, had died as a result of terrorism in the previous two years. Another situation cited by Evren as a reason for the coup was a crisis which arose after Fahri Korutürk's term as President was over, namely the inability of the TGNA, despite countless vote-taking, to elect a new President of the Republic. This had indeed degenerated into a major farce. The Justice Party and the RPP either were unable or chose not to agree on a suitable presidential candidate. It suited JP interests to refrain from accepting a compromise candidate, because according to the Constitution, İhsan Sabri Çağlayangil of the JP, as president of the Senate, was also acting President of the Republic. In any event, both parties had made it a matter of principle never to reach an understanding on any subject at all.

31

THE EIGHTIES

The 12 September 1980 coup

In the small hours of 12 September, the Turkish armed forces led by General Kenan Evren staged the third military coup in the history of the Turkish Republic. This coup was to be much more radical than the previous one. The government and Parliament were dissolved. The leaders of the main political parties—Demirel, Ecevit, Erbakan and Türkeş—were detained, and martial law was proclaimed throughout the country. The chiefs of staff of the four armed forces (army, navy, air force and gendarmerie), under their leader Evren, formed the National Security Council (NSC) and became the centre of supreme executive and legislative authority. By the end of 1981 the NSC had enacted 268 laws of which fifty-one were entirely new, the remainder being modifications of existing ones. On 16 October 1981 the regime was further stiffened by the dissolution of all political parties. It is said that if Demirel and Ecevit had made common cause at least after the coup, the military regime would have been forced to be more moderate. If this is true, their responsibility for their confrontational policies becomes much heavier.

The objective of the military regime was to end the 'state of anarchy' existing before 12 September. The assumption was that this condition was the result of the 'extreme' freedoms, the checks and balances established by the 1961 Constitution. It will be recalled that the same rationale lay behind the 12 March coup, which the military clearly thought had not been drastic enough. Now, with the complete overhaul of the legal system and a new constitution to crown it, an entirely new era of 'disciplined democracy' was to be initiated.

On 29 June 1981 a new law was enacted which established the constituent assembly, to be composed of two houses—the NSC and the Consultative Assembly. The members of the latter were to be chosen by the NSC from among non-partisan university graduates and would be in a consultative capacity. Its main function was to draft a new constitution, but the NSC was to give the constitution its final form. The resulting document strongly reflected the views of the junta. The executive was to be much stronger. Governments would now be able to issue decrees having the force of law (KHK), and the President of the Republic, while still remaining politically not responsible, was invested with a whole array of powers which his predecessors had lacked. The section concerning the rights and liberties of citizens seemed to emphasise not the rights and liberties, but the exceptions to them. The provision making religious courses in the schools compulsory was a blow to secularism. State universities, which for many decades had enjoyed academic and administrative autonomy, were now deprived of the latter. All universities were to be centrally administered by a Council of Higher Education (CHE) whose members were to be appointed by the President of the Republic (seven members), the council of ministers (seven), the Inter-University Council of rectors (seven) and the Chief of General Staff (one). The President of the Republic was to designate one of the Council members as president of that body, a kind of all-powerful 'super-rector'. University rectors were to be appointed by the President of the Republic, and faculty deans by CHE. (The details were filled out by the law of Higher Education—YÖK.) All chairmen, directors etc. were to be appointed, not elected, and all bodies, councils and faculty meetings were to be in a consultative capacity.

Another authoritarian aspect of the 12 September regime was the Law of Associations. The functioning of associations was subjected to strict and detailed rules, and all sorts of paperwork, with fines and other penalties in case of contravention. The fact that the police were charged with supervising the activities of associations further aggravated the situation. The net result was discouragement for those who wanted to form associations and for those who wanted to continue already existing ones.

The problem in Turkey is that, despite the twenty years that have elapsed, these undemocratic aspects of the legal system set up by the 12 September coup have more or less remained. The reason for this is the fact that the multi-party system, during its more than half-century history, has always worked in favour of the right. The left was never able to exceed the 41 % of the vote it obtained in the 1977 elections in the person of the RPP. The right has always had a rock-solid majority of about at least 60 %. Neither the RPP or any of the other leftist parties has ever been able to come to power except as a partner in a coalition with the right or by 'transferring' deputies from rightist parties, as in 1978, taking advantage of the divisions in the right. The right has never been much interested in democracy, except for the bare minimum of multi-party politics, which enables it to come to power. It hated the 12 March and 12 September coups which seemingly were against rightist governments, but was delighted by the rightist and authoritarian policies and measures which these coups ushered in, and has not been in the least inclined to reverse them when it came to power. Alpaslan Türkeş, leader of the Nationalist Movement Party (NMP), which appeared to take the Spanish regime of Francisco Franco as its model, and some of his colleagues spent four and a half years under arrest after the 1980 coup. They are said to have observed that they themselves might be behind bars, but their ideas were in power.

Lately, the European Union, taking advantage of Turkey's application for membership, has been forcing the Turkish government to democratise in conformity with the so-called 'Copenhagen criteria'. However, this democratisation has been piecemeal and been guided mainly by EU interests, so that many of the imperfections of the 12 September regime remain.

On 7 November 1982 a referendum was held for the new Constitution. It was ordained that a favourable vote for the Constitution would also signify the election of Evren as President of the Republic for a period of seven years. Propaganda in favor of the Constitution was allowed and Evren himself led the campaign, but propaganda against it was forbidden. Electors who did not vote were to lose their voting rights and eligibility for a period of five years. As for the presidency, Evren was the only candidate. 91% of the electorate voted in favour of the Constitution, and we can safely assume that a large proportion of these votes were cast in order to end Evren's military government.

The coup had ended the state of so-called 'anarchy' and the bloodletting that went along with it. But the human cost was high. Some of the figures are staggering: 650,000 persons were detained, 230,000 were tried, 517 received a death sentence, and forty-nine were executed. 171 persons died as the result of torture. About 30,000 people lost their jobs because they were considered 'unreliable', and 30,000 fled the country. Journalists were condemned to a total of 3,315 years in prison. With the knowledge and perhaps the cooperation of Professor İhsan Doğramacı, whom Evren had appointed President of the CHE and who had been the architect of the new university system, scores of academics, generally those known to belong to the left, were summarily dismissed by order of martial law commanders. Others were dismissed by university authorities, while a good number resigned in protest. As a result, universities lost hundreds of their best senior staff. Fortunately a good number of them were able to return years later. Trade unions fared no better. Two trade union confederations, DİSK and MİSK, together with their affiliated unions, were closed down. Many union members were prosecuted and convicted. As a result of this repression and IMF-style economic policies, the purchasing power of wages and salaries dropped drastically and began to pick up only towards the end of the 1980s. Commenting later on the sudden restoration of order on 12 September, Demirel voiced his suspicions, apparently suggesting that perhaps the disorder before that date might have been at least partly 'engineered' to provide a pretext for the coup.

There was an important ideological dimension to the regime. We saw earlier that during the 12 March 1971 coup there had been a left-right struggle within the army, with the right gaining preponderance. Apparently this swing had continued in the 1970s, with the result that Evren and most of the army were now thinking, probably with encouragement from the United States, that Islam was the best remedy for communism. Thus the suppression of the left was accompanied by an effort to fabricate a new ideology, the so-called 'Turkish-Islamic' synthesis. Compulsory religious education, building Sunni mosques in Alevi (a heterodox Islamic faith) villages, and the appointment of university rectors and other academic personnel from among extreme conservative groups (including religious brotherhoods) were implementations of that idea. Evren himself, a voluble speaker, often used religious references in his pronouncements while at the same time professing to be an enthusiastic and loyal Kemalist.

Indeed, it was decreed that all universities were to have a course entitled 'Principles of Kemalism and History of the Revolution' in every year of their programme. Hitherto this had been a course given during one year only of the whole academic programme. Handpicked rightists—therefore basically anti-Kemalists—were designated to teach the course. All this hypocrisy so exasperated Nadir Nadi, a well-known Kemalist and editor of the newspaper *Cumhuriyet* (Republic), that he published a book entitled *I am not a Kemalist*.

International reactions to the regime were varied. The US government, dismayed by the Soviet invasion of Afghanistan in 1979 and the Islamic revolution in Iran and fearful of developments in Turkey, welcomed the coup. The presence of General Tahsin Şahinkaya, commander of the Air Force, in Washington one day before the coup seems to indicate that the coup had the direct blessing of the United States. Europe on the other hand was cold towards it and the Council of Europe placed certain restrictions on Turkey's representation there.

On 1 January 1981, Greece was admitted to the European Economic Community (EEC). In spite of Turkey's unconditional acceptance of Greece's return to the military wing of NATO in 1980, the coming to power of Andreas Papandreou's PASOK in the same year exacerbated the thorny problems between Turkey and Greece. These were the questions of territorial waters, sharing the continental shelf (many Greek islands being on Anatolia's continental shelf), the FIR (Flight Information Region) line, and the arming of certain Greek islands which had been demilitarised under the Treaty of Lausanne in 1923. These were questions mainly concerning the Aegean region. Then there was the problem of minorities (Turkish in Eastern Thrace, Greek in İstanbul) and, of course, the Cyprus question. To prevent the extension by Greece of its territorial waters to 12 miles, Turkey declared that such an act would be cause for war. When intercommunal talks in Cyprus got nowhere and Greece began to increase its efforts to carry the question to international fora, the Turkish Cyprus administration proclaimed its independence (15 November 1983). Because the Evren administration was being shunned by Western Europe, it chose to develop relations with socialist and Third World countries, including those belonging to the Islamic Conference Organisation.

Return to party life

In the spring of 1983, the junta decided to end the freeze on political life. However, great care had been taken to ensure that the evils of the former era should not recur. To that end, for instance, the political freedom of the leadership of the former political parties was shackled. To prevent a proliferation of parties, a barrier of 10% was set up. Any party getting less than 10% of the national total of votes would not be represented in Parliament. This barrier, the nightmare of smaller parties, has remained until today. New parties were formed, but they encountered Sisyphean difficulties. Some were closed because they resembled the former Justice Party or the RPP. Many founders and many parliamentary candidates were vetoed and replacements had to be found. In the end three parties were able to take part in the election: the Motherland (Anavatan) Party led by Turgut Özal, the Populist (Halkçı) Party led by Necdet Calp, and the Nationalist Democracy (Milliyetçi Demokrasi) Party led by Turgut Sunalp. All these three party leaders could be considered close to the military regime. Özal had been a minister in the Ulusu government. Necdet Calp was a high-level bureaucrat in the Prime Minister's department. Turgut Sunalp was a retired general. Evren's preference was Sunalp's party, and just before the election he declared in a TV broadcast that people should not vote for the Motherland Party (MP). It is impossible to measure the exact effect of this pronouncement, but at any rate the MP got 45% of the vote and a little more than half the seats in the Assembly. The Populist Party got 30.5% and the Nationalist Democracy Party 23% of the vote. Özal, a great pragmatist, had no trouble embracing Evren when he went to visit him at the presidential palace. On the whole he and his government did not have too much difficulty getting along with Evren and the army. His too familiar manners and speech, his closeness to Islamism (in 1977 he had been a candidate of the Islamist National Salvation Party and his brother Korkut was one of the leaders of that party), his lack of interest in culture, his laxity towards corruption and his readiness to cut corners (he seldom held cabinet meetings) raised eyebrows in many quarters, but ideologically he was on the same wavelength as Evren.

In 1983 the last outrage perpetrated by the Armenian terrorist organisation ASALA took place, marking the end of its assassination campaign. However, the next year Turkey faced a new threat: the beginning of terrorism by the PKK (Kurdistan Labour Party). This was a Marxist group operating in a feudal, tribal environment, led by Abdullah Öcalan. It emerged as a small group in Ankara, but was soon engaged in terrorising certain Kurdish tribes and other left-wing organisations in southeastern Anatolia. After thus carrying out quite a number of killings, on 15 August 1984 it raided two towns, attacking army and police buildings. This was an attack on the state itself, but apparently the Özal government did not take the matter very seriously (he was having a holiday and did not deem it necessary to cut it short). In fact, the affair dragged on till 1999 and was the cause of over 30,000 deaths. The dead are only one aspect. There was also the misery of living under the threat of terror, the devastation of villages, the end of stockbreeding which was the mainstay of the eastern provinces, the curtailment of many freedoms under state-of-emergency conditions, the drain on the Treasury which could have been employed in development, a large-scale migration to the cities, and so on.

A state of emergency was declared only in 1987. The PKK operated in small groups in very rugged terrain, employing hit-and-run tactics and—astonishingly—enjoying safe haven in Syria and northern Iraq, and it was therefore difficult to bring the struggle to a speedy end. Öcalan was said to be living in a villa in Damascus, and he had training camps in the Bekaa valley which was in Lebanese territory controlled by the Syrians. There were other complicating factors: in certain circles in Europe there was a tendency to see the PKK not as a terrorist organisation but as an organisation fighting for freedom—a tendency strengthened by the restrictions on use of the Kurdish language and other imperfections of Turkey's democracy. Thus the PKK could easily get organised among the Kurds in Europe, securing every kind of support for its operations. Lastly, Operation Provide Comfort, while it gave comfort to the Kurds in northern Iraq, also seemed to give comfort to the PKK. Following the Gulf War of 1991 the Iraqis mounted an operation against the rebellious Kurds in northern Iraq, and in the ensuing panic half a million refugees flocked to the Turkish border. At Turkey's request the Operation mentioned above was organised to aid in the provision of food and shelter. Later the refugees were persuaded to return to their homes. However, it was thought necessary to continue the Operation (Operation-2) in the form of a US-British-French air force group which would patrol northern Iraqi skies (1991), but it became apparent that the Operation was not only encouraging the Kurds to take steps to form an autonomous Kurdish state, but was encouraging the PKK to step up its activities from camps in northern Iraq. Thus the number of terrorist incidents, which had been 160 in 1984 and 1,494 in 1991, jumped to 5,717 in 1993 and 6,357 in 1994.

On the internal political scene, the electorate started to undo what the military regime had done. In the local elections of 25 March 1984 the Motherland Party retained its percentage of the vote. But the Populist Party got only 8% and the Nationalist Democracy Party 6.5% of the vote. On the other hand, two 'new' parties, the Social Democratic Party (SDP) and the True Path Party (TPP), received 22% and 13% respectively. The SDP was being led by Erdal İnönü, a well-mannered, moderate physics professor and son of the well-known İsmet İnönü. With a leader with that family name the electorate had no trouble identifying the SDP with the RPP. Former JP voters, on the other hand, seemed divided between the MP and the TPP. The SDP and the Populist Party did what was sensible; at the end of 1985 the two united under the name of Social Democratic Populist Party (SDPP). Meanwhile the erstwhile RPP leader Bülent Ecevit's wife, Rahşan Ecevit, founded the Democratic Left Party (DLP) under her own leadership. Like Demirel, Ecevit—according to an article of the Constitution—had been banned from politics for ten years, but because of the high degree of factionalism within the RPP, he had decided to go his own way.

Pressure to lift the political bans was mounting. The SDPP took the initiative for a constitutional amendment. Özal could not resist the pressure, but he called for a referendum on the subject and he and his party openly campaigned against the lifting of the ban. Ending the ban, he proclaimed, was 'nostalgia for anarchy'. This was exactly Evren's line. The result was a very slender majority for lifting the ban (6 September 1987). The former political leaders flocked back into politics as the leaders of the new parties that their supporters had founded—Demirel, Ecevit, Türkeş, Erbakan. Özal then made two moves. He called for early elections (one year before they were due) and rigged the electoral law in his own favour. Elections were held on 29 November 1987. The MP got 36%, the SDPP 25%, and the TPP 19% of the vote. Özal must have been very fond of manipulation, for he called an extraordinary meeting of the Assembly in order to amend the Constitution, to enable local elections to be held five months in advance of when they were due. Because he could not muster a big enough majority, the issue had to be referred to a referendum which he lost in spite of his threats to resign (in the event, he did not). The downward slide of the MP was gaining momentum.

The local elections of 26 March 1989 confirmed Özal's fears. Despite his threat of resignation, the MP took third place: 28% of votes went to the SDPP, 26% to the TPP and 22% to the MP. The SDPP was in a state of euphoria. They had won the mayoralties of the most important cities: Ankara, İstanbul, İzmir, Adana.

With Evren's presidency nearing its end in November 1989, Özal executed another manoeuvre. Some wanted an amendment to the Constitution which would allow Evren a second term. İnönü was opposed to this. Demirel wanted the president to be elected by the people, instead of by the Assembly. As November drew near, Özal became a candidate. Given the MP's majority in the Assembly, he was sure to be elected. However, the idea that the president should be non-partisan and elected by a more or less consensual vote had circulated since the beginning of multi-partyism. Also the idea of Özal occupying the position once held by Atatürk scandalised many minds. At one point the TPP favoured the idea of the opposition deputies collectively resigning from the Assembly in protest. However, İnönü was opposed to the idea, although the opposition did boycott the election. It can be said that a collective resignation would have been somewhat contrary to the atmosphere of non-confrontational politics which had prevailed after 1980. Özal was elected on 31 October 1989.

With Özal in the presidency the leadership of the MP and the post of prime minister had become vacant. Özal designated Yıldırım Akbulut, President of the Assembly, as his successor. Akbulut was a rather insignificant, ponderous person; as İnönü put it, it was clear that Özal was going to continue his government by 'remote control'. The TPP boycotted the vote of confidence. As expected, Özal took a very active interest in the affairs of government—so active, in fact, that it is argued whether or not the Turkish system of government, which according to the Constitution was parliamentary, had not during his presidency been converted into a semi-presidential system (as in France) in practice. Özal's close interest in his former party continued, to the extent that in 1991 he had his wife Semra Özal elected chair of the party in the province of İstanbul. Eventually Özal himself came to the decision that Akbulut was not an asset for the MP, and at the Party Congress on 15 January 1991 he supported the candidacy of Mesut Yılmaz, who was elected leader and became Prime Minister. Yılmaz, sharper than Akbulut, was also more independent of Özal. However, public pressure for an early election was high, so that the government and the Assembly decided to hold early elections on 20 October 1991.

The economics of the 1980s

There were, and are, many who think that Özal was a genius, that he was one of the most remarkable statesmen to have come to power in Turkey. This admiration focuses on his economic policies. For many decades Turkey had lived in a more or less controlled economy. Privatisation of public enterprises, the lifting of exchange controls and the fact that you could buy or sell foreign exchange in any one of the myriad countless exchange 'buffets' which sprang up in the cities like newspaper and cigarette kiosks, the setting up of a major stock exchange in İstanbul (1986)—these were things which would not have been easy to imagine a few years before. Özal's courage and determination cannot be doubted, but what he did was not very original. These were the years of Reagan and Thatcher, globalisation and neo-liberalism. Coming as he did from the World Bank (1971–3), he was well aware of the formulas of the Bank and the IMF. His policies were new only in Turkey. As to their value, this has to be measured by the results for the Turkish people.

These policies started with the 24 January 1980 decisions described above. The 12 September regime prohibited strikes, abolished many trade unions and discouraged the rest, and wages were adjusted not through collective bargaining but through decisions of the High Council of Arbitration. Wages and salaries were more or less frozen while a wild inflationary process was under way. The same is true of agricultural subsidies. On the other hand, the freeing of interest rates in July 1980 caused an explosion of small banking firms trying to attract deposits with increasing interest rates. Rates became so high that many people sold their houses, land and other property to take advantage of these rates. In mid-1982 the whole system crashed, causing untold misery to thousands of people. This led to Özal's resignation from the military government. To keep the economy on an export-oriented course the Turkish lira was subject to devaluation on a daily basis. The result has been an endemic, very high rate of inflation that has lasted for more than two decades. At the time of this writing, a dollar is valued at about 1,600,000 Turkish liras.

Where investment was concerned, Özal's policy was to concentrate on energy, communications, motorways, and urban public works. The country's telephone system was remarkably improved and developed. The building of expensive motorways became a priority; Özal is said to have identified railways with communism, but the neglect of railways relative to motor roads has a long history in Turkey dating back to the 1950s. The second bridge across the Bosphorus, the Fatih Sultan Mehmet Bridge, was completed in 1988. The financial resources of municipalities were increased, enabling them to expand investment in public works. Like Menderes and Demirel before him, Özal was carefree in his financial policies: in addition to foreign debts, he stepped up domestic borrowing, issuing Treasury bonds at ever higher rates of interest, which were sold to the banks and the public. Naturally, foreign investors also took an interest in these bonds. Banking became an increasingly lucrative business. What is more, most of the income accruing from financial investments was (and is) tax-free. It is estimated that in 1993 over 40% of bank profits stemmed from investment in Treasury bonds. The same percentage for the 500 largest firms in 1991–2 was 45%. To increase their investments in such bonds some banks borrowed from abroad. It is often asserted that tax evasion is a widespread phenomenon, that tax controls are not very effective, that not enough personnel are hired to prevent evasion, and that they are not properly directed.

Because Turkey lacked a powerful capitalist class, much of the investment had to be made by the state. After 1980, when privatisation became a global fashion, Özal fell in step, and especially after

1985 a major effort was made to this end. Unfortunately results have often not been very positive. For example, some public concerns and factories have been undervalued and sold to favourites. In others the factory has been pulled down and its land used for real estate development, leading to unemployment and impoverishment. The fact that certain public concerns are making losses is often a poor excuse for privatisation, because these losses are often the result of the government's own mismanagement.

The resurgence of Kemalism

An important development towards the end of the 1980s was the resurgence of Kemalism as an ideology. As is to be expected, there is a lot of love and admiration for Atatürk in Turkey. Visitors who come to the country for the first time are often struck by his 'omnipresence'. His name is everywhere, and pictures, busts and statues are everywhere. That is because he is the sole symbol of the Kemalist Revolution, which brought modernity to Turkey. I referred to the love and admiration of the Turks for him. However, it is also true that love and admiration are an impediment to real understanding. Two developments raised the level of understanding of Atatürk. One was Evren's policy of presenting his un-Kemalist, even anti-Kemalist moves as Kemalism; as was mentioned above, this exasperated discerning Kemalists like Nadir Nadi. Secondly, a group of writers, first labelled 'proponents of civil society' and later 'second republicans', accepted Evren's understanding of Kemalism at face value and together with him they criticised Atatürk. Soon an alliance developed between these circles and the Islamists, their aversion to Atatürk being their common ground. This was very disturbing for Kemalists, and provoked them into making an effort to understand what Atatürk actually stood for. The result was the analysis given in Chapter 26.

This new consciousness did not stop there. Kemalism began to be forged into an ideology that would be a basis for social or political action. The concrete manifestation of this development was the founding by Professor Muammer Aksoy and his friends on 19 May 1989 of the Association of Kemalist Thought. About seven months later Aksoy was assassinated; apparently the crystalisation of Kemalism into an ideology and an organisation had been perceived as a

292 The Eighties

grave threat to the *status quo*. The same year Çetin Emeç, general coordinator of *Hürriyet* (a daily newspaper, usually with the highest circulation), Turan Dursun and Professor Bahriye Üçok were also assassinated. All were more or less Kemalists, and the assassins seemed to vanish into thin air. When in 1993 Uğur Mumcu, a well-known journalist who used to investigate cases of corruption, also fell victim to this wave of killings, his funeral in Ankara was transformed into a mammoth demonstration. In 1999 Professor Ahmet Taner Kışlalı was a new victim. Only in the year 2000, ten years after the death of Aksoy, was a group of rather miserable men arrested as the presumed assassins of these Kemalists. They have been convicted, but justice can only be considered to have been done when those who activated and shielded them through all those years are identified and brought to account. Meantime the Association of Kemalist Thought has become the country's largest civil society organisation with more than 500 branches and nearly 100,000 members (in 2002).

Aspects of foreign policy

Relations with Bulgaria rapidly deteriorated when the Zhivkov administration suddenly decided in December 1984 to stamp out the cultural identity of the country's Turkish minority (about 900,000 or 10% of the total population). They were forced to adopt Bulgarian names, Turkish publications and their sale were banned, and Turkish cemeteries were destroyed. The Bulgarian government also wanted Turkey to open its doors to the forced emigration of Bulgarian Turks. Özal, in defiance, complied and the result was a huge exodus of about 300,000 of them. This naturally created a big problem for Turkey, so that the border was again closed to immigration. The situation of the Bulgarian Turks improved only with the end of the Communist regime at the beginning of 1990. They were even able to form their own political party.

On 14 April 1987 the Özal government applied to the European Community for membership. The Commission report on the application, which came out at the end of 1989 and which was adopted by the EC Council of Ministers, was on the whole negative. It stressed the problems of the Turkish economy (inflation, unemployment, structural differences etc.) and the political problems (human rights, problems of democracy, unresolved issues with Greece). However, it did not close the door and suggested that a customs union would be an important step in the right direction. The sheer size of Turkey and the great cultural and religious differences from the European norm which it represented also probably played an important part in the European decision.

The breakdown of the Soviet system in 1989 had important repercussions for Turkey. In the first place it freed the Turkish psyche from an almost pathological obsession, the danger of Communism, which had been the result of intense internal and external 'cultivation'. In the second place, it opened up the perspective of warm and mutually beneficial relations with Russia in all areas. Thirdly, it opened the door of close cooperation with the Turkic republics of the former Soviet Union. These relations are not perhaps as close as some romantic Turanists had imagined. It was realised, for instance, that the peoples of these republics, with the exception of Azerbaijan, speak languages that are akin to Turkish but different from it. In this some have been disappointed but nevertheless these relations seem promising.

32

THE NINETIES

The Gulf War

On 2 August 1990 Iraqi forces occupied Kuwait, and as Iraq's neighbour Turkey was closely affected. Özal, who seemed all along to have toyed with the idea of expansion (named New Ottomanism), enthusiastically entered the fray. He is reported to have said laconically, in gambler's fashion, 'We shall place one, and we shall take five'. He declared that the map of the Middle East would be redrawn and he wanted Turkey to be present in that process. It is said that he had an eye on Mosul and its petroleum. This was a complete break with the Kemalist tradition of extreme caution in foreign policy and good relations with neighbours. When the Security Council decided on 6 August to impose an embargo on Iraq, Turkey was the first to respond (the next day) by closing down the Kirkuk-Yumurtalık oil pipeline and stopping commercial transactions with Iraq. On 12 August the TGNA gave its authorisation to the employment of the armed forces in operations beyond the borders. Curiously Özal felt the necessity to extract a similar decision from the TGNA on 5 September. Meanwhile, public opinion was being kept informed that Özal was conducting a very active telephone diplomacy with foreign statesmen, including President George H.W. Bush. Prime Minister Akbulut and Foreign Minister Ali Bozer were wellnigh non-existent during the whole affair. No Turkish official was allowed to be present during Özal's negotiations with the US Secretary of State James Baker in August and President Bush in November. The United States was asking for Turkish support in three matters. First, it wanted to use Turkish air bases against Iraq; second, it wanted a military concentration on Iraq's borders, to force Iraq to divide its forces; and third, it wanted Turkey to send a contingent to the Allied force assembling in Saudi Arabia. Turkey complied with the first two requests: it massed 180,000 troops on the border, thus tying down eight Iraqi divisions. Özal got bogged down in trying to comply with the third request. His unconstitutional, high-handed and adventurous conduct was causing an uproar. The opposition and many newspapers were criticising him. There was unrest not only in the cabinet, but also in the MP. Last but not least, the army was against him. In October first Ali Bozer and then the Defence Minister Sefa Giray resigned. On 3 December the Chief of the General Staff General Necip Torumtay resigned after announcing that he could not continue to serve since what he was being asked to do went against his principles and his conception of public service. This last resignation looked like a return of the military to politics after the end of the military regime. However, this was a protest rather then an assertion of power, and it had a good deal of popular support. On the whole the Gulf War was a disaster for Turkey. The UN embargo imposed on Iraq did not allow a restoration of commercial relations. An official source estimated Turkey's total economic losses in Iraq at US$100 billion in 2000. After the war a number of compensatory measures were taken by the United States and certain Arab countries vis-à-vis Turkey, but these were on a minimal scale. Perhaps even more important than the economic aspect, the war exacerbated the Kurdish problem, as was explained earlier.

The elections of 20 October 1991

After eight years in power the MP lost these elections and thus Turkey took one more step away from the 12 September regime, with which Özal had been more or less associated. The winner of the election was Demirel's TPP which received 27% of the vote. The MP was placed second with 24% of the vote and the SDPP only third with 21%. This result was an unpleasant surprise for the SDPP, which had won the local elections in 1989. It is not easy to pinpoint the exact causes of such a sudden swing, but an explanation might be a popular preference for Demirel over Erdal İnönü. Demirel, who was trying to project a father image, was a better speaker and a master of demagogy. He promised almost everything—two keys (for a house and car), green cards (free health care), reducing inflation to

10% in 500 days. The SDPP had made an electoral alliance with the People's Labour Party, which was understood to be a Kurdish party. This alliance may have increased the SDPP's vote in some quarters, but it may also have decreased its vote in others. What was worse, some of the People's Labour Party deputies turned their swearing-in ceremonies into manifestations of Kurdish nationalism. The SDPP was obliged to demand their resignation from the Party.

Demirel formed a coalition government with the SDPP—a momentous event. He and his party had chosen as partner not the MP, with which they had a strong ideological affinity, but the SDPP, because being co-victims of the 12 September regime was more important. The event was also historically important, because it was as if the TPP, heir to the Democrat and Justice Parties, was being finally reconciled with the SDPP as heir to the RPP. The programme of the government raised high hopes. A new constitution was to be prepared and all the legislation of 12 September was to be reviewed to democratise the regime, including the prevention of torture, restoration of labour and trade union rights, a more independent judiciary, the repeal of the Law of Higher Education and the restoration of autonomy in the universities. Unfortunately the record of the TPP-SDPP government was to be disappointing. Instead of a new constitution, it was only able to achieve one amendment, which dealt with the lifting of the state monopoly in radio and television. A few laws were amended, including the Law of Penal Procedure, and the parties dissolved by 12 September were revived. The resurrected RPP elected Deniz Baykal as its chairman. Özal made all sorts of difficulties for the government, and it responded by legislating certain 'by-pass' laws.

The presidency of Demirel, the premiership of Çiller
On 17 April 1993 Özal had a heart attack, as the result of which he died. About a month later (16 May) Demirel was elected President with İnönü's support. İnönü was criticised for not insisting on a more neutral person for the presidency, but apparently he thought he could not resist Demirel's desire for the position. However, it must be admitted that Demirel, although a classmate of Özal's from the İstanbul Technical University and having the same modest provincial background, was somewhat more correct in his observance

of constitutional rules. On the other hand Demirel often championed the view that a presidential system, with the president elected
by public vote, would be more appropriate for Turkey. Those who
knew Demirel's ambitious character had no difficulty in assuming
that he considered himself the most suitable candidate for such a
presidency.

With Demirel as president the question of the chairmanship of
the TPP arose. Hüsamettin Cindoruk, who had been chairman
while Demirel was debarred from politics, was considered the most
likely candidate, but he seemed unwilling. When party members
insisted on his candidacy, he consulted with Demirel, but apparently
he got no encouragement from him, so that he declared he would
not run. This meant that Tansu Çiller, economics professor from
Bosphorus University, who had been elected to the TGNA in 1991,
was to become the chairwoman of the TPP. Apparently Demirel had
for some time singled her out. She was a very ambitious, wilful
person who had spent many years in the US. Her husband had
gained public attention for being director-general of the İstanbul
Bank when it went bankrupt. After Çiller was elected chairwoman,
she was asked to form the cabinet. The coalition with the SDPP was
re-established.

As the Çiller government was about to receive a vote of confidence, a major tragedy occurred in Sivas. On 2 July thirty-five
persons, most of them artists and intellectuals among the many who
had gone to Sivas for a cultural festival, were burnt to death in their
hotel by fanatical Islamists after a siege of nearly four hours. Many
police, gendarmerie and army personnel were on hand but their
presence was ineffective. During the incident Demirel declared:
'State forces and people should not be allowed to confront each
other'. After the event Çiller tried to play down the situation, saying
'No harm whatever has come to our citizens encircling the hotel.' It
is not easy to believe, but 'people' and 'citizens' here referred to the
murderous mob. This attitude probably also explains the ineffec-
tiveness of the security forces. A lot was said about the 'provocation'
caused by the presence at the Festival of the free-thinking writer
Aziz Nesin, who had earlier voiced some sympathy for Salman
Rushdie, but this is more of an explanation than an excuse. Many
who had been glad to have for the first time a woman as prime

minister were disappointed by this her first performance. The Sivas incident is in many ways similar to the incidents of 31 March 1909 and Menemen in 1930. On 6 June Erdal İnönü announced his decision to quit politics. At the party Congress in September Murat Karayalçın was elected chairman and İnönü became honorary chairman. İnönü was reputed to be much more interested in physics than in politics, but RPP politicians always wanted to make good use of his famous surname. On the other hand he found their insistence difficult to resist, probably in part because he felt a certain responsibility. Later, when the RPP under Deniz Baykal failed to enter Parliament in the 1999 elections because it could not get the minimum qualifying 10% of the vote, Altan Öymen became leader. However, the next year Baykal was able to win back the leadership. His critics, disgusted and disappointed, turned to İnönü. Again he was unwilling, but also unable to resist. For about a year he toyed with the idea of playing some role in a new party and made conference tours, but in the end he announced that he would not play any role in the quest for a new party. Perhaps his realisation that he had no alternative to *status quo* policies except for his decency and civility, or perhaps a smear campaign in the newspaper *Hürriyet* concerning some irregularity in his family affairs, influenced his decision.

The premiership of Çiller was highly eventful. MP deputies brought to the TGNA a motion for a parliamentary inquiry into Çiller's property (1994); it was alleged that during her time as minister in charge of the economy in the last Demirel government she had made a fortune of US$7 million which had been invested in real estate in the United States. Apparently she had not disclosed this in her declaration of property in 1993. Because the SDPP was in coalition with the TPP and supported Çiller, nothing came of this motion. Other attempts were made to initiate parliamentary inquiries into allegations of corruption concerning her, but again they were fruitless because there were similar allegations concerning the MP leader Mesut Yılmaz (the two sides agreed not to press their motions) or because of the 'necessities' of coalition politics.

Another major event was economic disaster. The irresponsible economic and fiscal policies of Özal governments, involving deficit spending and heavy borrowing (between 1988 and 1993 the external debt rose from $41 to 67 billion), provoked a major crisis, the dollar suddenly rose from 15,000 to 38,000 liras and there was a run on the banks. The famous '5 April Decisions' were the result. The prices of products produced by the public sector were raised by an average of 50%. Inflation rose to over 100%, an extraordinary tax was levied, and the interest on Treasury bonds rose to nearly 400%. Bank deposits had to be insured by the state. To top it all, the IMF was called in and a stand-by agreement was made. The misery and dislocation caused by all these developments can be imagined. The SDPP, as a 'left-wing' coalition partner, apparently played no perceptible role either in restraining irresponsible policies or in trying to alleviate the burden on the middle and lower classes. This has continued in later years with other so-called left-wing parties in governing coalitions with right-wing parties.

On 27 March 1994 local elections were held with remarkable results. The TPP took first place with 21.4% of the vote, closely followed by the MP with 21%. What was remarkable was that the Islamist Welfare Party (WP), led by Necmettin Erbakan, was placed third with 19% and won the mayoralties of Ankara and İstanbul from the SDPP. The SDPP took only fourth place (13.6%), losing also the mayoralty of İzmir to the TPP candidate. This decline in the votes of the SDPP (and its successor, the newly-revived RPP) and the rise of the Islamist vote, a trend which was to be accentuated in the 1995 general elections, has to be explained. The decline can be explained by rather weak leadership and the fact that the SDPP seemed to be properly championing neither the welfare of the lower classes nor the principles of Kemalism. Even though İnönü had an aura, he, Karayalçın and Hikmet Çetin were on the whole rather weak political personalities. Deniz Baykal, leader of the RPP, seemed to have a strong personality, but he was out to please everybody and in the process he was turning his back on leftist policies, including Kemalism. This meant that he was pleasing almost nobody, because by enunciating rightist policies he could not hope to compete with rightist parties.

On the other hand, the rise of the Islamist vote may be explained first as a protest vote against the established parties for their failure in providing employment and economic and social benefits to the people. Secondly, thanks to the generosity of their supporters (in

Turkey and Europe) the Islamists had significant funds at their dis-
posal. They were alleged to be receiving financial aid from countries
like Saudi Arabia and Libya as well. Thirdly, they were successful in
organising their people locally and conducting door-to-door election campaigns, often supported by food gifts. Fourthly, they obviously also received many votes entirely for religious reasons, but
I think these votes alone would hardly have been enough to tip the
balance.

The year 1995 witnessed important developments concerning
the SDPP. This party and the RPP merged under the historic name
of RPP (18 February). Baykal, leader of the RPP, and Karayalçın also
agreed to Hikmet Çetin being chairman. However, this compromise
only lasted a short time, and Baykal was elected chairman on 10 September. Baykal wanted to show that he would not be a yes-man to
Çiller, and the result was that the two were not able to agree on
terms for the continuation of the coalition government. Çiller resigned, but was unable to form an alternative coalition, so that she
had to come to terms with Baykal—who wanted early elections,
which were held on 24 December. The result of these was a victory
for the WP, which won about 21% of the vote; the MP was placed
second (20%), the TPP third (19%), Ecevit's Democratic Left Party
(DLP) fourth (15%), and the RPP a poor fifth (11%). The RPP
barely managed to get the minimum 10% of votes necessary to be
represented in the TGNA.

Another important event was the signing of the Customs Union
treaty with the EU (6 March 1995). This was to enter into force on
1 January 1996. Çiller and Baykal had hailed the event as a great step
forward towards joining the EU as a full member, and in return had
expected to reap rewards in the elections. But apparently the electorate had been more impressed by the 5 April Decisions and had
voted accordingly. Critics had been quick to point out that in return
for Greece's acquiescence in a Customs Union with Turkey, Turkey
had not raised any objection to the EC announcement of a date for
the beginning of membership negotiations with southern Cyprus.
The date of the agreement being signed had coincided with the
announcement. The same critics charged that Northern Cyprus had
been 'sold out'. Since these developments caused uneasiness in
Northern Cyprus, President Demirel and President Denktaş signed

a Common Declaration confirming the continuation of the Turkish guarantee to Northern Cyprus (28 December 1995).

The WP's electoral victory posed a terrible dilemma for the regime. The earlier Islamist party, the NSP, had come to power in 1974 by forming a coalition with Ecevit's RPP, and many were scandalised by this. However, the NSP had then been the 'junior' partner in the coalition and Ecevit was Prime Minister. Now it was a question of Erbakan becoming Prime Minister, and this was generally considered unacceptable in the secular Republic of Turkey. Many were consoled by the fact that the WP had only 21% of the vote, leaving a solid 79% that was not Islamist, although many of the other parties had 'relations' with Islamist circles. The trouble was that there was a keen rivalry between Çiller and Mesut Yılmaz and the latter had all sorts of dossiers concerning Çiller's corruption with which he wanted to initiate parliamentary inquiries. On the other hand, the WP was ready to vote against such motions in return for the TPP being willing to form a coalition with it. Another problem was the sharp mutual dislike of Ecevit and Baykal, who could not get on together.

The Erbakan-Çiller government

At first Erbakan could not find a coalition partner, and a TPP-MP cabinet was formed under the premiership of Yılmaz. Later Çiller was to replace Yılmaz. However, the Constitutional Court ruled that the votes of confidence fell short of the quorum. This, and the news that the MP was tinkering with the problem of Çiller's personal wealth, ended the coalition (6 June 1996). Thus, when Erbakan was once more entrusted with the task of forming a government, the TPP was facing a motion for an inquiry into Çiller's use of the discretionary fund when she was premier. The WP voted against the motion and was thus able to persuade Çiller to take part in the coalition, in spite of her assurances during the elections that the TPP would be the guarantee of secularism. This decision provoked a minor rebellion in the TPP. Four deputies passed into the ranks of the MP, ten voted against the motion of confidence, five abstained.

There are some in the West who do not quite understand the reasons for the sensitivity that exists in Turkey *vis-à-vis* Islamism (Muslim fundamentalism). They tend to think that Islamist parties are more or less the equivalent of the Christian Democrats in

Germany and Italy. This view is mistaken, however, because it fails to take into account the great difference between the stages of development in Central and Western Europe and in Turkey. In most of Europe, the Middle Ages and institutions or practices like religious laws, the Inquisition and witch-hunts are things which existed centuries ago. Turkey experienced its Middle Ages in different, more moderate forms, but it can be said that in many respects it has not been able to distance itself from them. The tragedy in Sivas of people being burnt alive can be considered a terribly concrete example of medieval behaviour surfacing in 1993. In most of the West religious law is something belonging to the distant past, but in many places in the Islamic world the Sharia (Islamic canon law) is in force, and elsewhere (including Turkey) many Muslims actively demand its return. The stoning to death of women who have committed adultery is at present current practice in a number of Muslim countries. The great pressure that is exerted on the children of Islamists through their 'fire and brimstone' upbringing is in itself hardly a joke. Westerners who defend the political freedoms of Islamists in the name of democracy should take all this into consideration. In the twenty-first century there is not much that can be evaluated as democratic in the Sharia and hence in Islamism.

Anti-Kemalist Second Republicans, like some of the Western observers mentioned above, tend to think that the fear of the threat of Islamism in Turkey is very exaggerated, that Islamists are rapidly undergoing a process of 'softening' and 'civilisation' and are approaching or have reached the stage where their political parties can be compared to the Christian Democrat parties in Europe. The idea that Islamism will take over in Turkey and that Turkey will become another Iran is, according to these circles, paranoia: Turkey will never become another Iran. However, when one looks at history and at the big 'surprises' that one finds there, like the coming to power of Hitler in a country like Germany, like the takeover of Communism in Russia and its demise, like the Islamic Revolution in Iran, like the electoral success of Jörg Haider in Austria, one comes to the conclusion that definite predictions as to what will happen or what will not happen in a given human society in the future are at best hypothetical. If this is true, the insistence on precautions for certain eventualities cannot be so easily dismissed as paranoia.

In a country like Turkey, where the whole legal system is geared to secularism, it is not easy to carry on Islamist activities, especially in the political domain. Therefore Islamists have generally developed the art of dissimulation to a high degree. For instance, Erbakan was able to form two consecutive Islamist political parties, each of which was closed down. The third and fourth ones (the Virtue and Felicity Parties) were formed by his followers because the Constitutional Court had banned him from politics. Erbakan calls his political line 'the national viewpoint' (*Milli Görüs*). The word *milli* presently means national, but in Ottoman times it denoted a religious community, and one cannot be sure to which meaning Erbakan and his followers refer. Again, the name of Erbakan's fourth party ('felicity') might be a reference to the times of the Prophet Muhammad ('*asr-ı saadet*'). It is said that Islamists, when they are asserting their attachment, for instance, to Kemalism or secularism, are practicing *takiyye*, which means voicing a falsehood or blasphemy under duress—which is apparently not a sin. Of course, it is not easy to dissimulate all the time. Some of Erbakan's followers have been known to 'blow up', disclosing their real intentions. Erbakan himself once said that sooner or later they would prevail, and that the only question was whether this would happen by bloody or bloodless means.

Because the WP did not have a majority in the TGNA, and because of the Kemalist factor, Erbakan was far from having a free hand. He had often expressed his dislike for 'the Western Club', but he could not easily change the structure of Turkish foreign policy. However, he tried to develop an 'alternative track'. The ideas of developing a Muslim military alliance or a Muslim common market using a monetary unit other than the dollar were rather difficult to realise, but he did succeed in establishing the D-8 organisation. When he first announced the project in 22 October 1996, it was called, following the G-7 model, 'M-8' and included major Muslim countries, notably Turkey, Iran, Bangladesh, Egypt, Indonesia, Malaysia, Pakistan and Nigeria. Interestingly, it was Egypt that was rather unhappy about creating a group based on religion and after its objections the 'M' was changed to 'D' (standing for 'development' or 'developing'). The first summit meeting of D-8 was held in İstanbul on 4 January 1997. The aims of the organisation are various and include the promotion of democracy, economic development and commercial relations. Its main organ is the Council of Foreign Ministers. Erbakan also visited a number of Muslim countries, including Iran and Libya. The visit to Libya was a catastrophe: in front of TV cameras and the press Muammar Qaddafi gave him a dressing-down for Turkey's treatment of the Kurds. What was even more remarkable was that Erbakan, perceptibly perspiring and uncomfortable, did not have a word to say in response (6 October). Critics have charged that this was because of $500,000 financial aid that his party was alleged to have received from Libya in 1989, and/or because they were both alleged to belong to some Islamic organisation and Qaddafi held a position in it higher than Erbakan's. However, Erbakan was cautious enough not to want to antagonise the United States and so he sent one of his ministers to Washington with the proposal that the two allies should also be close economic partners (24 December). Erbakan had also been very keen on the creation of heavy industry by the public sector, but with the Treasury under a heavy burden of debt and a staunch neo-liberal like Çiller for coalition partner, such projects were not quite feasible.

Under Erbakan's government various spectacular events took place, like the sex scandals concerning two religious sheikhs, the Susurluk incident, some WP deputies and mayors 'blowing-up' and expressing their hatred for the Kemalist Republic, and an *iftar* banquet at Erbakan's official residence for fifty-one religious sheikhs (12 January 1997). What was more important, however, was the fact that the WP government stepped up the process of infiltration of public jobs by the Islamists—in the ministries, municipalities, public enterprises, schools and police. This had been going on for a long time and generally these persons were graduates of Imam schools. Imam schools had been started in the 1950s but nearly all governments were out to increase their number as proof of their religious credentials. The Imam schools were at two levels—intermediate (sixth to eighth years) and *lycée* (ninth to eleventh). Presumably their job was to educate imams, but girls, who were barred from the job, were admitted, and because the graduates could also go to any university and there were so many of them, these schools became a sort of alternative to general schools. In the 1990s there were about 400 Imam schools with about 120,000 students. Erbakan is reported to have described these schools as 'the backyard of our party'. Many parents, knowing that graduates from these schools were more likely to get into a public job, preferred them.

On 3 November 1996 a Mercedes car driven by Hüseyin Koca-dağ, the director of a police school, collided with a truck near Susur-luk. One of the passengers in the car, Abdullah Çatlı, was being sought by the Turkish police for being involved in the killing of seven students, members of the TWP, and for arranging the escape from jail of Mehmet Ali Ağca, who killed the famous journalist Abdi İpekçi and later attempted to assassinate Pope John Paul II. Interpol was also seeking Çatlı for drug trafficking and homicide. A third passenger was Sedat Edip Bucak, deputy of the TPP from Urfa, the chief of the Bucak tribe. The fourth passenger was Gonca Us, a model. She and Çatlı had assumed different names and were using false identity cards. They and Hüseyin Kocadağ died, while Bucak survived. Apparently their car carried a good number of guns with silencers. It was as if the occupants were travelling to fulfil some sort of dark plot. The affair at once became a major scandal involving the government itself. The TPP Minister of the Interior had to resign on 8 November; apparently he had been involved in providing false documents for 'their' criminals who were on the run.

There were a number of trials, two government reports and a par-liamentary inquiry. The story is rather complicated and apparently goes back to certain secret organisations, like the so-called Gladio in Italy, set up by NATO to organise resistance in the event of a possible Soviet invasion. 'Naturally' the elements chosen for this job were extreme right-wingers. In some cases, it seems, these groups became involved in illicit affairs. In Turkey they were apparently also used to conduct covert operations first against ASALA and then against the PKK. It appears that they began to be used extensively under the Tansu Çiller government and became involved in drug trafficking and similar mafia-type activities. For that reason the MP under Yılmaz was in the forefront of the accusers. In the end of the whole affair a number of persons have been convicted, but the general impression is that the bottom of the affair has not yet been reached. Nevertheless, there is no doubt that this type of activity has at least been strongly discouraged. It is also evident that the affair was an element in the downfall of the Erbakan-Çiller government, which tried to play it down. One remarkable aspect was an organised

popular reaction to corruption, the so-called 'One minute of dark-
ness for continuous light' campaign in all the major cities. From
1 February to 9 March 1997 lights were turned off at 9 p.m. for one
minute, sometimes supplemented by action such as the beating of
pans and blowing of horns.

The army steps in

On 28 February 1997, the army intervened, but this was a much
'subtler' intervention than those in 1960, 1971 and 1980. Indeed in
some quarters it was rather humorously dubbed 'a post-modern
coup'. 28 February was the date of a National Security Council
meeting where the Chief of the General Staff and the commanders
of the different forces demanded the implementation of eighteen
measures designed to check the growth of religious fundamentalism.
Apparently Erbakan, Çiller, Demirel had been informed of what was
coming. Nevertheless, the meeting of the Council was very tense
and lasted for nine hours. The military were courteous but very firm,
admitting only modifications in the wording of the document.
Among the more important demands were: the ending of schools,
residences and foundations operated by religious brotherhoods; a
reduction in the number of Imam schools to a level commensurate
with the need for imams; the ending of the infiltration of the
bureaucracy, the judiciary, schools and universities by fundamentalists; measures to stop subversive activities emanating from Iran;
and the extension of compulsory primary education from five to
eight years. The Council asserted that conduct contrary to the
secular principles enunciated therein would bring new tensions and
sanctions. Legally the eighteen measures were only recommen-
dations of the Council, but the government felt it had to comply.
The army also wanted to bring down the government, but this was
to be accomplished by applying psychological pressure.

Probably the most important, even epoch-making demand was
the extension of compulsory education. It meant that the whole of
the Turkish people were to be better educated; that girls, usually
those deprived of more advanced education, were to be culturally
and socially elevated; and that the intermediate Imam schools were
to be closed down. A law passed in 1973 had decreed that compulsory education would cover eight years, but a provisional article

had postponed its implementation. That provisional article had stood for nearly a quarter of a century, and it is a sad commentary on Turkey's politics that for all those years none of the parties, not even the party founded by Atatürk (the RPP), had pressed the issue. Islamist circles raised an uproar at the prospect of closing the intermediate Imam schools. Beginning religious education at fourteen years of age instead of eleven made a world of difference for them. However, many non-Islamists, both in Turkey and abroad, objected to military intervention because they deemed it undemocratic, without apparently considering how democratic theocratic practices and the under-education of children would be.

Thus the army began to monitor, on the one hand, the implementation of the 28 February decisions and, on the other, the activities of the Islamists. But with Erbakan in power the situation was very anomalous. It was disclosed later that the General Staff had formed a so-called 'Western Working Group' to study the activities of the Islamists. The information thus gathered was transmitted to various groups such as journalists, judges, prosecutors and diplomats in a series of briefing sessions. At the first of these sessions held on 29 April 1997 for journalists, which lasted three and a half hours, the new defence concept of the armed forces was also disclosed. According to this new concept, the external threat had receded and the internal threat from the PKK and Islamism, both equally dangerous, had gained priority. On 21 May the Chief Prosecutor of the High Court, Vural Savaş, made the momentous disclosure that he was bringing a suit against the WP at the Constitutional Court, asking for its dissolution because of its anti-secular activities. In mid-May a number of trade union and employers' confederations started a civil initiative to demand the resignation of the Erbakan government. Four TPP ministers resigned from their posts, and a number of deputies, from both the TPP and the WP, resigned from their parties. Faced with all this pressure and rumours of an approaching military coup, the government tried to save itself by an 'exchange' of premiership between Erbakan and Çiller. On 18 June 1997, Erbakan presented his resignation to President Demirel and at the same time handed him a declaration by the WP and TPP (as well as a third minor party) to show that a Çiller-Erbakan government would be assured of a vote of confidence. However, Demirel entrusted the job to Mesut Yılmaz on the grounds that the country needed a government to diminish tensions.

Yılmaz was able to form a coalition government with Ecevit's Democratic Left Party and Hüsamettin Cindoruk's Democratic Turkey Party. Baykal declared that the RPP would support the government on three conditions: the holding of early elections, implementation of the eight-year school programme, and lifting of the parliamentary immunity of certain deputies charged with corruption. The Yılmaz government was able to win a vote of confidence in July. On 16 August the TGNA passed the bill concerning eight-year compulsory education after a heated session lasting twenty-three hours. On 16 January 1998 the Constitutional Court decided by a 9–2 vote to dissolve the Welfare Party for anti-secular activities. By the same decision seven deputies, including Erbakan, lost their parliamentary seats and were banned from politics for a period of five years. Erbakan's followers had already prepared their new party, called the Virtue Party (VP) (Fazilet Partisi), to which they flocked under the leadership of Erbakan's fellow-student from the İstanbul Technical University, Recai Kutan. This party too was to be dissolved. The followers of Erbakan again formed a party—the Felicity Party. This time, however, there was a split, and the supposedly more progressive elements formed a different party—the Party of Justice and Development (PJD) led by Recep Tayyip Erdoğan. Erdoğan's motto became 'We have changed'.

Meanwhile the National Security Council in its monthly meetings continued to single out fundamentalism as the major threat to Turkey's security. The prohibition on the wearing of headscarves by women students began to be enforced at all universities, although this led to protest movements in many places. Some of these students took to wearing wigs in place of headscarfves. Many complied. Another important development was that the Imam-Hatip schools, now restricted to *lycée* level, experienced sharp drops in enrolment. Apparently many parents and students began to see an Imam-Hatip school diploma as a liability instead of an asset in terms of finding employment. On 21 April 1998, Recep Tayyip Erdoğan, then mayor of İstanbul and a leading figure of the WP, was sentenced to ten months' imprisonment for having made a militant speech in Siirt. The American Consul-General in İstanbul paid him a visit of sympathy. On the other hand, the State Council decreed that being convicted he was unqualified to continue in his position. Four years later in 2002, the High Electoral Council was to declare Erdoğan unqualified to lead the 'moderate' Islamist Justice and Development Party because of this same conviction. The Council also decreed that he could not run in the 3 November 2002 elections.

Collapse of the Yılmaz government, Ecevit in power

Charges of corruption against a Deputy brought about the end of the government. In the autumn of 1998 tapes of telephone conversations between a mafia leader and an MP minister found their way to the press. Their content indicated that the Deputy was trying to 'fix' the sale of a bank, using the services of the mafia for this purpose. The affair was brought before the TGNA. When the RPP supported a motion for an inquiry into the affair, Yılmaz resigned (25 November). After a prolonged crisis, Ecevit formed a minority cabinet with the support of the MP and TPP (11 January 1999). The intention was to hold early elections.

Starting from 28 February 1997, the army was a very active element in the political field. On 16 September 1998 its commander, Atilla Ateş, in a speech given near the Syrian border, declared how unacceptable it was that Öcalan should be given refuge in Syria. Thus at long last the intolerable nature of Syria's unfriendly behaviour was openly pronounced, with the implication of military action (why this did not happen earlier is an open question). The Yılmaz government supported this pronouncement, with the result that Syria had to deport Öcalan. In an agreement signed on 21 October 1998 in Adana between the two governments, Syria undertook not to support the PKK. Meanwhile Öcalan had gone to Russia, which was not willing to keep him; he then went on to Italy, and stayed more than two months there. Turkey's demand for extradition was turned down, but the Italian government could not give him indefinite refuge. Turkish public opinion was up in arms and relations with Italy were bound to suffer. Öcalan tried to obtain refuge in Greece, something that Greece was not prepared to face openly, but, hard though it is to believe, they secretly gave him refuge in the Greek embassy in Nairobi, Kenya. In a short while, his whereabouts were traced and, with some US help, he was lured out of the embassy and detained by Turkish agents who brought him to Turkey (16 February 1999). The ambivalent behaviour of the Italian government, and especially the behaviour of Greece and the fact that both countries are Turkey's allies in NATO, drew much comment in Turkey, Greece and elsewhere.

Öcalan's trial began in a State Security Court on 31 May 1999. Öcalan declared that he had not been maltreated and apologised to the families of the persons the PKK had killed (many of them attended the trial). However, he was also menacing, declaring that the PKK enjoyed the support of 140 countries, especially Italy, Russia, Syria, Greece and Germany. If he were to be executed, thousands of his supporters would shed a lot of blood. On the contrary, if he were spared he would do his utmost to stop the conflict. On 28 June the Court announced its decision: Öcalan was sentenced to death. The High Court approved the sentence, but it was not carried out because the government has judged it wiser not to submit it to Parliament, which has the final say over capital punishment. Meanwhile, PKK activity has come to a halt, but unfortunately this is not a dead halt. From time to time the PKK, based in northern Iraq, stages armed attacks, suggesting perhaps that persons and/or forces other than Öcalan control the PKK.

Riding high in the aura of victory over the PKK, Ecevit's DLP won first place in the general elections of 18 April 1999 with 22% of the vote. Baykal's RPP, with only 9%, was unable to win any seats at all, because of the electoral law's requirement of a minimum 10% of the overall vote in order to win any seats. Ecevit, in coalition with Devlet Bahçeli's Nationalist Movement Party (NMP) and Mesut Yılmaz's Motherland Party, formed the government. In forming this government Ecevit had to overcome some qualms about a coalition with the NMP and its ultra-nationalism, which were voiced by his wife Rahşan. But this was obviously better than joining up with the Islamist Virtue Party. A coalition with both the MP and the TPP was also out of the question in view of the incompatibility of Yılmaz and Çiller. This government was to remain in power until the 2002 elections. An important element in it was Sadettin Tantan, an MP deputy and a successful former police officer, who became Minister of the Interior. Thanks to his leadership, the police began to crack down on crime and corruption. About thirty 'operations' with colourful names were conducted, some of them involving well-known businessmen and politicians. One of them involved Yahya Murat Demirel, grandson of Süleyman Demirel's brother, who was charged with 'emptying' his own bank. One piece of evidence was a security camera recording of him carrying sacks of money out of his bank at night. Yılmaz could not for long tolerate Tantan's activity, especially when it began to touch his interests. On 5 June 2001 Tantan was moved to a state ministry. Tantan retorted by resigning both from his post and from MP membership.

The new GNA was remarkable in two ways. For the first time in the history of the Republic (if we exclude the 12 September episode) Atatürk's RPP was not represented there. RPP electors had preferred to vote for the DLP. This was apparently a preference for Ecevit's reputed honesty and patriotism over Baykal's superficiality. In Turkey party leaders generally dictate the nomination of candidates at all levels, with the result that they are all-powerful. Likewise, electors usually vote for the leader, rather than the party. Also, party leaders are generally not much affected by electoral defeats, but in the case of the RPP, being supposedly the most 'educated' and most 'democratic' party, it was considered 'natural' that Baykal should resign his leadership. This he did, unlike Çiller and Yılmaz, who had experienced dramatic drops in their party's vote but had managed to squeeze into the Assembly. Nevertheless, probably because Altan Öymen, the party's new leader, proved to be very weak as a leader and because of the party organisation's undemocratic structure, Baykal was able to return to the Party's leadership fifteen months later in the year 2000, to the chagrin of many Kemalists.

The second remarkable thing concerning the new Assembly was the presence of Merve Kavakçı, a rather good-looking young woman who was elected deputy from the lists of the Virtue Party and who wore the Islamist headscarf and tunic. There was no precedent for that attire in the Assembly and no female public employees or female students are allowed to wear it. Nevertheless, Kavakçı came to the first swearing-in session of the Assembly in that dress. The DLP deputies thereupon did an unprecedented thing: clapping their hands in unison and chanting for her expulsion, they staged a protest. The president of the Assembly gave a recess, and after it Kavakçı chose not to reappear. It was later discovered that she had adopted a second citizenship, not that of an Islamic country but, interestingly, that of the United States. This she had done without receiving the requisite consent of the Turkish authorities. She was therefore expelled from Turkish citizenship. The suit which she brought forward in the State Council was disallowed.

That summer a major calamity struck Turkey. On 17 August 1999, an earthquake of the magnitude of 7.4 centred in Gölcük devastated one of the most important heartlands of industry (İzmit, Adapazarı, Gölcük, Yalova). Thousands of homes and factories were destroyed. The fact that it occurred at 3 a.m. when nearly everybody was asleep resulted in many deaths. An estimated 16,000 people died, and 40,000 were injured. This staggering loss of life was also in large part due to corruption and neglect. Many of the destroyed buildings were built on land which should never have been used for building unless very special precautions were taken, and many others had been built with no regard for standard building specifications.

At the end of the year the EU at its summit meeting in Helsinki decided to invite Turkey as a candidate for membership (10 December 1999). This was a reversal of earlier EU policy. As late as 11 July the Chairman of the EU's Foreign Relations Committee, Tom Spencer, had openly declared that the EU had no intention of admitting Turkey as a member. It was dishonest not to say so for the sake of extracting benefits from Turkey. Instead of full membership, he said, some sort of formula involving very close relations could be adopted. At the Luxembourg EU summit in December 1998 it had been declared that for the moment full membership was out of the question. Apparently, Turkey's earthquake disaster played some role in softening the EU's attitude in this matter. More specifically, Greek aid for the victims of the disaster had been the occasion to develop a certain cordiality between the two governments, especially between the Foreign Ministers, İsmail Cem and Georgios Papandreou. However, the mention of the Cyprus and Aegean problems in the EU statement gave rise to grave misgivings. Was this intended as an encouragement to facilitate the solution of these problems, or was membership to be conditional on their solution? Javier Solana and Gunther Verheugen were rapidly despatched to Turkey to allay these misgivings. After their talks with Ecevit, the government, already under pressure from the pro-EU media not to 'miss the train', accepted this invitation. Ecevit flew to Helsinki to take part in the so-called EU 'family portrait', the photograph of all the participants.

33

IN THE NEW MILLENNIUM

A new president and economic catastrophe

Süleyman Demirel completed his seven years in office as President of the Republic. Since no single party had the majority in the Assembly, the issue of who would replace him became important. Demirel, since his election to the leadership of the Justice Party in 1964, and even when not in power, had been continuously in the forefront of Turkish politics. Over the years he seemed to have mellowed somewhat and assumed some of the characteristics of statesmanship, and it therefore appears natural that the idea of changing the Constitution in order to allow him to run for a second term gained currency. The proponent of this formula was no other than Ecevit, his erstwhile bitter opponent. When it came to the vote, however, the motion was defeated; many deputies apparently thought that Turkey had had enough of Demirel. The government then came up with an uncontroversial candidate for the presidency: Ahmet Necdet Sezer, president of the Constitutional Court. Sezer—a quiet, modest, serious person—was elected (5 May, 2000). But if anybody had thought that Sezer would be easy to manage, they were to be proved wrong, since he turned out to be a principled and determined president.

Economic catastrophe was triggered by a row between him and Ecevit in a National Security Council meeting in February 2001. Since December 1999 the Turkish economy had been managed in accordance with an economic stabilisation model imposed by the IMF, involving fixed rates of exchange. As usual, after the crisis, there were many who declared that the model had been wrong. In any case the value of shares traded in the stock exchange fell by 29.3 in three days. During the year the Turkish lira was devalued by 130%, the rate of inflation rose to 90%, and 1.5 million people lost their

313

jobs. In the face of this misery and chaos, Ecevit invited Kemal Derviş, a Turkish economist whom he had known from earlier times, and who was one of the assistant directors of the World Bank. It turned out that he was coming not only as an expert. At the beginning of March he was appointed Minister of State, and armed with new IMF credits, which were made to look like his personal achievement, he became the 'Tsar' of the economy. He was able to dictate to the Assembly the passage of 'fifteen laws in fifteen days'. Governments had lately been quite docile about complying with IMF instructions and introducing new laws, and the same can be said for EU demands. But the servility shown by the government and the Assembly in this instance was remarkable. Some of these laws doubtless brought certain improvements, but it can safely be said that many of their provisions mainly served the interests of the 'global powers'. They wrought havoc among peasants (45% of the population), leaving them with little public support, whereas the agricultural sector in most of the developed countries is more or less subsidised. All this is a sad commentary on Turkey's multi-party regime as well as on the globalisation process. For, come election time, the same parties that were throwing agriculture to the wolves would be soliciting votes from these very same people. Another astonishing feature of the affair was that Derviş became the darling of the big press. His tennis games, his strolls, his American wife made the headlines. It would not be an exaggeration to say that he was treated like a national saviour.

On 22 June 2001 the Constitutional Court decided to dissolve the Virtue Party. A month later Erbakan's followers, under the leadership of Recai Kutan, founded the Felicity Party (FP). However, a number of followers under the leadership of Recep Tayyip Erdoğan and Abdullah Gül founded a different party, the Party of Justice and Development (PJD). Erdoğan's close followers had all once been Erbakan's followers, but the PJD claimed to be a 'different' party. It asserted that it had 'changed'. Now that the PJD is in power and commands a parliamentary majority of about two-thirds it will be seen how far this is true. The only major difference, to this writer, is that Erdoğan and Gül have abandoned Erbakan's anti-imperialist tone and are much more ready to please the West. Otherwise there is little doubt that the PJD is an Islamist party ultimately seeking to bring in the Sharia. Naturally, this is not an easy objective and has to be achieved piecemeal and gradually. Secular public opinion in Turkey as well as the EU and the US have to be 'managed'. In many EU circles a 'moderate' Islamist regime might be considered a salutary development, since it would rid them of the problem of accepting Turkey for full membership.

The end of the Ecevit government

Ecevit was seventy-seven years old in 2002. Much more serious than that, according to one theory he is said to be suffering from a muscle weakness called myasthenia, which means that he cannot endure physical activity for any length of time without taking heavy doses of cortisone. However, because it is dangerous to prolong such treatment or to stop it abruptly, the doses have to be gradually lightened. It seems probable that, in order to be able to cope with a rather heavy programme during his official visit to the United States, Ecevit had to take heavy doses of cortisone. This visit began on 14 January 2002, culminating in talks with President Bush on the 16th.

Whether or not the above supposition is accurate, it is a fact that on 4 May Ecevit was taken ill and had to be hospitalised. Throughout May and the beginning of June he had to cancel his public activities. The wildest rumours concerning his incapacity began to circulate in the press, together with calls for his resignation; he was charged with irresponsibility, for holding on to a job he could not perform. Earlier, in mid-March, the press had reported that the US Ambassador in Ankara, Pearson, had visited the three leaders of the coalition to ascertain how much support there was for Kemal Derviş and his policies. It was said that Pearson was dissatisfied to find that this support was not very enthusiastic. Soon after Ecevit's illness, on 9 May, Derviş declared to a journalist that the existing political uncertainty was harmful, and that holding early elections would not adversely affect the economy—in fact, they would clarify the situation. In the mean time Ecevit changed his doctors and his treatment, and a marked improvement was seen in his condition. From later developments it might be surmised that this improvement was not foreseen, that Foreign Minister İsmail Cem was preparing to succeed him as leader of the DLP and as prime minister.

When this did not materialise, apparently after some hesitation, it was decided to break away from the party. .

On 8 July resignations from the DLP began, led by ministers Hüsamettin Özkan (Ecevit's right-hand man), İsmail Cem and Kemal Derviş. In a political party based almost entirely on personal allegiance to the person of Ecevit and his wife, it was a remarkable sight. It is not clear how many resignations the rebels were expecting in the Assembly, but at any rate they stopped at sixty-three, out of a total of 136 deputies. The sixty-three deputies formed under the leadership of İsmail Cem the New Turkey Party. After this heavy haemorrhage the coalition lost its majority in the Assembly. Moreover, the DLP had been reduced to the smallest party in the coalition. Therefore it would be 'natural' for Devlet Bahçeli, leader of the NMP, to assume the premiership. But even before the break-up of the DLP—in fact only one day before, on 7 July—Bahçeli, as if taking his cue from Derviş, declared that if there was political uncertainty (presumably due to Ecevit's health) early elections could be held on 3 November 2002. Perhaps Bahçeli was thinking of taking electoral advantage of the DLP's disarray by holding elections before the DLP could properly put its house in order (for instance, by an orderly change of leadership). Public opinion polls were showing the PJD in the lead, but with blind optimism all the parties, with the exception of the DLP, rushed towards the 3 November elections without even thinking of lowering the minimum 10% threshhold for admission to the Assembly. The behaviour of the suave Derviş in this affair was remarkable. After having abandoned Ecevit, he also abandoned İsmail Cem, and on 23 August, after staying aloof for a while, he joined the ranks of Baykal's RPP. If his action was not very principled, there is no doubt that it was astute. He probably studied public opinion polls and acted accordingly. There is not much doubt that Baykal regarded the accession of Turkey's 'financial saviour' as a great asset for his party, in spite of widespread consternation among his followers and sympathisers.

To understand these developments fully it might be useful to take the international situation into consideration. After 11 September 2001, the Bush administration declared war on terrorism. It appears that the Bush administration was all along thinking of using the Turkish army as an important auxiliary ground force for its purposes.

It also appears that Erdoğan and Gül were willing to fulfil this expectation not only in Iraq, but in other foreign policy issues as well. The Ecevit government, on the other hand, was very docile about fulfilling economic and social demands. But when it came to pitting Turkey against Iraq or making important concessions over Cyprus and the Aegean, it was more or less clear that this government would not be very accommodating. Therefore, the US government had every interest in the seeing Ecevit and his government emasculated and in the holding of early elections. How actively they worked to promote this objective is something that future research will uncover.

The end of moderate politics?

When the DLP split, Ecevit replaced İsmail Cem with Şükrü Sina Gürel and Kemal Derviş with Masum Türker. Thus the cabinet acquired a more national character, more in keeping with Ecevit's erstwhile image.

The elections proved a real earthquake. Only two parties were able to pass the 10% threshold and enter the Assembly. One was the PJD, the other the RPP. The first got 34% of the vote and won nearly two-thirds of the seats, enabling it to make constitutional changes. The second presumably harvested the 'Kemalist' votes with 19%. With 1% the DLP was completely flattened. To date, however, Ecevit is still leading the party. The TPP got 9.5%, the MP 5%, and the NMP 8% of the vote. Çiller and Yılmaz resigned from the leadership, while Bahçeli promised not to stand again in the next party congress, but was nevertheless elected Chairman.

How is this earthquake to be explained? There is little doubt that it is a reaction to the economic crisis and the misery that ensued. It also seems that what are called 'IMF policies' are blamed. None of the major parties came out openly against 'IMF policies' in their programmes, but some of them spoke out in their campaign speeches. This is especially true of the Young Party, led by Cem Uzan. Uzan is the name of a family owning some eighty-odd companies and often accused of corrupt practices. Cem Uzan decided to found the Young Party, and thanks to an active anti-IMF campaign and his family's ownership of newspapers and TV channels he was able to get 7% of the vote. Research would probably show that the PJD emphasised anti–IMF attitudes and/or that the electorate somehow associated that party with anti–IMF policies. On the other hand, it is to be noted that socialist parties in general, including those with a strong, sincere anti–IMF platform, again received only marginal votes. This anti–IMF tendency and the electorate's reluctance to vote for the real anti–IMF parties is a dilemma of Turkish multi-party politics.

Turkey's two fixations in foreign policy are another important problem for the country. One is the EU membership fixation, which allows the EU to impose its policies on Turkey, oblivious of Turkey's 'real' interests. The second fixation is the determination not to allow the creation of a Kurdish state on its borders, which is considered a great danger to Turkey's stability because of the Kurdish population in the southeast of the country. This, it seems to this writer, is an irrational fear in view of the fact that Turkey has also long had an Arab population in the same region and two independent Arab states on its borders, with no resulting problems. This second fixation, together with Turkey's indebtedness, allows the United States to impose many of its policies on Turkey.

Turkey's EU perspective

Turkey's accession to the EU is progressing, but the process can be described as tortuous at best. The attractions of such a relationship for both sides are evident. For the EU the strategic location of Turkey in command of the Straits and a bridge to the Caucasus, Central Asia and the Middle East is important. Economically its large market, its mineral wealth and its potential as an area for investment draw attention. Turkey's army is also cited as an asset.

For Turkey, on the other hand, membership in the EU is perceived as a solution to its economic problems, a prospect of social, cultural, educational development, and a guarantee for the proper functioning of its democracy. Especially since the application by Turgut Özal when Prime Minister for full membership in 1987, it has become a Turkish dream, a panacea for all ills.

However, the objective difficulties in the way of Turkey's European integration are gigantic. One major difficulty is the underdevelopment of the economy. A very large section of the economy is 'unregistered'—for instance, tax evasion and illicit (informal) employment are widespread. Officially unemployment is around 10%, but real unemployment is much higher. Per capita income is low (2,232 euros in 2004) and very unevenly distributed. Agriculture is generally underdeveloped and staggering under the impact of neoliberal policies. Another factor is Turkey's underdevelopment in terms of education: many children, especially girls, are not sent to school. Until 1997 compulsory education was only for five years, now it is for eight years. Classes are overcrowded, teachers underpaid, schools ill-equipped, and school and public libraries too few and inadequate. A third objective difficulty is the fact that Turkey is Muslim and the EU Christian. There are many who think that because the EU and Turkey are secular, this is no problem. But it is obvious that despite secularism and perhaps a weakening of religious feelings, the EU is culturally Christian and Turkey culturally Muslim. A fourth difficulty is Turkey's great size. With a rapidly growing population of 70 million its representation in the European Parliament would be second only to Germany's—for a while.

This is not the place to go into the age-old prejudices of Europe towards Muslims and towards the Turks in particular. But they obviously play an important part. At any rate, for those with eyes to see the EU's reluctance to admit Turkey to full membership is evident. In the autumn of 2005, with the beginning of negotiations which are scheduled to last for at least ten years, there were important signs of this reluctance. Unlike the negotiations with all the other candidates, they are to be 'open-ended'. Already free circulation of Turkish labour in the EU has been ruled out for the foreseeable future. France and Austria have indicated that even if negotiations are concluded in favour of full membership, they will submit this decision to a referendum in their own countries. It has to be remembered here that the defeats of the European Constitution in the 2005 referendums in France and the Netherlands were to some extent due to the electorates' aversion to the membership of Turkey. But it has to be noted also that, however reluctant it may be about full membership, the EU has already ruled out any outright refusal. The idea now being aired quite frequently, for instance by Angela Merkel, is to attach Turkey to the EU in a 'special relationship'. Hitherto most EU statesmen have pretended that Turkey was to become a member, probably because of the opportunities it gave them to control Turkey and extract concessions.

For many years most Turks, warmly encouraged by the Turkish media, considered EU membership a rosy dream which would surely come true. With the passage of time, however, this mood has darkened considerably because of some of the demands made by the EU. It is becoming evident, especially with the admission of the Greek Cypriot state to EU membership, that sooner or later the EU will demand the end of the Turkish Republic of Northern Cyprus and of the presence of the Turkish army there. This is also viewed as an indication that Turkey will not be admitted to the EU. Because if Turkey were really to be an EU member, the insistence on sub-merging the Turkish Republic of Northern Cyprus in the Greek Cypriot state would lose its meaning and the Cyprus 'problem' would thereby be solved.

A second source of uneasiness is the EU's demand to turn the Kurds and Alevis into legally recognised minorities. According to the Turkish conception, consecrated by the Lausanne Treaty, only non-Muslims are 'minorities'. The Kurds and Alevis may have certain problems but these are to be solved by democratisation and social and economic development, not by 'minoritisation'.

Thirdly, the European Parliament has passed a resolution to press Turkey into recognition of the so-called 'Armenian genocide'. This is coupled by the 'inevitably' rising number of Western parliaments passing resolutions to the same effect. The Turkish viewpoint (shared by the great majority) is that, yes, there have been mutual massacres, but the charge of genocide has not been verified even after all these years and is therefore most unlikely to be verified today. As to the forcible transfer in 1915 of many Armenians from Anatolia to Northern Syria and Iraq (which were Ottoman provinces at the time), this was a necessity dictated by the betrayal of many Arme-nians in joining the enemy side (Russia) in time of war.

Despite all these ominous developments, Turkish governments in recent years have stolidly continued to declare their faith in the country's EU membership. There is a suspicion in many quarters that these governments were and are aware that theirs is a false optimism, but they use it, first, to prevent army influence in politics, and secondly, and more important, because if they can show that they are successfully carrying the country towards EU membership, they can get electoral support. Thus, it appears that Turkey's membership has perhaps become a two-sided 'game' played by European and Turkish statesmen.

To many Turks these developments are very alarming and smack of a revival of the Sèvres Treaty, Turkey's 'death warrant'. To them the 'Europe at all costs' attitude is self-destructive. They dream of a much more independent Turkey, self-reliant, freed from the shackles of indebtedness and keeping its foreign policy options open. Then, perhaps, a healthier relationship, on a footing of equality, can be established with the EU.

Thus it can be said at the time of writing that Turkey's progression towards European integration has become somewhat confused. A certain stretch of time is needed to see clearly where Turkey will be going.

CONCLUSION

As a final analysis let us first examine the areas in which Turkey's development could be said to have been lacking.

Since 1950 Turkey has to a certain extent shelved the integral development model applied during the Atatürk administration and in its stead followed the material development model. As a result of this revised strategy, major advances have been made in the spheres of infrastructure and production. By contrast, education, culture and public health have stagnated or regressed. In the 1994 United Nations Human Development Index (HDI) Turkey is accorded 68th place among 173 countries. Not having attained the high degree of human development of the first category of fifty-three developed countries, Turkey is placed in the second category of sixty-five countries that have developed to a medium degree. According to that HDI the time spent in school by the average Turk is 3.6 years. The equivalent is 5 years in Iraq and Azerbaijan, 3.9 years in Iran, 4.2 years in Syria, 7 years in Greece and Bulgaria and 9 years in Russia. These statistics reveal that in the field of education Turkey is behind all its neighbours. The quality of education imparted to the average Turk during this 3.6 years in school is in itself problematical. The primitive conditions in village schools—over-crowded classrooms, lack of libraries or cultural and sports facilities in primary and secondary education—are well-known facts. Giant steps must be taken nation-wide to catch up where, owing to an over-concentration on material development, Turkey has lagged behind.

The public health service is equally in need of major improvement, qualitatively and in making it more accessible to the public. The fact that the population explosion has lost some of its impetus may have a positive effect on the national health situation.

The emergence of a strong Islamic-fundamentalist movement has opened the way to a schizophrenic split in Turkish society. In future this current could gain sufficient momentum to endanger national consensus and threaten the achievements of the Atatürk Revolution. This development may have weakened Turkey's chances of becoming a developed country.

For Turkey to achieve its aspiration of becoming a developed country, its politicians must become more statesmanlike and responsible, more ready to compromise. If the political ranks had left aside their minor disputes and acted with less emotion and more rational deliberation, it is very probable that there would have been no need for the three military takeovers that the country endured in its recent history and it would by now have reached a far higher level of development.

In 1999 the armed insurgency in eastern Anatolia was brought to an end, resolving to a great extent the long-outstanding Kurdish question. We should now look at the positive aspects of Turkey's development.

Although the Turks are relative latecomers on the stage of history, they have made great advances. Turkey today, despite its many faults and deficiencies, seems to have a well established secular and democratic social and political structure. A glance at its history is enough to show what great progress has already been made. Thanks to the secular system, society has to a great measure been freed from the bonds of medievalism. The multi-party system, which from 1946 to 1980 was often a dictatorship of the majority party, has given way to acceptance of both the concept and application of pluralism. The equality of male and female before the law is the highest achievement of secularism. The laws propagated in 1926 and 1934 ensuring equal rights have been, in time, implemented and have changed the fabric of Turkish society. Although there may still be a way to go, the distance travelled thus far is great.

As argued, secularism has largely freed Turkey from its medieval bonds. Through secularism and its complement, the revolution of enlightenment, Turkey now has an appreciable intellectual establishment along with cultural, scientific and artistic institutions. Thanks to these institutions, Turkey is on its way to reaching a high level of international esteem. It is now home to established publishing houses, serious newspapers, periodicals and magazines, flourishing theatrical companies, a cinema industry, a variety of good radio and television programmes, universities, conservatories, opera, ballet and an artistic and scientific community. A hundred years ago Turkey had few or none of these. In 1934 1,530 books were published, in 1994 the number was 7,224.

Turkey has also made great advances in the fields of agriculture, industry and public works. A capitalist class has developed, which, though not yet on a par with its Western equivalents either culturally or in capital accumulation, has begun to make its mark in international markets. Only time will tell whether Turkey's 'Yes' to the European Customs Union is based on its weakness or strength, that is to say whether Turkish capitalism can compete with its rivals in the EU.

BIBLIOGRAPHICAL NOTE

There are a number of sources available in the English language concerning the Ottoman Empire. A popular recent book giving a general view of the Ottomans is Jason Goodwin's *Lords of the Horizons* (2000). Other books in this category are Lord Kinross' *The Ottoman Centuries* (1977) and Justin McCarthy's *The Ottoman Turks: An Introductory History to 1923* (1996). For the earlier Ottoman centuries comprehensive studies are by Stanford J. Shaw, *History of the Ottoman Empire and Modern Turkey* (vol. I, up to 1808) (1976), and Halil İnalcık, *The Ottoman Empire: The Classical Age 1300–1600* (1973). A useful work of reference for general Ottoman history is Selçuk Akşin Somel's *Historical Dictionary of the Ottoman Empire* (2003). The monumental *Encyclopaedia of Islam* (2nd edition) is, of course, an invaluable source. *Histoire de l'Empire Ottoman* (1989), edited by Robert Mantran, is a general Ottoman history written by various French scholars. In Turkish, a general history of the pre-Tanzimat period is that by İsmail Hakkı Uzunçarşılı, *Osmanlı Tarihi* (vols I–IV). For those interested in economic and social history, *An Economic and Social History of the Ottoman Empire, 1300–1914*, edited by Halil İnalcık and Donald Quataert (1994) can be recommended.

The best-known source in English for the nineteenth century and the first half of the twentieth in Turkey is Bernard Lewis's *The Emergence of Modern Turkey* (1961). Stanford J. Shaw and Ezel K. Shaw's *History of the Ottoman Empire and Modern Turkey*, vol. II, brings Turkish history to 1975. Both volumes of Shaw's work contain valuable and extensive annotated bibliographies for those wishing to further their studies. A general appraisal of Turkish history from the viewpoint of modernisation is Niyazi Berkes' *The Development of Secularism in Turkey* (1964, 1998).

The Tanzimat period can be studied in Roderic Davison's *Reform in the Ottoman Empire, 1856–1876* (1963). The intellectual and political history of this period has been examined in Şerif Mardin's *The Genesis of Young Ottoman Thought* (1962), which deals with the revolutionary movements of the 1860s. His other study, in Turkish, *Jön Türklerin Siyasi Fikirler i, 1895–1908* (1964), examines the Committee of Union and Progress before 1908. The standard work in Turkish for the nineteenth century is Enver Ziya Karal's *Osmanlı Tarihi* (vols V–VIII).

The First Constitutional Period (1876–80) can be studied in Robert Devereux' *The First Constitutional Period* (1963). For the reign of Abdülhamid II (1876–1909) a popular study is Joan Haslip's *The Sultan: The Life of Abdul Hamid II* (1958). Sophisticated analysis can be found in Selim Deringil's *The Well-Protected Domains: Ideology and the Legitimation of Power in the Ottoman Empire, 1876–1909* (1998). A good study has lately been published in French: François Georgeon's *Abdülhamid II. Le Sultan Calife* (2003).

The history of the Second Constitutional Period, except for its last years (1908–14), has been covered in Feroz Ahmad's *The Young Turks* (1969). Another source is Naim Turfan's *Rise of the Young Turks* (2000). A compact general history of the period in Turkish is Sina Aksin's *Jön Türkler ve İttihat ve Terakki* (1980). The standard source in Turkish for Turkey's pre-Republican revolutionary past is Yusuf Hikmet Bayur's *Türk İnkılabı Tarihi* (3 vols).

For those interested in the Armenian issue the Turkish viewpoint can be found in Kamuran Gürün's *The Armenian File: The Myth of Innocence Exposed* (1985). The Armenian side is extensively studied by Richard Hovannisian, *The Republic of Armenia* (4 vols).

The war of National Liberation is comprehensively examined in five volumes by Stanford J. Shaw's *From Empire to Republic: The Turkish War of National Liberation, 1918–1923* (2000). A remarkably detailed chronology of this war is Zeki Sarıhan's *Kurtuluş Savaşı Günlüğü* (4 vols, 1993). My *İstanbul Hükümetleri ve Milli Mücadele* (2 vols, 1976, 1992), partly based on British archival material, deals with the first part of this period (1918–20). The standard study in Turkish on the War of Liberation and the history of the Republic (up to 1960) is Şerafettin Turan's *Türk Devrim Tarihi* (4 vols, 1991).

Two objective works that concentrate on the Greek side of the conflict are Michael Lewellyn Smith's *Ionian Vision: Greece in Asia Minor, 1919–1922* (1973, 1998) and Dimitri Pentzopoulos' *The Balkan Exchange of Populations and its Impact on Greece* (1962, 2002).

Atatürk, as founder of the Turkish Republic, occupies a central position in research dealing with modern Turkey. An early popular biography is H.C. Armstrong's *Grey Wolf* (1932). Lord Kinross wrote the first comprehensive biography, *Atatürk: The Rebirth of a Nation* (1964). Now we have a major achievement, Andrew Mango's *Atatürk* (1999). In French there is A. Jevakhoff, *Kemal Atatürk. Les chemins de l'occident* (1989). A good biography in Turkish is Şevket Süreyya Aydemir's *Tek Adam* (3 vols, 1963). A cultural reflection on the period of Atatürk's ascendancy is provided by Saime Göksu and Edward Timms' *Romantic Communist* on the life and work of the poet Nazım Hikmet (1999).

Feroz Ahmad picks up the thread where Bernard Lewis stopped. His *The Turkish Experiment in Democracy, 1950–1975* (1977) is a good detailed study of those years. The Turkish version of the book, *Demokrasi Sürecinde Türkiye 1945–1980* (1994), expands this history by ten years. A compact and analytical study, Andrew Mango's *The Turks Today* (2004), brings Turkish history (in English) up to 2003. In Turkish we have *Türkiye Tarihi* (Cem Yayınevi) (vol. 3: 1600–1908; vol. 4: 1908–1980; vol. 5: 1980–2003). Erik J. Zürcher's *Turkey: a Modern History* (1993) is a compact handbook.

For those interested in Turkey's foreign policy William Hale's *Turkish Foreign Policy, 1774–2000* (2002) is a reliable source. In Turkish we have two massive volumes, *Türk Dış Politikası* (2001), edited by Baskın Oran. At the time of going to press, this work is being translated into English. Philip J. Robins' *Suits and Uniforms: Turkish Foreign Policy since the Cold War* (2003) focuses on a number of specific case histories.

INDEX